Households and Families of the
Longhouse Iroquois at Six Nations Reserve

Studies in the Anthropology of North American Indians

Editors
Raymond J. DeMallie
Douglas R. Parks

HOUSEHOLDS AND FAMILIES

of the

LONGHOUSE IROQUOIS

at

SIX NATIONS RESERVE

Merlin G. Myers

Foreword by Fred Eggan
Afterword by M. Sam Cronk

PUBLISHED BY THE UNIVERSITY OF NEBRASKA PRESS • LINCOLN AND LONDON
In cooperation with the American Indian Studies Research Institute, Indiana University, Bloomington

Foreword © 1989 by Fred Eggan ¶ "Households and Families of the Longhouse Iroquois at Six Nations Reserve" ¶ by Merlin G. Myers © 2006 by Alice Fay Brady Myers, Trustee of the Alice Fay Brady Myers Family Revocable Trust ¶ Preface and afterword © 2006 by the Board of Regents of the University of Nebraska ¶ All rights reserved ¶ Manufactured in the United States of America ¶ ⊗ ¶ Library of Congress Cataloging-in-Publication Data ¶ Myers, Merlin G. ¶ Households and families of the Longhouse Iroquois at Six Nations Reserve / Merlin G. Myers ; foreword by Fred Eggan ; afterword by M. Sam Cronk. ¶ p. cm. – (Studies in the anthropology of North American Indians) ¶ Includes bibliographical references and index. ¶ ISBN-13: 978-0-8032-3225-9 (cloth : alk. paper) ¶ ISBN-10: 0-8032-3225-X (cloth: alk. paper) ¶ 1. Cayuga Indians – Ontario – Six Nations Indian Reserve No. 40 – Kinship. 2. Cayuga Indians – Ontario – Six Nations Indian Reserve No. 40 – Dwellings. 3. Cayuga Indians – Ontario – Six Nations Indian Reserve No. 40 – Social life and customs. 4. Matrilineal kinship – Ontario – Six Nations Indian Reserve No. 40. 5. Six Nations Indian Reserve No. 40 (Ont.) – History. 6. Six Nations Indian Reserve No. 40 (Ont.) – Social life and customs. I. Title. II. Series. ¶ E99.C3M84 2006 ¶ 306.83089'97554071352–dc22 ¶ 2005035674 ¶ Set in Quadraat by Kim Essman. ¶ Designed by R. W. Boeche. ¶

To Professor Meyer Fortes
In memoriam and with gratitude

Contents

Illustrations

Photographs

Figures

Maps

Tables

Foreword

Fred Eggan

This volume, *Households and Families of the Longhouse Iroquois at Six Nations Reserve*, represents a long-awaited publication of Merlin Myers's doctoral dissertation at Cambridge University. Myers applied the research methods learned from his mentor, Meyer Fortes, to the Six Nations Longhouse Iroquois in Ontario. Although most of the tribes of the Iroquois Confederacy were split in their decision to ally themselves with Great Britain during the American Revolution, the greater part of the Iroquois nations remained loyal to the British Crown and as a result saw their villages in New York State destroyed by General Sullivan. Later, portions of all tribes of the League fled to Canada with Joseph Brant, along with remnants of the Tuscarora, Delaware, and other adopted tribes, and were settled on a reservation on the Grand River in Ontario, Canada.

Dr. Fortes had come to Cambridge as professor of anthropology in 1950, where he had introduced social anthropology, learned from Malinowski and Radcliffe-Brown, to the postwar generation of students in England. How Merlin Myers was recruited is a story he should tell, but he proved an apt pupil and was sent to Canada to study the Iroquois, using the models derived from Fortes's African studies of the Tallensi and Ashanti, along with insight derived from Lewis Henry Morgan's pioneer accounts of Iroquois kinship.

Merlin Myers carried out his field research on the Grand River Reserve in 1956–58, concentrating his attention on the Longhouse sector rather than the Christian populations. The Longhouse religion is well described in Anthony F. C. Wallace's *The Death and Rebirth of the Seneca* (1970). In essence, Handsome Lake, a Seneca chief, led a cultural revival around AD 1800 that has become the "old religion" for the Iroquois. During his fieldwork, Merlin Myers came to the University of Chicago for a period to prepare preliminary reports and to present seminars on various problems of Iroquois social organization and cultural change.

The present volume (after the introduction, which summarizes the historical background of the Iroquois and gives an overview of the Longhouse people within the reservation setting) concentrates on the composition of the household group and its economic features, and on the political-jural and ritual aspects of matrilineal descent, with special reference to kinship and marriage. Myers analyzes the basic data derived from a census of some 150 households from the Longhouse sector, representing all five tribes of the original Confederacy. From this we clearly see the continuing importance of the matriline, despite the efforts of the Canadian government to install their own cultural conventions with regard to citizenship and inheritance. The variations in household composition are also seen as representing different points in the "developmental cycle" of household groups, one of Professor Fortes's major contributions to the study of household organization.

In the external domain, the Longhouse people organize their social structure on the rule of matrilineal descent and utilize uterine kinship as the basis for forming corporate groups. Agnatic kinship has also been recognized from the time of Morgan but is concerned with interpersonal relations only—not as a basis for corporate descent groups. In Longhouse thinking, the mother supplies "blood" and the father furnishes the substance from which the body is formed, notably the bones. Of these two, blood is the more important and thus provides closer relationships.

Lineages are the basic units in contemporary reserve life among the Longhouse sector and still control membership in the Council of Hereditary Chiefs, although some of the fifty sachem names have had to be reassigned to new lineages. Lineages may be divided into sublineages, based on three-generation units of mother, daughter, and daughter's children associated with households. However, the larger matrilineage is the corporate group controlling the key political and ritual offices in the society, providing names to the newborn, conferring "citizenship" in Longhouse society, looking after the welfare of lineage ancestors, and providing continuity between the living and the dead. Lineages are still exogamous, and kinship behavior is reflected in the unity of the lineage. The father's lineage, "the people of my father's sister," and the spouse's lineage, are both important, each using a single kin term for the entire lineage.

Merlin Myers noted some thirty to thirty-five such matrilineages, some tracing descent back to ancestors present on arrival in Canada. These are related to the "clans" and "sides," or dual divisions, represented in Longhouse ritual, but the relationship now is apparently somewhat arbitrary. There are four "longhouses," each with a dual organization made up of sets of lineages on the model of matrilineal descent groups, but with transfers recognized to keep the "sides" in balance. The "sides" are named (Wolf and Turtle or Wolf and Deer) and are fully corporate groups, each with a set of officers from the constituent lineages and with reciprocal services and ritual gift exchanges.

With this background, Merlin Myers looks at kinship and marriage. I once wrote that Morgan's view of kinship was forever complicated by the fact that the Iroquois system of terminology, with its balanced bilateral character, did not rest conformably on a matrilineal clan system, as he supposed. Myers clears this up in part by showing that Iroquois kinship terminology (given here in the Cayuga language) is built up not only on the basis of matrilineal descent, but in addition, on the complementary recognition of filiation with the father. Institutionalized *personal* relations on the basis of agnatic relationships give its "balanced" bilateral character. He calls the latter a "kind of shadow lineage."

In the early historic period, the Iroquois lived generally in longhouses of bark, which were occupied by a matrilineage segment with matrilocal residence, which carried out the horticultural activities, while the men were hunters and warriors. Lafitau reported a kinship system in 1724 that is similar to Morgan's discoveries in the middle of the nineteenth century. In the meantime, Handsome Lake's reforms around 1800 were designed, in part, to accommodate Iroquois customs to American norms. More recently, the Canadian government recognized the importance of the father and played down matrilineal tendencies.

Whether the Iroquois had a form of double descent at anytime in the past is not clear. Perhaps the present kinship terminology is old and the changes have affected mainly the behavioral patterns. Today personal names have taken the place of kin terms for one's own and descending generations in many cases, and terms for father's brother's children, formerly classed with siblings, now tend to be cross-cousin terms.

Marriages were formerly arranged by the mothers and mothers' mothers of the couple, but individual choice is now the rule, sometimes with a period of "trial marriage" before the actual ceremony. Marriage within the matrilineage is forbidden, and marriage with agnatic kin seems to be rare. There are further restrictions against marrying into the Christian community, or outside the reserve. Marriages between second cousins may occur when the couple is descended from a brother and a sister, respectively, which may suggest possible cross-cousin marriage at some earlier period.

The marriage ceremony is relatively simple. The bride and groom are seated together at the bride's parents' house or the longhouse and listen to speeches from the officiating chief, along with other chiefs and elders, prior to partaking of a feast with all officiators, relatives and friends. Husband and wife have equal jural status, there is no transfer of rights, and rights in *genetricem* remain vested in the woman's lineage. The wife also has a claim on the husband for economic support. Ideally termination of the marriage should be by death, with the surviving spouse being returned formally to his or her own lineage; but about half of all adults in the census had had previous unions.

The League or Confederation of the Iroquois tribes has lost much of its significance now that the tribes have been reduced to "dependent domestic nations." However, each such nation was, in 1958, still represented by hereditary chiefs and other officials who, through their lineages, were affiliated with Longhouse organizations, wherein they attended to ritual matters and dealt with internal problems while they attempted to regain sovereignty in the larger world.

Merlin Myers's account of the Six Nations Longhouse people provides a model that should be applied to studies of the major Christian and other factions on the reserve, as well as other Iroquois settlements and other tribal nations. We may then make comparisons with some assurance of success. With regard to kinship, for example, the Iroquois kinship system has often been equated with the Dakota system without regard to differences in the underlying social structure, so that the worldwide classification of Murdock and others will need to be reassessed.

Meyer Fortes was pleased with this analysis of the Iroquois and arranged for its publication in the Cambridge Papers in Social Anthropology, but Merlin Myers delayed release of his work for publication. Recently pressures from colleagues and students at Brigham Young University have been effective. The present contribution will add an important component to the Iroquois studies of recent years, both in terms of Professor Fortes's methodological contributions and the new data on the Longhouse Iroquois at Six Nations Reserve. Here is an account that emphasizes Iroquois social structure as exemplified in the household or domestic organization and the political-jural organization based on the lineage and the Longhouse organization, which once controlled the League of the Iroquois. Here Iroquois kinship acquires a new dimension and opens the possibility of new knowledge of its development through comparison of the several systems.

Preface

Alice B. Myers

Introduction
Teaching and Research History

My husband, Merlin Gilbert Myers (1923–91), was professor of anthropology at Brigham Young University, Provo, Utah, from 1964 to 1990. There he established a program for social and cultural anthropology, as well as chairing the Department of Anthropology and Archaeology for fourteen years. He was lecturer at McMaster University (Hamilton, Ontario, Canada), summer 1964; consultant for the Rough Rock (Navajo) Demonstration School (Chinle, Arizona), 1966–68; consultant for the Macy Public School (Omaha Indian Reservation, Macy, Nebraska), 1969; lecturer at the University of Nebraska (Omaha), summer 1969; and visiting professor of anthropology at the University of Waterloo, (Waterloo, Ontario, Canada), summers 1970–73.

It is certainly true that one of the best measures of personal success for any teacher is found in the achievements and quality of his or her students. Merlin chose not to create a graduate degree program at Brigham Young, because he felt it best to focus on building and maintaining an intensive, quality undergraduate curriculum that would prepare its students for successful placement in the top PhD programs in the United States and England. The success of this endeavor was realized as a considerable number of his students received doctorates from graduate programs at Chicago, Columbia, Cornell, Harvard, Michigan, Wisconsin, Cambridge, and Oxford, among others, engaging in fieldwork in many different regions, including Africa, East Asia, South Asia, the Middle East, North, Central, and South America, and Europe. These individuals now work in a diverse range of occupations: university professors, museum directors, political and business analysts and consultants, and attorneys; and several have established or work for nonprofit humanitarian organizations around the world.

Merlin's research interests were varied. He had a lifelong personal and scholarly engagement with the Longhouse Iroquois at Grand River Reservation in Ontario, Canada, and also developed lasting relationships within Navajo and Hopi communities in the American Southwest. Toward the end of his life he traveled to East Asia, as well, conducting research in South Korea, which led to consultations concerning Korean reunification. Most of his research appeared only in his lectures and notes; his heavy teaching load, and finally diminishing health, precluded publishing. The only completed written materials that he left are the doctoral dissertation that constitutes this publication, the 1975 Karl G. Maeser Distinguished Teaching Award Address, *Kinship, Religion, and the Transformation of Society*, and an unpublished paper on beliefs and practices concerning the dead among Six Nations Longhouse people, which he delivered at the University of Chicago in December 1973.

Over the course of his career, Merlin continued to find structural-functionalist models learned at Cambridge useful. However, like his mentor, Meyer Fortes (1978, 11), he was a "pluralist" and recognized the value and necessity of interpreting field data from various frames of reference. Merlin's courses at Brigham Young University, and his later research in the American Southwest and East Asia, drew liberally from the insights of historical, interpretive, and structural approaches, as well as perspectives found in more recent semiotic, poststructural, and postmodern perspectives. A number of Merlin's students have remarked that their first encounters with the central concepts and issues of contemporary social and cultural studies came from Merlin's critiques of colonialization, industrialization, and various other features and problems of modernity. Merlin did not, however, evidence much concern over the "identity crisis" and consequent reflexive practices that emerged within social and cultural anthropology during the 1970s and 1980s. To him this seemed a natural and necessary consequence of the expansion and growing sensitivity and sophistication of the discipline. He maintained that the most useful and honest approach to the ethnographic endeavor critically engaged and built upon the insights from both established and current perspectives.

Initial Training and Fieldwork: From Cambridge to Grand River

Merlin came to the discipline of anthropology by chance. In the fall of 1953, on our way to Scotland, where he intended to pursue graduate studies in political science, he found a Cambridge University catalogue at the British Museum in

London that outlined a course of study in social anthropology, which provided a holistic approach to the study of human behavior that, while including political organization and practice, went further to encompass economic, kinship, religious, and ritual topics as well. He saw in this approach not only a means to broaden his perspective of political theory but also an opportunity to explore a lifelong interest in the rich diversity of the world's peoples. He set out at once for Cambridge to investigate the possibility of enrolling in the program. After a two-hour conference with Meyer Fortes, head of the Department of Anthropology, he felt assured of being accepted as a graduate student and redirected our course toward Cambridge, not realizing that only one in seven applicants was accepted for graduate study at that time; however, by the week's end he was enrolled in the program.

Registering to read for a master's degree, he embarked on learning the fundamentals of British structural-functionalism under the tutelage of Meyer Fortes, Edmund Leach, Audrey Richards, and later Jack Goody, among others. It was a new world of thought for him and highly stimulating, especially during this period at Cambridge when the polemical debates between Fortes and Leach were at their peak. The physical setting of this ancient seat of academia was also quite inspiring, as was the social and intellectual environment, which, as Goody describes it (83), was structured on both "scholarly authority" and an atmosphere "of camaraderie, of solidarity [and] of *communitas*."

At a social gathering of faculty and graduate students at his home, Fortes asked me how Merlin's studies were going. I replied that he was developing some very good ideas for research, to which Fortes counseled, "No, no, now is not the time for ideas. First he must understand and test current theories and methods; then, he can develop his own models."[1] After gaining a solid foundation in the fundamentals, Merlin settled his focus on the subject of Iroquois research, first brought to his attention by Fortes, who had long been impressed with the apparent comparability of various facets of Iroquois social structure (found in Lewis Henry Morgan's writings) with the findings of British social anthropologists in African societies. He proceeded to study Morgan and other Iroquoian ethnographers and examined Fortes's works on the Tallensi and Ashanti tribes in Africa, as well as his theoretical essays, as guides to research and later as models for exposition. Thus grounded, he presented his proposal for study among the Six Nations Iroquois of Ontario, Canada, in June 1955. The proposal was accepted, the master's thesis requirement was waived, and as a candidate in the PhD program, he prepared for initial research in Albany, New York.

Here Dr. William N. Fenton of the New York State Museum and Science Service generously made his own unpublished field notes on the Iroquois available and gave other aid in library research that preceded fieldwork. He also made funds available for a period of the fieldwork, beginning in May 1956, and gave important assistance by introducing us to members of the Six Nations community. Although Merlin's theoretical and methodological interests differed from Fenton's, he held a lifelong appreciation for this early assistance. Yale linguist and ethnographer Floyd Lounsbury also rendered much appreciated assistance and encouragement throughout the course of the initial fieldwork and writing.

Merlin wrote in the original preface to his dissertation, "A great debt of gratitude is due all those Longhouse people who have honestly and earnestly sought to help a white man understand the intricacies and genius of their way." This is true; we were received warmly and graciously into their homes at times of joy or sorrow, on occasions of great ritual importance, and during activities of everyday life. They, in turn, would often visit and share food with us in our home on the reserve.

It was our great pleasure, in April 1957, to host one of the condolence ceremony rehearsals of the hereditary chiefs (Three Brothers moiety) for the upcoming installation of Cleveland General to the chiefly title of *Deyotowe'hgǫ*. On another occasion, the Six Nations Mutual Aid and Singing Society (comprised of Lower Cayuga, Onondaga, and Seneca Longhouse male and female ritual singers) came to our home to practice.

We were welcomed at Onondaga, Seneca, and Sour Springs Longhouses; and participated for two years with the members in their ceremonial cycle, rites for the dead, personal and lineage medicine rites, condolence and installation ceremonies, and the preaching of the *Gaiwhio*. There was some disagreement among the faithkeepers at Lower Cayuga Longhouse at that time as to whether a white man and woman should be admitted, so respecting the sacred nature of their desire for privacy, we did not participate with this group, except for Merlin's attendance at a *Gaiwhio* convention. Nevertheless, members of this ritual group were cordial and friendly in day-to-day contact. We were quite astonished and gratified one afternoon, in November 1957, while visiting with Edward Johnson (the Lower Cayuga faithkeeper who had earlier been most opposed to our entry), when he remarked amiably that he had not seen us at an *O'hgiwe* feast recently held for a Lower Cayuga member; nor had he seen us at *Hǫnahidos* held at Lower Cayuga Longhouse the day before. It was apparent that he no longer objected to our participation in activities at Lower Cayuga.

It occurs to me now, as I read our journals from this time, that Edward Johnson's response was characteristic of a general increase in joviality and warmth extended to us by all our Longhouse friends and acquaintances, dating from the autumn of 1957. To Merlin's surprise and pleasure, Esther Jamieson, head matron of the lineage of Howatsadęho, expressed the desire to give him a name; and on September 29th, the second day of Gakowanę held at Sour Springs Longhouse, she arranged for him to be ceremonially adopted and receive the name Kadiyo (Good Forest) from her lineage set of names. Gilbert Thomas assisted him by singing his adǫwa'h song; and during the four pauses in singing, Merlin spoke the four parts of his ritual prayer in the Cayuga language. Thereafter, as a member of the Big Bear lineage, Oneida Nation, he sat on the Turtle side of the longhouse and next day was one of the players representing his moiety to good advantage in Gayędowanę (the peach pit bowl game).[2] I, and later both of our daughters, received a name from the lineage of Dyǫhyǫgo, Wolf lineage, Cayuga nation, Wolf moiety. As certain Longhouse women say, my husband became "one lonely Turtle among all us Wolves!"

Later, our third and youngest child, Christopher, had the distinction in the family of receiving a name "hung about the neck." On a visit to the reserve when he was five or six years old, while playing with two of Esther's grandsons, we heard him call out, "Let's play cowboys and Indians. You guys be the cowboys, 'cause I'm the Indian!" This was both amusing and pleasing to Esther, and she took a special liking to him. Although he rightfully should have received a name from my lineage, she desired to give him a name "hung about the neck" from her name set, there being precedent for that option.

I characterize this matter in terms of "belonging" simply to illustrate how prevailing Longhouse attitudes of charity and generosity engendered mutual feelings of kinship. Merlin and I both felt, and were treated by Esther and the wider family, as though we did belong. Esther addressed Merlin as "hi-h-ha-waak" (son) in her letters and signed them "kno-ha" (mother); and throughout the remainder of Esther's life Merlin made his contribution to carry out lineage responsibilities in connection with such things as deaths of lineage members. Likewise, when Merlin became ill in 1969, Esther demonstrated her care and concern for him by "putting through" a feast for the dead on his behalf. Even a person whom we had never met (who calls the members of Esther's matrilineage "father's kindred") felt free to contact me several years after Merlin's death for genealogical data and assistance with a ritual matter.

At the beginning of our time at Grand River, one area of concern was apparent wherever we went visiting: we had no children. One day when Esther came to our house to work on some legal aspects of matrilineal descent, she brought with her a potato, which she had Merlin plant in our garden. It had small potatoes growing at each eye instead of the usual sprouts. It was apparent what she had in mind. In due time, I became quite ill and pale, and a number of people came to Merlin asking what was wrong, to which he in turn asked them what they thought might be the problem. Some of them speculated that I was possibly being witched; however, when we learned that I was expecting our first child, word got around about the potato incident and their concern disappeared. We went home to Utah for the birth, and when we returned with our three-month-old baby girl, she was passed from hand-to-hand among the women of each longhouse and was fed and cuddled as if she were their own. Violet (Lickers) Thomas could not get over it. With her characteristic good humor, she asked, "How long did you say you'd been married? Five years? Ga-a-a, it's a pretty good place after all. You've been married all that time, and you had to come way up here to get a baby!"

Prior to our departure for the birth, Longhouse friends from all parts of the reserve came by for farewell visits bringing gifts and good wishes, and a sub-lineage group in the Sour Springs area gave me a baby shower. The members of Seneca Longhouse surprised us with a farewell feast and traditional social dancing (which the members of the Sour Springs Longhouse duplicated later upon our return to the reserve). All the people came in shifts to eat with us; and in our entire time on the reserve, we had never eaten so much corn soup, corn bread, pie, cake, doughnuts, and scones. When the meal was finished and the dancing was over, everyone filed by, the women to hug me, the men to shake hands goodbye. Then we were invited to speak and tell them what we thought of their community and how we had been treated. I thanked them for their hospitality and kindness. Merlin expressed appreciation for their patient willingness to teach him their way of life and pointed out Longhouse practices he felt were valuable for people everywhere to understand and emulate— for example, the way in which the two sides of each longhouse dedicated themselves to serving and caring for one another by performing reciprocal services in the ceremonial cycle, in curing ceremonies, in condolence rites, in carrying out wakes for one another, and in burying each other's dead, as well as participating in recreational activities together. "What a 'Great Peace' could be accomplished," he said, "if the nations of the world could serve each other in a similar way." Finally, two men were appointed to take up a collection in their hats. It came to $28.68, which they brought to us and said, "This is for lunch money on the way home." This gift meant a great deal to us not only because our finances at the time were almost depleted but also because the gift represented a notable sacrifice on their part, given the reservation economy of the 1950s. It was a generous gesture, symbolic of the goodness of their hearts, and much appreciated, for when we drove down Parley's Canyon into Salt Lake City a few days before Christmas 1957, our gas gauge registered empty, and only twenty-five cents remained in my husband's pocket.

Following the trip home, Fred Eggan and the Department of Anthropology at the University of Chicago provided Merlin a research assistantship, from March through May of 1958, which allowed him to do preliminary work with the data and to give lectures on his findings. This afforded him invaluable experience, as well as helping to make the concluding five and one-half months of fieldwork (June through mid-November) financially possible. Also of great value were the lifelong friendships established with Eggan, Ray Fogelson, Sol Tax, and others at the University of Chicago.

Finances are the bane of many, if not most, graduate student fieldworkers. We were no exception. Coming from a farming family of seven children in rural Utah, Merlin had relied on the GI Bill (received from his service as a pilot in World War II) to obtain his Bachelor of Arts degree in political science from Brigham Young University. To further maintain ourselves during graduate studies abroad I taught grade school at the American air base at Lakenheath, and we both taught summer high-school courses to American servicemen at Wimpole Park Hospital Base. Since most postwar anthropological funding had come to an end by the time Merlin entered the discipline, we had to take a working break in order to finance the major part of his fieldwork.[3]

Now, with fieldwork completed, proposals for further funding to analyze and write up the data and for the return to England were unsuccessful. British sources were not interested in research with a North American focus, and American sources were not interested in research based on British methodology. Therefore, Merlin temporarily left his studies in December 1958, working for three years as a carpenter and construction foreman in Utah, to acquire the necessary savings for our return to Cambridge in January 1962. Analyzing and writing up the data took longer than anticipated; but with additional financial help from our families at home, the dissertation, which comprises this publication, was finally completed, and the oral examination passed in London in January 1964, under examiners Darryl Forde and Jack Goody.

The Dissertation

Merlin's original intention was to conduct a structural-functionalist analysis of the politico-jural domain of Longhouse Iroquois society. He soon realized, however, that one could not elucidate the political structure without first examining the corporate structure of the matrilineages, from which hereditary officers are derived and longhouse ritual centers function. Because the household is the generative source of the matrilineage, it was the structure of the household that became the emphasis of the present publication, intended as the groundwork for a later, detailed exposition of the politico-jural system.[4]

It can be said of this study, as Goody (99) says of Fortes's work, that it is an "example of an individual going to the field not with a definite hypothesis as such but with a defined topic, with adequate training, with a series of ideas and with methods of collecting the data he required to examine them." The methods Merlin used in fieldwork include: (1) plotting Longhouse dwellings in relation to other reserve households, as well as schools, churches, longhouses, stores, and so on, to help determine the effect of locality on Longhouse social structure; (2) visiting and helping families at work on fruit farms, as well as interviewing owners of other workplaces off the reserve to assess economic factors in relation to the household; (3) collecting genealogies to learn how social relationships were connected to biological relationships at various levels of the social structure; and (4) compiling a household census covering (a) name, birth date, and birthplace of household head and spouse, and household structure; (b) group affiliation, including lineage, lineage eponym (clan), longhouse, medicine societies, lineage or other offices held; (c) nuclear family of origin and ancestry; (d) personal history; (e) marriage; (f) children; (g) economics, including property ownership, occupations, wells, gardens, pensions, child allowance, and so on.

The data necessary for a structural-functionalist analysis of the household does not lend itself to single-informant inquiry. Even when researching the politico-jural and ritual aspects of matrilineal descent, Merlin had multiple instructors: head matrons of chiefly lineages, hereditary chiefs, and other hereditary and non-hereditary officers. Hereditary officers most helpful in studying and confirming aspects of the politico-jural and ritual systems were hereditary chiefs Alexander General (*Deskahe'h*, Cayuga), Levi Jacobs (*Hǫwatsadǫhǫ*, Oneida), William Johnson (*Gadjinǫdaohe'h*, Cayuga), Joseph Logan Sr. (*Tadodaho*, Onondaga), Joseph Logan Jr. (*Ha'hstawędrota*, Mohawk), Alexander Nanticoke (*Hadyatrǫne'h*, Cayuga), and David Thomas (*Hahihǫ*, Onondaga); *haǫdanǫh*—chief's runner or messenger—Howard Skye (Cayuga); and head matrons, Louisa Key Bomberry (Cayuga), Emily John Curly (Onondaga), Susan Isaacs Fraser (Onondaga), Esther Jacobs Jamieson (Oneida), Margaret Green Johnson (Onondaga) and *kogiwe*—lineage officer in charge of *O'hgiwe* feasts for the dead—Susan Johnson (Cayuga), among others. Ariel Johnson Harris provided invaluable assistance in plotting the residence map, and Lorna Jamieson Thomas Hill spent many hours patiently teaching Merlin the intricacies of the Cayuga Language.

Besides English (which was spoken by all but a few elderly Longhouse people), Cayuga, Onondaga, and Mohawk were the principal Iroquoian languages spoken on the reservation at the time of fieldwork. Since Cayuga was commonly understood in the Longhouse households of the various nations represented in this study, fieldwork was carried out in a kind of hybrid English and Cayuga.[5]

During the Albany period, W. N. Fenton introduced Merlin to Iroquoian linguist Floyd Lounsbury, who gave him instruction in a Cayuga phonetic orthography and advised him to glean lexical content of the language from the people themselves rather than rely on a Cayuga dictionary available in the early 1950s. This instruction was not intended to prepare Merlin for rigorous structural linguistic analysis, but it was well suited to his objective, which was to derive the meaning of language from social context. It was also sufficient to highlight variations among Cayuga-speaking persons on the reserve. There was variety in pronunciation from Upper Cayuga to Lower Cayuga speakers and from person to person within the two areas—a strong Onondaga influence "down below," and a Mohawk influence "up above." Intermarriage among these groups was so pervasive that speakers of each of the three principal languages lived in both vicinities and attended each of the four longhouses. For these reasons, Merlin quite frequently listed two or three phonetic spellings for the same word; and when he finally settled on a single spelling, regardless of pronunciation, the decision was purely arbitrary.

Occasionally, there was also variation in meanings, as noted in the glossary. Terms such as *agadǫni, keyadawę, he'hyadawę, agadǫnihonǫ*, and *sahǫwędrǫhʌs* held meanings for many elders of Longhouse society that were unknown to younger people. The elders remembered institutionalized social events from their childhood in connection with these terms; whereas for younger people they have been recontextualized, taking on related but, to varying degrees, different meanings.

Regarding the orthography used in this publication, I have turned to three sources: Merlin's initial Cayuga teacher, Lorna Hill; a team of Six Nations linguists and teachers involved in the Iroquois language-immersion programs on the reserve; and the recently published *English-Cayuga/Cayuga-English Dictionary* (2002).[6] I have outlined in an introduction to the glossary the way in which I have employed each of these sources.

An effort has been made in this publication to render the case data anonymous, sometimes with the use of randomly selected pseudonyms, sometimes with no reference to names at all; therefore, a wide range of persons may be read into many of the cases included, making accurate identification unlikely. This has been done in an effort to honor the concerns and wishes of several participants.

Although many years have passed since this material was written, Merlin elected to retain the use of the present tense in much of the exposition as an ethnographic present, referring to conditions that pertained at the time of fieldwork. This style has been adhered to, except where further clarity seemed necessary.

This monograph is the study of a single sociological problem, the household structure of Longhouse Iroquois living on the Six Nations Reserve in Ontario, Canada, (1956–58) and is based on original field research; however, where reference to other works has been necessary or desirable, acknowledgement has been made at the place in the text where the reference occurs. A number of these acknowledgements refer to works of British social anthropologists Meyer Fortes and A. R. Radcliffe-Brown (largely unfamiliar names in Native American studies), because a number of their methods and theories are explored throughout this study. Very few studies of North American Indians have been carried out by ethnographers trained in the British structural-functionalist tradition, and Merlin's work is the only example of this perspective applied to the Iroquois. With this in mind, it will be useful in the remainder of this introduction to discuss some of the differences between a structural-functionalist perspective and those American approaches utilized in most Iroquoianist anthropology, highlighting these differences with examples drawn from several prominent American Iroquoianists and from Merlin's fieldwork.[7]

Approaches to Iroquois Studies
Background and Central Concepts

Any attempt to compare and contrast British and American anthropological perspectives should acknowledge several important facts. First, these categories are largely conventional. Even a cursory analysis reveals that neither school fits comfortably within this dichotomy, resting as it does on assumptions and implications situated within nationalist discourses and narrow, even polemical, histories. Second, these conventions often obscure the considerable theoretical and methodological tensions and variations *within* each "tradition."[8] Finally, the degree to which "national" anthropologies penetrate or cross-fertilize one another is too often overlooked.[9]

That said, it would nonetheless be helpful to maintain the dichotomy to some extent, in order to familiarize the reader with the assumptions that inform Merlin's methods, objectives, and theoretical concepts that appear in this monograph vis-à-vis those that inform the anthropology of several prominent Iroquoianists.

American anthropology is primarily concerned with the concept of culture, while British concerns often focus on society or social structure and social relations. American Iroquoianist W. N. Fenton (Speck 1995, ix) describes *culture* as "a seamless web of activities. Officials, foods, musical instruments, and other ritual props that pertain to particular ceremonies, or are shared by many, belong together and comprise conceptual units." A. L. Kroeber (1948, 8) defines culture as "the mass of learned and transmitted motor reactions, habits, techniques, ideas and values—and the behavior they induce." These are only two definitions among many of a highly contested yet central concept in American anthropology. In addition to the central importance of culture to their work, American anthropological studies of the Iroquois during the twentieth century seem to utilize a Boasian perspective. This approach is primarily diachronic. It seeks to *describe* individual phenomena in meticulous detail and is not particularly interested in any universal behavioral laws such descriptions may reveal. Rather, the focus is on the phenomenon for its own sake, its own internal nuances, not its place in a larger network or system of relations. This approach favors inductive over deductive methods (Stocking 1989, 1–20). Monographs from this perspective are often concerned with tracing "traits," "themes," and usages over time, to establish the roots of a cultural item or trace its diffusion through cultural contact. One other important characteristic of these Iroquoianists is that when the terms *structure* and *function* appear in their work, *structure* typically refers to a description of some item of *culture*, while *function* refers to the general use made of that particular item.

In contrast, the methods of British structural-functionalism at Cambridge were set in the frame of *social structure* rather than that of *culture*.[10] Meyer Fortes (1978, 23) expressed the analytical distinction between the two when he defined *culture* as "the totality of the customary resources available to a community for the management of its existence" and then explained that "the most distinctive rule of empirical field research and theory building in the framework of the structural-functionalist method . . . is the necessity of envisaging every happening, every activity, intellectual, affective, social, or physical of individuals or groups, in the context of the *social relations* in which it occurred." Structural-functionalist studies evidence particular characteristics based on these methods and objectives. Monographs are tightly focused on single topics such as kinship, economics, law, politics or ritual and tend to emphasize a synchronic rather than historical orientation. This perspective seeks to explain phenomena in terms of universal social norms, rules, and regularities. It is fundamentally concerned with human behavior at the level of society and is often characterized as a deductive science. The objective, according to A. R. Radcliffe-Brown, "was to formulate generalizations about the common features of all human societies" (Kuper 1997, 51) based on empirical evidence, in order to arrive at social laws that would have the same validity as the natural laws of science (Fortes 1978, 10–11). When the terms *structure* and *function* appear in the text of British monographs, *structure* refers to "an arrangement of 'parts' brought about by the operation through a period of time of principles of social organization which have general validity in a particular society" (Fortes 1949, 83). *Function* refers to the "performance by the 'parts' of particular tasks which are necessary for the maintenance of the form" (Radcliffe-Brown in Kuper 1997, 52).

Perhaps it is best now to position the conventions "British anthropology" and "American anthropology" in the background of this discussion, focusing instead on particular individuals and their work, not merely as examples of one perspective or the other but also as unique scholars, often in dialogue, as well as tension, with one another, who draw to varying degrees from the basic assumptions of a particular tradition.

With this in mind, a comparison of Merlin's methods, analyses, and conclusions with those of several prominent American Iroquoianists will further illuminate the contribution of his monograph to Iroquoian studies.

Political-Jural Aspects of Iroquois Society and
the Four-level Segmentary System of Social Organization

American ethnographer Frank G. Speck, in his work *Midwinter Rites of the Cayuga Long House* (1995), exemplifies some of the early ideals of American cultural anthropology and is concerned with "Cayuga cultural history, approached through the treatment of religious rites of the Sour Springs Long House" at Six

Nations Reserve (1995, i). Speck avoids what he calls "ornate embellishments of theory" and avowedly does not elaborate on psychological implications or implications of historical change (5). His aim is simply to describe "the raw material" (5), and his method is to work "intensively with a single informant, coupling the interviews with observation of 'the doings' . . ." (viii). The bulk of his text is given to detailed descriptions of the following items of culture: the hierarchy of spirit forces, the sacred rites of the annual ceremonial cycle, ceremonial officiants, foods, instruments, and costumes, the midwinter ceremony, medicine societies and their rites, social dances, and the family condolence rite of the Sour Springs Band.

Three points of comparison between Speck's and Merlin's findings occur at the levels of social organization of the longhouse and the "sides" or moiety divisions within each longhouse. First, at the level of the longhouse, Speck simply records the fact that each longhouse is represented by a band of wampum (19). In contrast, Merlin identifies these bands, in their theoretical context, as the corporate property of each longhouse group, symbolic of the corporate identity of each. Second, in connection with the level of the sides, Speck notes eponyms, officers, and custody of ceremonial property (20–28), but does not provide a jural context to show their interrelation. Merlin, on the other hand, recognizes the politico-jural aspect of the sides as corporate bodies. The eponyms, corps of officers, and ritual paraphernalia constitute the corporate estates of these bodies. Third, also at the level of the sides in the Midwinter rites bowl game, Speck describes the paired stakes, suggesting that they symbolize the principles of sacrifice and blessing (142–143), whereas Merlin, emphasizing the structural context, concludes that they are "a ritual gift exchange by which the two sides renew their standing, 'contractual' relationship for reciprocal services" (chapter 5).

Speck views his purpose as the "first stage of systematic investigation—the recording of observations and facts" (5). In this endeavor he generally avoids subjecting the data to close analysis or theory. Rather, he either simply describes it (sometimes including stories of origin), or he classifies phenomena hierarchically (as in the case of controlling spirit forces) or groups ceremonial acts in tables by time (of year), duration, purpose, and composition, as in the case of the annual ceremonial cycle (ix). His objective is to produce a study that will serve as a foundation for future ethnographers to build upon.

Merlin's purpose, on the other hand, is to closely analyze and theorize about his data; and crucial to this concern is the question of what constitutes the units of social organization. He identifies four segments above the level of the household: the sublineage, the lineage, the sides or moieties of the longhouse, and the longhouse itself. Having identified this basic social structure, he turns to what constitutes the underlying basis of these segments. Here Merlin employs Meyer Fortes's paradigm of the "corporate lineage" (1978, 12–13; 1969, 304). This concept identifies the lineage as a corporate descent group; that is, a body politic formed and authorized by law to act as a single person and endowed by law with the capacity of succession. The lineage, as this "perpetual juristic person," comprises one segment of an overall segmentary system, and other segments of the system may also be corporate in nature. After examining the four segments of Iroquois society, Merlin concludes that all but the sublineage have properties of a corporate group.[11] In the comparative examples given here, at the levels of the sides and longhouse, such items as wampum, eponyms, corps of officers, ritual paraphernalia, and so on, constitute part of the corporate estates of these two groups.

Iroquois Naming Practices: Framework and Functions

Another example of an American approach to Iroquois studies is Annemarie Shimony's *Conservatism among the Iroquois at the Six Nations Reserve* (1994). This work is significant for comparison because, among other reasons, the fieldwork for both her study and Merlin's was done among the same group of people during approximately the same period of time. Shimony's primary concern was to identify the "means by which so much of Iroquois culture [had been] preserved at Six Nations in spite of intense acculturative pressure" (xi). Her methods include informant interviews and attendance at all but one event in the ceremonial cycle, as well as attendance at most of the curing rites described (xi). The subject matter of her text is devoted to thorough descriptions of the structure of the orthodox Longhouse community (including the social organization, Longhouse membership and organization, Longhouse functionaries, and the hereditary chiefs) and the content of the orthodox culture (including longhouse ceremonials, the orthodox life cycle, and a consideration of medicine and witchcraft).[12]

One point of comparison between Shimony's and Merlin's findings concerns Iroquois naming practices. Shimony looks at this phenomenon in the context of the life cycle of the Longhouse individual. With this focus on the individual she describes almost all aspects of naming, such as citizenship, official status, ritual, and medicinal importance, and so on. She does not, however, identify either the contextual framework in which names function or the jural rights and obligations that are associated with them. For instance, the jural aspect of the names regarding rights in *genetricem*, which accrue to the matrilineage, is entirely overlooked.

In contrast, Merlin looks at name sets in the context of the social relations and structure of Longhouse society and thereby is able to distinguish their jural aspect. Focusing on the social group rather than the individual, he perceives that the name sets are one of the constituent elements of the unit of social organization called the matrilineage, which is a corporate entity (as described above). They are part of the corporate estate of this lineage, having perpetuity in time and partaking of the nature of *corporation sole*; that is, a legal entity composed of a single person and his successors, being the incumbents of a particular office, or in this case of a particular name (Black 1968, 410). The names function to define citizenship in Iroquois Longhouse society, rights in *genetricem* of lineage female members, and to delineate all offices within the lineage, as well as being central to the physical, social, and psychological well-being of its members. As a result, they also function to help maintain the entire social system. For lineage offices that are traditionally known to be named, these names also have perpetuity in time; and even where some names have been "lost," the "offices themselves continue on as part of the corporate estate of the possessing lineages" (chapter 5).

Lineage and Clan: Clarifying an Essential Feature of Social Organization

Another contrast between Merlin's findings and Shimony's appears in the way each is used to address the distinction between the terms *clan* and *lineage*. Many American Iroquoianists use *lineage* and *clan* interchangeably when elaborating Iroquois social organization, thereby obscuring the fact that the two are entirely different and that for the Iroquois *lineage* is preeminent. This misunderstanding of the nature of Iroquois social organization has led to errors in American Iroquoianist academic findings (including Shimony's) as well as confusion in certain Longhouse communities. Merlin's use of a model of social organization based on corporate groups identifies the underlying locus of confusion and a means of clarification.

Before comparing Shimony's and Merlin's approaches to this matter, it will be necessary to draw a clear distinction between *lineage* and *clan*. A *lineage* is defined as a descent group having a *known* common ancestor (Fox 1996, 49). In the case of the Iroquois, it is an actual, matrilineal, corporate descent group whose common ancestress is known. Whether the depth of the matrilineage is only one person or several generations, this is a unit of Longhouse social organization in which social structure and function can be seen and empirically demonstrated. It is the matrilineage (in the case of chiefly lineages) that is the corporate group possessing a corporate estate of name sets, *otgǫa'h* (wampum), an eponym, hereditary offices, lineage charms, and medicine rites, that has responsibilities toward lineage dead, and whose elders (men and women) meet in council.[13] Non-chiefly lineages are organized on the same model, looking to their oldest woman as *kogiwe* in charge of responsibilities toward lineage dead, having lineage charms and medicine rites, possibly lineage names, and sometimes claiming the ritual offices of faithkeepers.

Merlin found that it is the corporate Iroquois *matrilineage* that has perpetuity in time, not the clan, as Fenton suggests (1998, 27). In the case of a chiefly matrilineage, if lineage personnel die out, it retains its corporate functions and estate and is replenished with new personnel, either in the form of a flourishing non-chiefly lineage group or in the form of a sublineage segment of an existing chiefly lineage. In the latter case, the "mother lineage," so to speak, simply continues on as a corporate lineage holding one chiefly title; while its previous sublineage is established as another corporate lineage holding another chiefly title (Myers Journal 1h, 30–31).

A *clan* is defined as a social unit "often consisting of several lineages whose common descent is *assumed* but cannot necessarily be demonstrated" (Fox 1996, 49). That is, *clan* is an imagined connection linking two or more lineages that have a common eponym.[14] Based on this shared eponym, these different, individual lineages assume they have a common, single point of origin in an ancestor in the distant (forgotten) past. The members do not know precisely *how* (or even *if*) they are related.

Evidence used by early American ethnographers in constructing the concept of the Iroquois clan derives in part from the legend that chief titles of the ancient League were placed in extended families or matrilineages that were identified by particular eponyms (animal, bird, etc.) and that, since those ancient eponyms survive today alongside the chief titles, they point to the existence of another, higher level of social organization—the clan (Fenton 1998, 25–27). However, both chief titles and eponyms were (in legend) and are now part of the corporate estate of single *matrilineages*, not clans; and some of the eponyms connected to certain chief titles have correspondingly changed along with necessary changes in *lineage* personnel (Shimony 1994, 107, 112, 115, 116).

The fact that moiety seating in the longhouse is ordered according to an eponymous arrangement has also been deemed by ethnographers as evidence pointing to the existence of clans; however, it is *lineage* eponyms that have formed the basis of moiety seating in the longhouse, both on the level of group assembly and the naming of the sides. Individuals who have no organized matrilineage to determine their seating (such as wives from other reserves or children of non-Iroquois mothers) may arbitrarily, with no prescribed rule, decide to sit on a spouse's or father's side of the longhouse and thereafter identify themselves with the eponym of that particular side or the eponym of the spouse's or father's matrilineage.

The concept of "clan" was first applied to the Iroquois by early American ethnographers, including Lewis Henry Morgan and A. A. Goldenweiser, who were categorizing the units of Longhouse social organization in an historical frame. Morgan was the first to cast the Iroquois *lineage* in the mold of the Greco-Roman *gens* or Gaelic *clann* (Morgan 2000, 62–68), which was not the best fit (Fox 1996, 49–50). Morgan rightly states that the Greco-Roman *gens* was comprised of several lineages, each of which could trace its individual genealogy back to a known ancestor, but collectively were allied through an assumed common ancestor or shared eponym. This alliance, or *gens*, had considerable social and political power, rights, privileges, and obligations (Morgan 1997; 2000). However, in the literature on Iroquois social organization produced by Morgan and subsequent ethnographers, there is little if any concrete evidence supporting the claim that the Iroquois clan *ever* had the same kind of social function seen in the Greco-Roman *gens*. Merlin's findings in 1956–58, in fact, provided considerable evidence to the contrary, since for the Iroquois it is the single matrilineage with a known common ancestress that possesses these rights, privileges, and obligations.

Fenton (1998, 26), referencing Goldenweiser and utilizing Morgan's concept of the *gens*, which he calls *clan*, adds to the general confusion when he states: "These lineages, which later formed the segments of clans [Morgan's *gens*] with which they shared their functions, were the building blocks of the social system." Two claims made in this statement are misleading. The first characterizes Iroquois lineages as "building blocks" (units of a lower order, presumably possessing less social power and status) that later became segments of clans (units of a higher order, possessing greater social power and status), mirroring the Greco-Roman *gens*. However, it is impossible to show this "evolutionary" order for the Iroquois. Early literature on this topic (first published by Morgan in 1870 and 1877) is largely speculative, relying on the assumption that at the peak of its complexity the Iroquois system of social organization matched that of the Greco-Roman tradition. It is problematic to assume, without considerable empirical evidence, that the Iroquois system, *rather than possessing its own unique structural organization*, so closely resembled that of the Greeks and Romans.

The second misleading claim is the assumption that lineages "share" their functions with clans. It may be assumed that lineage and clan share *personnel*, because of the assumed genealogical connection between the two. However, rights, duties, and functions pertaining to the politico-jural domain are not shared. According to Merlin's analysis, Longhouse Iroquois society is a segmentary system of corporate groups based on matrilineal descent, each corporate segment being vested (or endowed) with exclusive jural rights, duties, and functions. Single Iroquois *matrilineages*, past and present, are vested with such rights, duties, and functions. Iroquois *clans* are not. It appears that these American Iroquoianists produced an unnecessary category of social organization for Longhouse society, ascribing the same functions, power, and privileges to both the single lineage and the clan.

The clan does not appear in Merlin's model of social organization featuring the four orders of segmentation above the household of sublineage, matrilineage, "sides" or moieties of the longhouse ritual group, and the longhouse ritual group itself. One reason for this is that what Fenton and other ethnographers call *clan* is not a demonstrable corporate group having social power; nor is it a noncorporate group, such as the sublineage, having moral and educational influence on the household. However, the primary reason clan does not appear in Merlin's model is that Longhouse people, themselves, gave evidence that the unit they had been taught to call *clan* was in reality their individual *matrilineage* descended from a single known ancestress; which, according to oral tradition, was the unit originally endowed with (or affirmed as having) social power by *Deganawida* himself. This became clear to Merlin both in conversation and in studying their genealogical charts with them in connection with rights, duties, and functions of persons and groups.

In one instance, both the confusion between lineage and clan and its source became evident. David Thomas (Onondaga hereditary chief Hahihǫ, who also preached the *Gaiwhio* on circuit) quite often turned to the topic of confusion existing between *clan* and *family* (which he identified as an extended family or a single matrilineage).[15] Over and over again, he would say, "One *gawhadjiia* (family), one clan; one *hoyane'h* (chief), one clan; one *goyane'h* (head matron), one clan" (Myers Journal 1h, 30–31). He was saying, in effect, that since there is only one lineage per so-called clan, and this unit possesses one chief and one head matron, then *lineage* and *clan* are one and the same unit.

It was a troubling issue for Chief Thomas, because of practices he had witnessed at St. Regis. He explained that in this community the Longhouse people were trying to reestablish their old system and "get the chief titles working the way they should." However, to accomplish this they were reading descriptions of their social organization produced by non-Iroquois ethnographers, who proposed that the Mohawks had three clans, each possessing three chief titles. In keeping with this information, three head matrons had been established representing the three clans, and three chief titles had been assigned to each matron. "This is all wrong," he said. "Each clan mother has one chief title and no more: one 'clan mother,' one chief; one family, one chief." Again, he stressed that one *goyane'h* (the so-called clan mother) and one *hoyane'h* (chief) belong to one *gawhadjiia* (family or matrilineage). In this case, there should have been nine *godiyanesǫ* from nine different families (or lineages) each choosing a single *hoyane'h* (chief). He felt that since the ethnographic literature had not clarified this, the St. Regis community was confused (Myers Journal 1e, 69–70). He also cited a similar problem at Syracuse.

Shimony, in contrast to Merlin's segmentary model, uses a modification of Goldenweiser's vertical segmentary model for the exposition of data on Longhouse social organization. Her model features nuclear family, extended family, father's kindred, lineage, clan, moiety, tribe, and League (20–21). One of her objectives is to show how and why confusion has developed concerning "delineation, function, and linguistic identification" in connection with units such as lineage, clan, phratry, and moiety (21). In this endeavor, with respect to the clan and lineage, she attributes changes in each of these to factors such as: (1) transfers of function (such as adoption being transferred from extended family *and* clan to nuclear family [24, emphasis added] and citizenship being transferred from the clan to the father in the nuclear family by the Canadian government [23]); (2) a breakdown in passing on clan and lineage affiliation to children (27); (3) some lineages dying out (27); (4) some immigrants establishing new lineages or claiming connection to chiefly lineages (28); (5) flexible or weakening sanctions for moiety seating of clans (21); and (6) depletion of clans (28).

Throughout her enumeration of these insightful reasons, however, there is never a clear structural or functional distinction made between lineage and clan. To the contrary, confusion persists. Consider the following statements:

At present, however, the lineage is an important social unit, *since a chief is chosen from a matrilineage*" (27, emphasis added).

Some attributes of the clan nevertheless remain intact, for the clans are named units, *they determine the seating with the appropriate moiety, they own sets of names, and they have chiefs associated with them*" (34, emphasis added).

These two statements taken together are unsettling when it is clearly demonstrated that not only is it single *matrilineages* rather than *clans* that possess chief titles but it is also single matrilineages rather than clans that are the eponymous units that determine seating with the appropriate moiety and have their own sets of names.

A further example of this problematic issue is found in Shimony's discussion of how modern "clan functions" have changed from those recorded earlier by Goldenweiser, in 1914, and by Morgan, in 1877. Since Shimony highlights Morgan, I show here only his list of ten rights, duties, and privileges of the Iroquois descent group he calls the *gens*.[16] Morgan equates *gens* with *clan* terminologically, but his *gens* of the 1800s mirrors the Six Nations single *matrilineage* of the 1950s, with only two modifications. The list reads as follows:

1. The right of electing its sachem and chiefs.
2. The right of deposing its sachem and chiefs.
3. The obligation not to marry in the *gens*.
4. Mutual rights of inheritance of the property of deceased members.
5. Reciprocal obligations of help, defense, and redress of injuries.
6. The right of bestowing names upon its members.
7. The right of adopting strangers into the *gens*.
8. Common religious rites, query [sic].
9. A common burial place.
10. A council of the *gens*.

Shimony, in conformity with both Morgan's and Goldenweiser's assumptions, equates *gens* with clan. Addressing the issue of the loss of "clan function" over time, she states (30) that of the ten items on the list, "only the first, second, and sixth functions still belong to the clan, *and the first and second are strictly not so much clan as lineage characteristics*" (emphasis added). From this point of view, she perceives the *gens* or clan to have suffered severe losses in function since 1877. However, as we have seen, only a lineage (not a clan) can be characterized as being a corporate group whose structure and function can be seen and empirically demonstrated as possessing the politico-jural rights, duties, and functions listed. This confusion on her part can be better understood if one recognizes the problem inherent in trying to map Gaelic or Greco-Roman practices, terms, and concepts directly onto an Iroquois practice that possesses its own unique system of social organization.

In contrast to Shimony's use of Morgan's list, Merlin references the section from *Ancient Society*, in which the list appears, with this footnote: "*This [the single Iroquois matrilineage] is the unit Morgan designates by the term 'gens'*" (emphasis added). Merlin equates *gens* with individual *lineage* rather than with *clan*, because he recognizes the rights, duties, and privileges of the *gens* to be those of the corporate matrilineage in the Longhouse segmentary system. Looking at the list from this point of view, the percentages are reversed; all but numbers five and nine were still functioning in 1958.[17] Merlin's model demonstrates that the lineages were still viable and strong after eighty-one years of further acculturation.

It appears, then, that the problem of distinguishing lineage from clan is not, as Shimony suggests, because almost all "clan" functions have been "lost" or transferred to longhouse or lineage since 1877. Rather, the problem appears to arise from the fact that the lineage, having always possessed its estate and functions, has been inaccurately portrayed by early ethnographers as "sharing" its identity with (or ascribing its identity to) the concept of a clan.

In summary, *lineage* and *clan* are, by definition, distinct from one another. A *lineage* is a descent group having a known common ancestor. At Six Nations it is the corporate seat of the politico-jural domain and possesses social power emanating from its corporate estate and functions, which can be seen and empirically demonstrated. The ethnographic process of the American perspective, however, has revealed neither the corporate nature of Iroquois matrilineages nor their corporate estates and politico-jural functions. A *clan* is a largely informal collective, in which common ancestry is *assumed* rather than known. At Six Nations it is not a corporate group having a corporate estate or functions that can be seen or demonstrated. Merlin's segmentary model avoids confusing comparisons and indicates that the level of social organization called the "clan," although applicable to Greco-Roman and Gaelic societies, likely had little efficacy in the past and certainly has no major observable political, economic, ritual, or moral function in present Iroquois society.

The Sublineage: Mapping the Subtleties of Household Organization

Merlin's segmentary model establishes another point of contrast with Shimony's work at the level of the sublineage. In his attempt to discover the relative weight of paternity and matrilineal descent within the household,

Merlin turns to Fortes's theoretical concept of the "developmental cycle of the domestic group," which is useful in understanding what happens to the structure of the household over time. Applying this concept to Longhouse Iroquois household structure, Merlin identifies the presence of the sublineage. It does not have the characteristics of a corporate group, but as "a kind of domestic subdivision of the lineage," it serves structurally as an "intercalary unit between the household group and the lineage."

This sublineage may be a three- or four-generational unit consisting of a woman, her daughters, and their children, living in separate households at one stage of the cycle or living in the same household at another stage. Or it may consist of a woman, her daughters, and sister's daughters, and their children, or of several sisters and their daughters and daughters' children, living in various stages of household development, who look to one of the older women as a focus of their group unity (see figures 1 and 2). As a group they mitigate the strength of the conjugal ties of the members, cooperate in economic, domestic, and ritual activities, and serve to support each other and to educate and instill Longhouse values among the children of the group. Shimony (26–27), is only able to observe the household as being "synonymous with the nuclear family." In her view, "the coresident matrilineally extended family does not exist (except in the fortuitous event that adjacent houses and land are divided among daughters only)." She seems unaware of the social complex of the sublineage and its importance to the endurance of Longhouse society.

The "Shadow Lineage": Complementary Filiation and the Problem of the Bilateral Nature of Unilineal Kinship Systems

Another instance for comparison of the American Iroquoianist and structural-functionalist perspectives is found in William N. Fenton's *The Great Law and the Longhouse: A Political History of the Iroquois Confederacy* (1998).[18] In this study Fenton makes reference to the bilateral nature of the Iroquois kinship system, evidenced in kinship terminology and social behavior.[19] (Shimony, too, makes such references, as did Lafitau.[20]) However, Fenton's methods provide only a descriptive approach to this phenomenon. They do not solve the problem of how the Iroquois kinship system could be a *unilineal* descent system and at the same time have *bilateral* characteristics.

Merlin, collecting and studying current and past Iroquois kinship terminology and weighing the respective household influences of matrilineal descent and paternity, found that the Iroquois practices he witnessed bore notable resemblance to a central theoretical concept of the structural-functionalist perspective. This was a theory posited by Meyer Fortes in answer to the dilemma of unilineal descent groups of certain African societies, which also exhibited bilateral characteristics. Fortes noted that besides the principle of the "unity of the lineage" at work in unilineal societies, there was also a web of kinship operating that cut across the descent group. He called this web "complementary filiation." He noted that kinship is always bilateral, even in unilineal descent systems, the descent group (matrilineage among the Iroquois) being defined by politico-jural imperatives, and the complementary group (paternal kin among the Iroquois) being defined by amity and moral norms and usages (Fortes 1978, 15; Kuper 1997, 167–8; Fox 1996, 133).

Observing this principle in action in Longhouse society, Merlin applied the principle of complementary filiation to an analysis of the Iroquois kinship term *agadǫnihonǫ* (literally, father's sister's people). Whether this term is perceived as inclusive of only ego's father's matrilineage or father's bilateral kindred (Fenton 1998, 32; Shimony 1994, 21), the theoretical conclusion remains the same: "One is linked with, but never becomes a member of a corporate group within Longhouse society on the basis of paternal kinship, and this is the essential difference between kinship through the father and that through the mother" (chapter 6). Although this "linking" with a Longhouse person's paternal kin does not give him descent status (that is, it is not of a politico-jural nature), it is significant to him in its complementary, moral, and interpersonal nature (Fox, 231–32). University of Chicago anthropologist Fred Eggan (1975, 319–20), saw the value of the theoretical articulation of this distinction, which Merlin calls a "shadow lineage," when he stated that Merlin's identification of the Iroquois practice of complementary filiation with the father cleared up some of his own questions regarding the balanced bilateral character of the Iroquois system of terminology, which exists within their matrilineal descent system:

> I once wrote that Morgan's view of kinship was forever complicated by the fact that the Iroquois system of terminology, with its balanced bilateral character did not rest conformably on a matrilineal clan system, as he supposed. Myers clears this up in part by showing that Iroquois kinship terminology . . . is built up not only on the basis on matrilineal descent, but in addition, on the complementary recognition of filiation with the father.

To date there seems to be no better theoretical portrayal of the bilateral character of the Iroquois kinship system than Merlin's application of the concept of complementary filiation.

The analytical method formulated by Fortes (1969, 308–09) and applied here by Merlin is based on the premise that in the social structure of every society there is a distinguishable, irreducible dichotomy, which is manifested in a particular balance of social relations in any specific society at a given time and place. The aspects of this dichotomy are characterized by Fortes as polarizations between moral order and legal order, institutions and norms, kinship and polity, or familial domain and politico-jural domain, depending on the emphasis under consideration. Merlin's analysis of complementary filiation versus matrilineal descent illustrates the particular balance between the familial domain and political-jural domain, as these affected the households of Six Nations Iroquois society in 1958.

As Fortes points out, this analytical method is not designed to reveal historical origins or underlying cause and effect. However, it may be used to illustrate social structural balance in both modern and earlier times when applied to the Iroquois kinship terms *agadǫni*, *keyadawę*, and *he'hyadawę*, associated with the term *agadǫnihonǫ* (father's sister's people).[21] On the interpersonal level, in 1958, affective practices connected to all four of these terms demonstrated bonds of amity characteristic of complementary filiation. These were balanced against practices connected to kinship terms demonstrating jural bonds characteristic of matrilineal descent (see chapters 5 and 6).

Two examples from Fenton's *The Great Law and the Longhouse*, examined in the light of Merlin's findings, illustrate this structural balance in earlier times. First, Merlin's findings provide an alternative to Fenton's assessment of the "*agadoni/kheya'tawenh*" relationship at the level of Iroquois League moiety division. Fenton (1998, 27–28) characterizes the Three Brothers moiety as the symbolic male principle of nature represented in the kinship term "*agadoni*," which he interprets as "sires." He characterizes the Two Brothers moiety (often called Four Brothers since the Cayuga adoption of the Tuscarora and Delaware) as the female principle of nature represented in the term "*kheya'tawenh*," which he interprets as "offspring" or "nephews." However, other interpretations given to Merlin by elders of the Longhouse community reveal that *agadǫni* and *keyadawę* are female terms: *agadǫni* being father's sister (to state it simply) and *keyadawę* being the reciprocal term that *agadǫni* uses for her brother's daughter.[22] *Agadǫni* does not call her brother's son *keyadawę* but rather *he'hyadawę*, using the male prefix. Yet it is the two terminological females, *agadǫni* and keyadawę, who symbolize the moieties forming Deganawida's League of the Iroquois. The ascendant politico-jural influence of matrilineal descent is seen here, at the level of the League in ancient times, in the use of female terms to symbolize the two groups of male officers (hereditary chiefs) who have a reciprocal politico-ritual relationship with one another. However, balance is achieved, since these are female terms associated with complementary filiation (agadǫni, father's sister, and keyadawę, brother's daughter) rather than terms associated with matrilineal descent (knohaʌ, mother's sister, and kehawakʌ, sister's daughter). This is not only a matter of gender balance but also of the basic societal balance between kinship (filiation with the father) and polity (matrilineal descent).

Second, Merlin's insights into the agadǫni/he'hyadawę relationship help clarify contradictions concerning the structure and directionality of this relationship and misleading implications regarding the range of legal authority held by lineage matrons found in Fenton's discussion of the practice of "mourning-wars." Mourning-wars, which influenced societal balance in earlier times, were raiding parties undertaken to replenish Iroquois extended matrilineal households or lineages, which had been reduced in population by warfare, disease, and other causes (Richter 1983, 530–31). An extended matrilineal household or lodge contained sons whose fathers were married to women of the household. According to Lafitau, each of these sons had a mourning-war obligation to his father's matrilineal lodge to obtain captives to replace his father's deceased lineage members.[23] The head matron of the father's lodge (possibly his sister) could require her brother's son to go to war to capture such a replacement. Fenton (1998, 28), quoting Lafitau, states that "a father's sister held her brother's son under special obligations to replace losses in her family." However, as Fenton (32) continues he contradicts the relationship described in his first statement: "Since manpower was their only asset, the loss of a single person created the demand for his replacement, which entailed an obligation not of his household or lineage but of the agadoni (persons related to him as father's kin). The obligation extended to their offspring, who were thus duty bound to their father's lodge, to which they were strangers."

What Fenton claims here, in effect, is that a replacement for the deceased must be obtained by one of his father's sister's sons. According to Merlin's findings, however, this is incorrect, since in the mourning-war practice (as described by Lafitau in Fenton's own translation) the obligation to replace the deceased falls not on his father's kin but on his mother's brother's sons. They are each he'hyadawę to the deceased's mother, whom they call agadǫni. The deceased is he'hyadawę to his father's sister and, being deceased, could never perform a mourning-war obligation.

Fenton's contradictory statement is confusing because it reverses the directionality of the mourning-war obligation. Merlin's research, in contrast, supports Lafitau's assertion that this duty lay in one direction only—the direction of complementary filiation. A young warrior was morally obligated to replace the deceased son (or other lineage member) of his father's sister, and the warrior's mother's brothers' sons were obligated to replace him should he die. The obligation did not apply in reverse order. Additional comments in Fenton's text concerning the matron's role are likewise confusing, because these various contradictions conceal the matron's true relationship to both the deceased and the warrior who must provide his replacement.

A further critical point of confusion is Fenton's use of the word "agadoni" to mean "father's kin" in general. Although, as noted above, agadǫni may be applied metaphorically to a group, Merlin's research revealed that agadǫni was primarily singular, denoting primarily father's sister, as well as applying individually to other agnatic women specified as father's classificatory sisters (see figures 3 and 4). A son called his father's sister (or classificatory sister) agadǫni, and she in turn called him he'hyadawę. Agadǫnihonǫ (father's sister's people) denoted primarily the father's sister's (likewise, father's) matrilineage and also included the matrilineages of father's classificatory sisters, but at the time of fieldwork was sometimes used to include father's general kindred as well (Myers Journal 1g, 30).

In any case, in this striking example of complementary filiation, the deceased individual is the mediating factor between his mother and his mother's brother's son (who are agadǫni and he'hyadawę to each other). It is he whom his matrilineal lodge mourns and who, in death, exerts a moral influence that reaches beyond his own lineage to other independent lineages or households. The application of the principle of complementary filiation to the custom of mourning-wars highlights the particular balance between the legal order (matrilineal descent) and the moral order (complementary filiation) in seventeenth-century Iroquois society. This brings into clearer perspective a questionable legal implication in the concluding sentence of Fenton's statement on the mourning-war practice (32): "The matron of the lodge of the deceased could *force* persons so related to her to go to war to make up the loss, or she could keep them at home to prevent further losses" (emphasis added).

The word *force* here implies that the matron of the deceased person had legal authority over her brother's son. However, although the matron represented the legal entity of her distressed matrilineage, it is doubtful that she could enforce any kind of legal sanction upon he'hyadawę, her brother's son, who belonged to another completely autonomous matrilineage.

As Richter (532) relates: "[Y]oung men who were related by marriage to the bereaved women but who lived in other longhouses [other lineages] were obliged to form a raiding party or face the matron's accusations of cowardice." Her sanctions of "force," exemplified in this statement, are sanctions of complementary filiation: sanctions of moral expectations, an appeal to right conduct, personal honor, and dignity in order to shame he'hyadawę if he considered disregarding this serious filial norm.

Perhaps it is the very principle of sacrifice involved in the mourning-war relationship that Deganawida chose as a fitting symbol for the degree of loyalty and reciprocity necessary to unify the moieties of the League. In any case, the symbolic kinship terms he applied to the moieties suggest that just as he'hyadawę (brother's son) is morally rather than legally bound to agadǫni (father's sister), so are the keyadawę and agadǫni moieties of the League bound by moral rather than legal imperatives. This further suggests that although the constituent lineages comprising the separate tribes retain their legal autonomy inherent in matrilineal descent, they nevertheless willingly submit to bonds of moral obligation embodied in the agadǫni/he'hyadawę relationship of complementary filiation in order to facilitate League solidarity.[24]

In conclusion, both perspectives have much to offer those interested in the lifeways of the Six Nations Longhouse Iroquois. The American Iroquoianists provide a wealth of carefully catalogued historical data and detailed descriptive analyses of various elements of culture. Merlin's approach reveals many of the structural nuances of Iroquois society and the specific functions of these social features and relationships. Together they provide a solid body of data and analyses that will prove useful to contemporary ethnographers who wish to continue historical or structural inquiry, or even to those who wish to use these findings to engage in the decentering endeavors of current poststructuralist and cultural studies perspectives.[25] Regardless, it is my hope, and I feel confident that it is Merlin's as well, that this publication is useful, first to the Six Nations people themselves, and second to all those involved in the worthy endeavor of First Nations studies.

If I understand correctly the essence of Deganawida's mission to the Iroquois (that is, to denounce war and proclaim peace through the instrumentality of the League of Peace), then I must conclude that my husband and I were privileged to come under the influence of that essence. We were permitted the reciprocal pleasure of making friends and enlarging our family circle, of connecting with Longhouse people on various levels of understanding, of bridging cultural differences in the spirit of mutual good will and respect. Nor did the effect of our experience end with us. Merlin imparted his respect for the Longhouse way of life to his family and to his university students. They, in turn, have imparted it to families and students of their own, and so on for yet another generation. Who can say how far-reaching this essence of the "Great Peace" may extend?

Notes

1. For studies of British anthropological theory and methods see Fortes 1969; Goody 1995; Kuper 1997; and Stocking 1995.

2. Esther Jamieson (head matron for the lineage of Hǫwatsadęhǫ) informed Merlin that their lineage eponym was the Black Bear, rather than the Big Bear usually assigned to their lineage in the literature.

3. One of our good Longhouse friends, Onondaga hereditary chief Freeman Green, had once forthrightly asked Merlin if the Canadian government was paying him to do research on the reserve. Ironically, on another occasion Clifford Styres, chief of the elective council (established by the Canadian government), expressed the council's concern that Merlin might be in the employ of interests that were trying to turn the hereditary chiefs against the government. Merlin's honest reply to both concerns was that he had not come to the reserve to instigate actions of any kind, but rather was merely a student with limited funds, who had come to observe and learn the Longhouse way. He always felt obliged to assist the people with whom he worked, in return for the time and service they gave him, by taking them places in the car, giving them vegetables from our garden, helping them fill out government forms, assisting in wood-cutting and house-raising bees, helping to put new siding on Seneca Longhouse, or expressing his gratitude in whatever way he could. It was reassuring when Joseph Logan Jr. (ritualist and hereditary chief, Ha'hstawędrota) and later Howard Skye (ritualist and hereditary subchief for Deyotowe'hgǫ) each expressed approval of Merlin's interaction with Longhouse people in the spirit of reciprocal service, rather than hire for money.

4. It would have been informative to read the insights emerging from a structural-functionalist study of the politico-jural aspect of Longhouse life; but Merlin, unfortunately, was unable to finish his intended project. However, W. N. Fenton's publication, *The Great Law and the Longhouse: A Political History of the Iroquois Confederacy* (1998), provides a wealth of information on early Iroquois political history. Also in the framework of the American tradition, Annemarie Shimony gives some attention to recent political history and the status of hereditary chiefs at Six Nations (1994, 91–123). Regarding the role of hereditary chiefs in Longhouse ritual matters, both Shimony's and Merlin's data are in agreement; however, their analyses produce different conclusions. Shimony argues that lineage chiefs, having been stripped of political power to govern under the auspices of the Canadian Government, are now making an innovative attempt to establish a legitimate role for themselves in the ritual sector of Longhouse society. Merlin's analysis, on the other hand, indicates that ritual functions concerned with presiding and holding custody have long been an integral part of chiefly office. There is, characteristically, little division between the political and ritual domains in a segmentary, "stateless" society like that of the Iroquois, which historically has been organized on principles of unilineal descent. (Similarly, intrinsic Iroquois politico-jural functions do not necessarily resemble those of a society built on principles of "the state.") Claims made to this effect in 1958 by many

Longhouse people were consistent with these findings. In this context, innovation would appear to arise, not from the chiefs, but rather from certain Longhouse officials from some of the more fragmented families, mainly at Lower Cayuga Longhouse, who (invoking Handsome Lake) initiated changes in keeping with the principle of separation of church and state and contributed to the "breakdown of the matrilineage as the effective basis of ceremonial life" (Myers Journal 1d, 62–63; 1e, 74). Historical events, of course, have necessitated both the emergence and the imposition of a "state" overlay on Longhouse society; however, the fact that underlying governing principles of matrilineal descent were still evident in politico-ritual (and politico-jural) matters in 1958 is quite remarkable.

5. Calculated on matrilineal descent, the heads and spouses of the households studied represented the following groups: 29 percent Cayuga, 20 percent Onondaga, 19 percent Mohawk, 5 percent Oneida, 4 percent Seneca, 3 percent Wyandot adopted by Cayuga, 2 percent Tuscarora, 0.7 percent Delaware, 0.4 percent Shawnee, 0.4 percent white, and 16.5 percent unknown or uncertain.

6. Those interested in Iroquoian language and culture should benefit from the forthcoming Cayuga dictionary by Michael K. Foster, for whom Lorna Hill has been a consultant.

7. While notable ethnographic and ethnohistorical contributions by Native Iroquois scholars like Ely Parker, Arthur Parker, David Cusick, Alexander General, John A. Gibson, Seth Newhouse, and Jacob Thomas, among others, did see publication, most early ethnographers working in this field were non-Iroquois, and their work often received more attention than that of their Iroquois contemporaries. Fortunately, this seems to be changing. A solid and growing body of critical, insightful and provocative literature is coming directly from Iroquois and other First Nations scholars across North America. M. Sam Cronk (one of this new generation of Native scholars) provides more detail on these scholars and their work in the afterword to this volume.

8. In the United States, strong tensions existed between the Washington DC–based Bureau of American Ethnology and Franz Boas and his followers and students (Stocking 1982). Later conflicts arose between many of Boas' students (for example, between Kroeber and Sapir). Others such as Leslie White and Julian Steward, both trained in the Boasian tradition, mounted strong arguments against many of its basic assumptions (Stocking 1989). Benedict, Mead, Sapir, and, later, Clifford Geertz, Marshall Sahlins, and Eric Wolf, among many others, illustrate the considerable variety of voices and orientations in American anthropology. The British tradition has its tensions and variations as well—Leach's critique of Fortes and the assumptions of the structural-functionalist school, for example, as well as the range of perspectives exemplified in Gluckman, Douglas, Reo Fortune, Gregory Bateson, and others.

9. Some examples include Lewis Henry Morgan's influence on perspectives as divergent as those espoused by Marx and Engels, Tylor, or Radcliffe-Brown and the structural-functionalist school, or the considerable impact Franz Boas, and the German philosophical and scientific concerns that he brought to the United States, had in shaping a significant and pervasive chapter in American anthropology. Radcliffe-Brown, Malinowski, and Levi-Strauss—British, Polish, and French nationals respectively—have had far-reaching impacts on both sides of the Atlantic.

10. See Fortes (1969, 11–13) for a comparison of L. H. Morgan's and Sir Henry Maine's influences on British structural theories versus E. B. Tylor's influence on American cultural theories.

11. This is not in the sense of the Weberian model of corporateness, dealing with the administrative order in modern capitalistic business enterprise. For a thorough exposition of various dimensions of corporateness, as these apply to anthropological studies, see Fortes 1969 (especially chapter 14, "Descent and the Corporate Group," 276–310).

12. Shimony (290–92) loosely employs a structural or functional frame of discourse to show how the interconnections of various Longhouse institutions serve to support each other as well as maintain the society as a whole. However, an analysis of the principles involved in the politico-jural determinants of kinship and descent, which are basic to Iroquois social structure, cannot be achieved without a more focused and rigorous application of structural-functionalist methods. Fortes (1969, 309), in fact, has shown that the emergence of institutional patterns themselves largely reflects the balance between matrifiliation and patrifiliation in a given social system. One outcome of Merlin's study reveals how these fundamental elements are balanced in Six Nations Longhouse social structure, as they affect the household.

13. Compare Shimony (34): "Finally, a council of the clan does not meet today . . . and appointments are not made by a democratic assembly of males and females, as Morgan (1877, 85) would have us believe." This refers to Morgan's council of the *gens*, which Merlin recognizes as the corporate Iroquois *matrilineage*, not the clan.

14. There are ten eponyms (sixteen, including possible subdivisions), such as Bear, Wolf, Turtle, and so on, extant on Six Nations Reserve (Shimony, 55–56). When one considers Iroquois adoption practices, population dynamics, as well as the limited number of animal, bird, and reptile eponyms that have been used repeatedly among Iroquois and other Woodland nations, accurate genealogical connections, in many cases of a shared eponym, seem difficult to establish with certainty. At Six Nations the only observable manifestation of clan occurs when persons from different reserves, having the same eponym but no known genealogical connection, treat each other with friendly interest or joke about being related.

15. A corporate Iroquois matrilineage ("family") may be as small as one person or two uterine siblings; or it may be as large as several generations of offspring descending laterally through females from a known ancestress. The term o'hwadjiʌ is applied to this "family," whatever its size, as well as to its perceived, noncorporate component parts, such as extended families or sublineages. Six Nations persons who also applied the term o'hwadjiʌ to the nuclear family almost invariably added that the father did not really belong to the group. This term is not applied to persons or groups who have the same or similar eponym only, who cannot trace their relationship to a known common ancestress (e.g., it does not apply to an assumed "clan" relationship as defined above).

16. Morgan, *Ancient Society*, 71. Also see Fox, *Kinship and Marriage*, 49–50, for explanations of other confusions arising from the use of terms such as *gens*, *clan*, *sib*, and so on.

17. Concerning number 4, although Canadian inheritance rules for the dispersal of *real* property at death has displaced lineage inheritance practices, the single matrilineage, in 1958, still exercised the right to oversee the dispersal of *personal* property of the deceased at the Tenth Day Feast.

18. Merlin comments on the descriptive and historical nature of Fenton's studies, in which he (Fenton) provides detailed accounts of certain ceremonies and feasts or employs what he calls "historical upstreaming," a method that establishes certain "traits," in order to trace origins of cultural items, or establishes "ritual complexes" as guides to reconstitute the past.

19. Fenton (1998) comments on this in several places: "These terms derive from the fireside family, which in essence was bilateral . . ." "Thus the *agadoni/kheya'tawenh* principle had its operating base in the bilateral family and a symbolic projection in the confederacy" (28). "Lafitau is the only writer for centuries afterward to discuss this bilateral relationship" (32n).

20. Shimony (1994): "In fact, however, the group designated by this term [*agadǫnihonǫ*] is the father's bilateral kindred" (21). "The group of persons termed *agado'nih* includes all bilateral relatives related to ego through an initial ascending agnatic link . . ." (31).

21. See kinship charts fig. 3, male ego, and fig. 4, female ego, listing both old and new usages.

22. Among Merlin's instructors who elaborated on these kinship terms were: Libby (Isaacs) Green, Hannah (Isaacs) Jacobs, Levi Jacobs, Esther (Jacobs) Jamieson, Margaret (Green) Johnson, Joseph Logan Sr., Joseph Logan Jr., Emma (Powless) Longboat, Patrick Longboat, Alexander Nanticoke, Howard Skye, and Mabel (Doxtater) Skye.

23. Fenton, *Great Law and the Longhouse*, 32n. "Lafitau wrote: 'the children of these different marriages [by men of other lodges who have marriage links with a particular household] become obligated to their father's lodge, to which they are strangers, and contract the obligation of replacing them [those who are lost] so that the matron who has the principal authority in this household, can force these children to go to war . . . or keep them home.' "

24. Commenting on the genealogical basis of metaphorical kinship words, Fortes (1969, 53) emphasizes that "kinship terms designate not individuals but status relations between persons"; or in this metaphorical usage, status relations between two groups.

25. As Fortes points out (1969, 14), "We must never forget that 'structure' and 'culture' stand for indissociably conjoined frames of analysis in our studies. What matters is how they are mutually balanced in any particular kind of inquiry."

References

Black, Henry Campbell. 1968. *Black's Law Dictionary*. 4th ed. St. Paul MN: West.

Eggan, Fred. 1975. *Essays in Social Anthropology and Ethnography*. The University of Chicago Studies in Anthropology, vol. 1. Chicago: Department of Anthropology. (Chapter titled "Lewis Henry Morgan's Systems: A Reevaluation" is from P. Reiming, ed. 1972. *Kinship Studies in the Morgan Centennial Year*. American Anthropology Society of Washington.)

Fenton, William N. [1949] 1995. Introd. to *Midwinter Rites of the Cayuga Long House*. Repr., Philadelphia: University of Pennsylvania Press.

———. 1998. *The Great Law and the Longhouse: A Political History of the Iroquois Confederacy*. Norman: University of Oklahoma Press.

Fortes, Meyer. 1949. "Time and Social Structure: An Ashanti Case Study." In *Social Structure: Studies Presented to A. R. Radcliffe-Brown*. Oxford: Clarendon Press.

———. 1978. "An Anthropologists' Apprenticeship." In *Annual Review of Anthropology 1978*. Palo Alto CA: Annual Reviews.

———. 1969. *Kinship and the Social Order: The Legacy of Lewis Henry Morgan*. Chicago: Aldine.

Fox, Robin. [1967] 1996. *Kinship and Marriage: An Anthropological Perspective*. Repr., New York: Press Syndicate of the University of Cambridge.

Froman, Frances, Alfred Keye, Lottie Keye, and Carrie Dyck. 2002. *English-Cayuga/Cayuga-English Dictionary*. Toronto: University of Toronto Press.

Goldenweiser, A. A. 1914. "On Iroquois Work, 1912." *Summary Report of the Geological Survey [of Canada]—Department of Mines for the Calendar Year 1912*. Sessional Paper no. 26, Anthropological Division, 464–75. Ottawa: C. H. Parmelee.

Goody, Jack. 1995. *The Expansive Moment: Anthropology in Britain and Africa, 1918–1970*. Cambridge: Cambridge University Press.

Kroeber, A. L. [1923] 1948. *Anthropology*. Rev. ed., New York: Harcourt Brace.

Kuper, Adam. 1997. *Anthropology and Anthropologists: The Modern British School*. New York: Routledge.

Morgan, Lewis Henry. [1877] 2000. *Ancient Society*. Repr., New Brunswick NJ: Transaction Publishers.

———. [1870] 1997. *Systems of Consanguinity and Affinity of the Human Family*. Repr., Lincoln: University of Nebraska Press. (Originally published as vol. 218 of the Smithsonian Institution series: Smithsonian and Contributions to Knowledge.)

Myers, Merlin G. 1956–58. *Journal*. Unpublished fieldwork journals.

Richter, Daniel K. 1983. "War and Culture: The Iroquois Experience." *The William and Mary Quarterly* 11 (4).

Shimony, Annemarie Anrod. [1961] 1994. *Conservatism among the Iroquois at the Six Nations Reserve.* Repr., Syracuse NY: Syracuse University Press. (Originally published as Yale University Publications in Anthropology, no. 65.)

Speck, Frank G. [1949] 1995. *Midwinter Rites of the Cayuga Long House.* Repr., Philadelphia: University of Pennsylvania Press.

Stocking, George W. Jr. 1995. *After Tylor: British Social Anthropology, 1888–1951.* Madison: University of Wisconsin Press.

———., ed. [1974] 1989. *A Franz Boas Reader: The Shaping of American Anthropology, 1883–1911.* Repr., Chicago: University of Chicago Press.

———., ed. [1968] 1982. *Race, Culture, and Evolution: Essays in the History of Anthropology.* Repr., Chicago: University of Chicago Press.

Acknowledgments

Foremost on this list are the people of the Longhouse community with whom we shared so many rich experiences. Among these are Louisa Bomberry, Emily Curly, Susan Fraser, Elizabeth Green, Dorothy Green, Ariel Harris, Esther Henry, Lorna Hill, Hannah Jacobs, Esther Jamieson, Margaret Johnson, Susan Johnson, Verna Logan, Emma Longboat, Mabel Skye, Mary Skye, Teenie Skye, Daisy Thomas, Doris Thomas, Mabel Thomas, Mary Thomas, Violet Thomas, Ruby Williams, Alexander General, Joseph Logan Sr., Joseph Logan Jr., Patrick Longboat, Huron Miller, Alexander Nanticoke, David Thomas, Howard Skye, Jacob Skye, Albert Thomas, Gilbert Thomas, Jacob Thomas, William Thomas, and Fred Williams, along with many others. Those in each of the 150 households we came to know not only served as valuable instructors but welcomed us as friends. It is impossible to do full justice to their kindness, good humor, patience, and the beauty and depth of their way of life. Other members of the Six Nations community, like Joseph and Florence Hill and Elliot and Ethel Moses, also became close friends and instructors.

Considerable thanks are due Merlin's mentor, Meyer Fortes, along with a number of other professors at Cambridge. This gratitude must also be extended to American anthropologists Fred Eggan, William Fenton, Floyd Lounsbury, and Sol Tax, who provided assistance, friendship, guidance, and support.

Anthropologist John Hawkins of Brigham Young University patiently convinced Merlin to release his dissertation for publication and provided unremitting assistance in locating a suitable publisher. Readers Jason Jackson and M. Sam Cronk made discerning, thoughtful reviews of the manuscript, which are greatly appreciated, as is Cronk's afterword noting changes on the reserve since 1958 and issues relevant to contemporary Iroquois life. Coeditors Raymond DeMallie and Douglas Parks were consistently courteous and helpful in response to my enquiries. When I was reluctant to elaborate various issues in the preface, DeMallie's encouragement enabled me to proceed. Appreciation is also extended to the acquisitions and publication staffs at the University of Nebraska Press, who have made this process a pleasant experience—Gary Dunham, Jeremy Hall, Beth Ina, Sandra Johnson, Sara Springsteen, and Joeth Zucco. Copyeditor Karen Brown has been meticulous, instructive, and congenial; ever a pleasure to work with.

Lorna Hill played an integral role in Merlin's Cayuga language training from the beginning of his time in the field, and it seems particularly fitting that her work should feature in this publication. Her expertise in editing and converting Cayuga words and sentences and in editing and expanding translations made the glossary possible. She gave generous permission for the use of photographs as well. Ariel Harris, close friend and correspondent for almost fifty years, her sister, Ruby Williams, and niece, Diane Johnson, have been valuable consultants in the final stages of preparing the manuscript. Ariel also granted permission to use photos in this publication. The transcriptions of a number of Six Nations linguists, who wished to remain anonymous, are a welcome contribution to this study as well.

I am grateful to my daughter-in-law, Jennifer Myers, who took keen interest in the project and typed the electronic copy of the dissertation without complaint, later revising the Cayuga orthography in the text, adding the glossary and preface, and typing the final version of the manuscript sent to the publisher. My son, Christopher Myers, made significant contributions to the preface. He convinced me to engage the project more comprehensively than just providing Merlin's curriculum vitae, became an encouraging but demanding coach and editor, and drawing on his own anthropological training, enabled me to contextualize Merlin's work with an eye to both historical and contemporary issues.

Finally, I must thank the members of Merlin's family, all of whom fostered courage and hope throughout Merlin's graduate work, particularly his sister, Helen M. Gardner, his brother, Newell, and his parents, Edna and Wilford Myers, who contributed financially to its completion. My parents, Verl and Feurman Brady, also provided financial assistance. Even now, in their mid-nineties, they have often patiently awaited by attention while I have pursued this project. To all I extend heartfelt thanks from Merlin and myself.

Attempts to locate the copyright holders for *Grand River* by Mabel Dunham (Toronto: McClelland and Stewart Ltd.) and *A Geography of Canada*, edited by Donald F. Putnam (London: J. M. Dent and Sons, 1952) were unsuccessful. Map 1 is adapted from Dunham; maps 3 and 4 are adapted from Putnam.

Alice B. Myers

Households and Families of the
Longhouse Iroquois at Six Nations Reserve

I

Plowing competition at Ohsweken fair. Photo by author.

Onondaga Longhouse, 1956. One of four ritual centers of the Longhouse people at Six Nations Reserve. It also served as council house for Confederacy lineage chiefs. Photo by author.

Roger Logan watches Elijah Harris take aim along a newly prepared snow snake track in the Onondaga Longhouse field. Photo by author.

Upper Cayuga (Sour Springs) Longhouse, 1956. Although each longhouse is known by a specific tribal name, members and officiators at all longhouses are of mixed tribal affiliation. Photo by author.

Etịnose ("our uncles"), Hubert Cusick and Huron Miller, on their rounds to announce ganahaowi, "stirring the ashes day," for Midwinter rites at Seneca Longhouse. Photo by author.

1. Introduction

The descendants of the five original tribes—Mohawk, Oneida, Onondaga, Cayuga, and Seneca—that made up the Iroquois Confederacy now live on some fifteen separate reservations in the United States and Canada (Morgan 1851, 29–35; Fenton 1951, 39–40). This study is concerned only with the group living on the Six Nations Reserve in Ontario, Canada.[1] More specifically, it is concerned with the group on this reserve commonly referred to as Longhouse people. In this part of the study an effort is made to outline briefly and generally the historical background to settlement in their present habitat and the establishment of the reserve, to define some of the critical factors of identity for the group to be studied, and to note some features of their physical and sociological environment that influenced the systematization of their social life at the time of fieldwork.

Historical Background

The removal of fragments of each of the five tribes of the Iroquois Confederacy to the area of the present Six Nations Reserve and their establishment there of a model of their former League was the culmination of a series of events spanning nearly two centuries of relations with Europeans.[2] The Dutch traders who founded Fort Orange (afterward Albany, New York) in 1615 were the first to establish friendly relations with the Iroquois and carried on a trade with them in which awls, hatchets, knives, guns, fabrics, and other European goods were exchanged for furs. When the British took over the Dutch colonies in the New World in 1664, they continued to ply this trade and established a "covenant chain of friendship" with the Iroquois as a check on the expansion of French interests from centers at Quebec and Montreal. Recognizing the great value to their own interests of maintaining good relations with the Iroquois, the British government, in 1749, removed the conduct of Indian affairs from colonial officials and traders at Albany and established a separate office for this purpose, appointing Sir William Johnson Indian commissioner.[3] Johnson displayed an adroitness in dealing with the Indians, especially the Iroquois, which has probably never since been equaled. He succeeded in winning a good deal of support from them against the French in the action that eliminated the latter as a power in the New World in 1760, and it was the confidence in him, although he died in July 1774, that influenced the greater part of the Iroquois to join the British forces during the American War of Independence; however, most of the tribes of the League were split over this decision (Stone 1838, 1:104; 2:37–40). Thus, the alliance between the Iroquois and the British government continued for more than a century. Indeed, even today, as will be seen below, these ancient treaties remain a factor to be reckoned with by the Canadian government in dealing with the Iroquois at Six Nations Reserve.

Removal to Canada

As the War of Independence drew to a close, the Iroquois, whose settled places of habitation had been destroyed, retired to the Niagara River near what is now Lewiston, New York; and it was from here that Joseph Brant, the Mohawk war captain and former aide to Sir William Johnson, went to Quebec to claim from Governor Frederick Haldimand the fulfillment of a pledge made to him first by Sir Guy Carleton in 1775, and confirmed in April 1779 by Haldimand himself, that the Iroquois would be "restored to their former positions with regard to lands" at the expense of the British government. Brant first sought a concession at the Bay of Quinte on the north shore of Lake Ontario, and some of the Mohawk people actually settled at this place. But the Seneca, who were remaining in their own Native domain, expressed dismay at having the other tribes of the League at so great a distance (in the event of future trouble with the Americans) and urged Brant to seek land nearer at hand. Deferring to the desires of the Seneca, Brant journeyed a second time to Quebec and was granted a tract six miles wide on each side of the Grand River from its source to its mouth totaling some 1,200 square miles (map 1). In 1784 Haldimand reiterated this grant in the name of the Crown, identifying the land as "upon the banks of the River Ouise, commonly called Grand River, running into Lake Erie, of six miles breadth from each side of the river, beginning at Lake Erie, and extending in that proportion to the head of said river; which the Mohawks, and others of the Six Nations who had either lost their possessions in the war, or wished to retire from them to the British, with their posterity, were to enjoy forever" (Stone 1838, 2:240; Sparks 1848, 258).

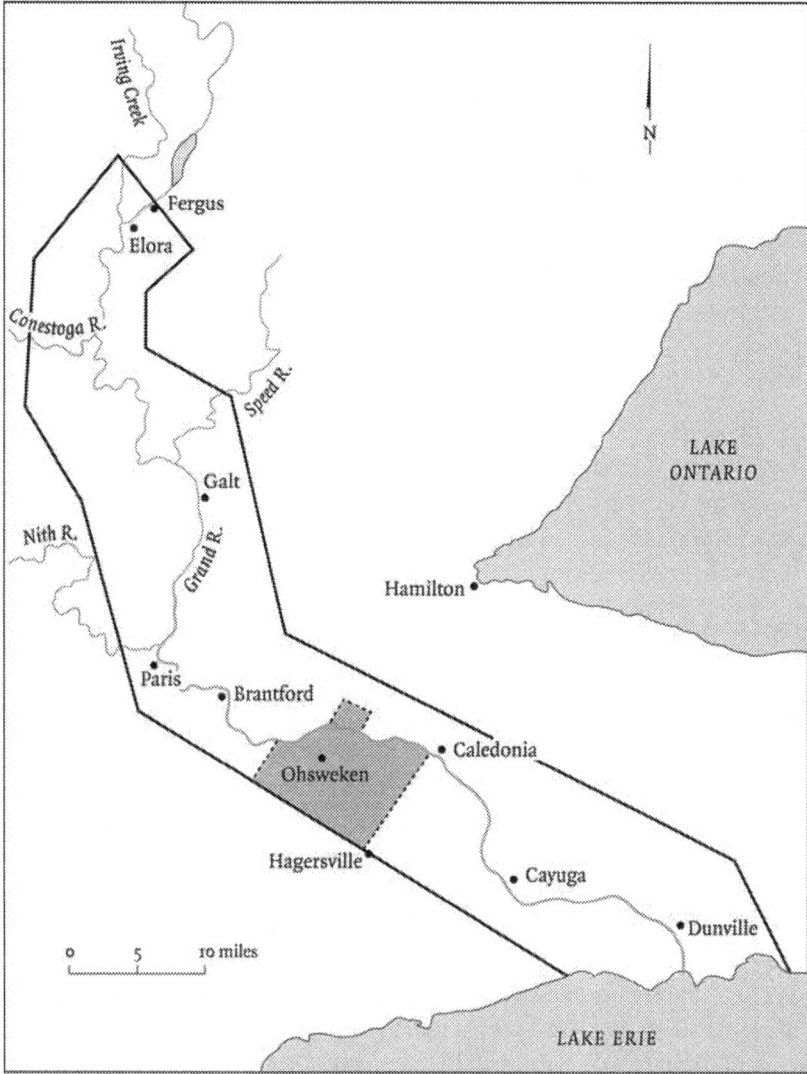

1. Area of original Haldimand Grant, also showing present Six Nations Reserve (adapted from Dunham 1945)

It is difficult to find explicit data on the departure of the groups of Iroquois from their encampment on the Niagara and their settlement within the area of the Haldimand Grant. It is supposed that migration began soon after Brant returned from Quebec after his second conference with Haldimand. At any rate, Major E. B. Littlehales, secretary to Governor J. G. Simcoe, in 1791, and Captain Alexander Campbell, in 1792–93, made note of the fact that Cayuga, Onondaga, and Mohawk villages had arisen along the banks of the Grand River near the present site of Brantford, Ontario, by that time (Reville 1920, 37–44).

The Sale of Lands

Less than a decade after their settlement in the area of the Haldimand Grant, Joseph Brant, avowedly recognizing that the area was too small for the continuance of the hunting-gardening economy native to the Iroquois system and that the area would be further diminished by the almost certain encroachment of Europeans and Loyalists, who had begun already to be attracted by the fertility of the area, set out to sell some of the land to establish an annuity to ensure the future welfare of the Six Nations people. This raised protests from the colonial government, and Governor J. G. Simcoe issued a new deed in 1793, denying the right of the Iroquois to alienate any part of the territory of the Haldimand Grant and defining the Crown's preemptive right to the land. Brant and the people of the Six Nations rejected the Simcoe deed, and it appears that the colonial government did not at first base its policy on it. Brant was appointed by the Six Nations Council in 1796 to negotiate with the government for the disposal of a large portion of their lands in his own name.[4]

Notwithstanding the provisions of the Simcoe deed, the colonial government consented to the proposed sales, and Brant promptly concluded eight separate land transactions involving 352,707 acres at an average selling price of seventy cents per acre. White squatters continued to encroach upon the remaining lands, and a welter of litigation grew out of their attempts to make good their irregular titles. In an effort to alleviate the conflict, the government proposed to settle the Iroquois on a reservation created out of a small part of their original grant and thus separate them entirely from the squatters. Accordingly, under this policy the government began to negotiate with the separate tribes to buy up land outside the reserve area. By 1840 all were living within this area, and by 1841 all remaining lands outside the reserve area were conscripted, surveyed, and resold to white settlers (Reville 1920, 345–46). The proceeds from the sales, amounting to more than eight hundred thousand dollars, are at present held in trust by the Canadian government for the Six Nations people.

The Six Nations Reserve
Physical Characteristics

The reservation thus established is laid out from a point located at 43°6' north latitude and 80°32' west longitude, near the modern city of Brantford, Ontario. Except for 1,600 acres of land lying north of the Grand River (map 2), the reserve is a roughly rectangular area nearly seven miles wide and ten miles long containing 70.15 square miles or 44,900 acres.

Of this area, 36,000 acres lie in Tuscarora Township and 1,600 in Onondaga Township, Brant County; and the remaining 7,300 acres adjoin Tuscarora Township on the east, but lie in the township of Oneida, Haldimand County, Ontario. The reserve has one natural boundary, the Grand River, on its northeast side, and gravel roads form the boundaries on the remaining three sides.

There are no physical geographical features peculiar to the reserve distinguishing it from the surrounding area. The land itself is flat to gently undulating, and drainage is affected by five or six small creeks that flow into the Grand River. Although about three thousand acres of the natural mixed forest coverage remains, most of the land, with its excellent soils, ranging from lacustrine clay to sandy loam types, has been cleared. The region has four distinct seasons in the year, with 170 to 216 frost-free days. The mean annual temperature is forty-six degrees, with January the coldest and July the warmest months. Great fluctuation in temperature is modified by the presence of the Great Lakes to the south, west, and east. Annual precipitation ranges from twenty-six to forty inches (Putnam 1952, 222–25). Soils and climate combine to make ideal conditions for agricultural pursuits.

The interior of the reserve has been laid out in grid pattern, having rectangular blocks one and one-half miles long by one and one-quarter miles wide, each containing twelve hundred acres. The lines forming the grid have been turned into roads, many of which become veritable quagmires for a period each year with the coming of spring, but which are being gradually improved from the natural clay surface to gravel. About ten miles of roads connecting the center of the reserve with the Brantford Highway were paved with asphalt during the summer of 1956. The building of roads on the reservation caused dwelling houses to be moved from along the creeks and springs to the roadside, and

HOUSES UNCHARTED

MOSTLY CHRISTIAN HOUSEHOLDS

-N-

0   I   2 miles

S

S

S

S

G

Sour
Springs
Longhouse

Ohsweken

S

SC   E   H

G   R

G

C

C

C

C

S

Onondaga
Longhouse

S

New
Credit
Missisauga

C

Seneca
Longhouse

S

C.

S

Lower
Cayuga
Longhouse

G

G   G   G

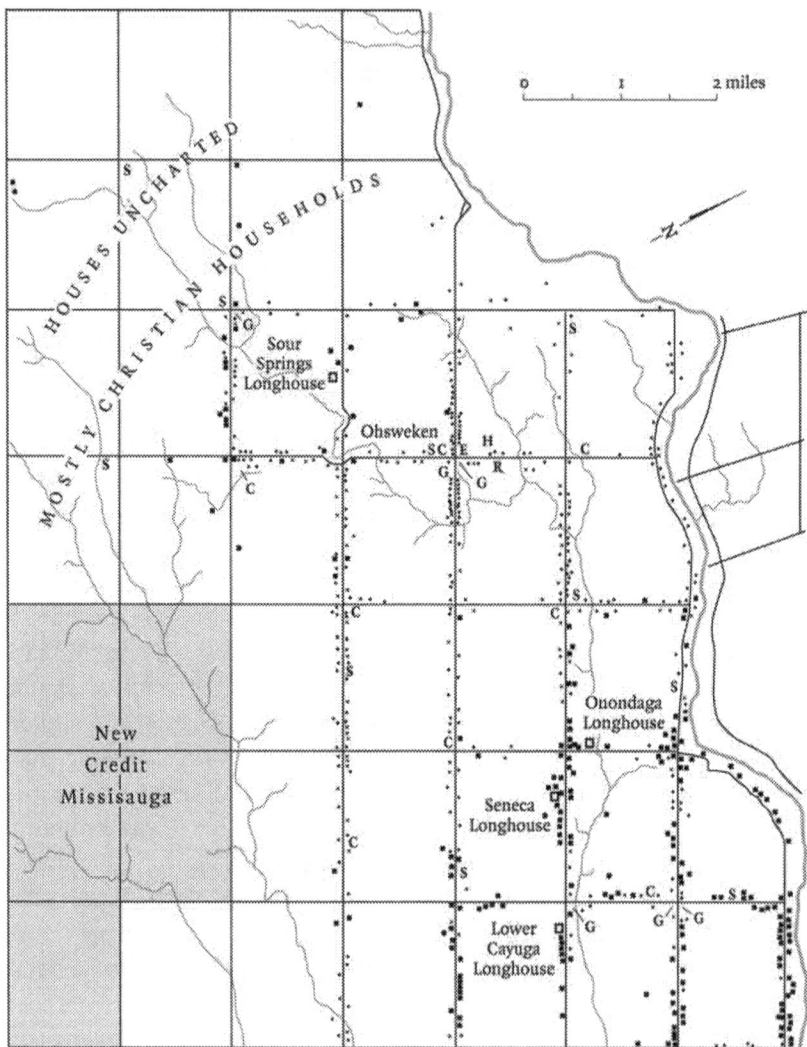

•   Longhouse households   C   Christian churches
·   Other households   H   Hospital
E   Elective council house   R   Royal Canadian Mounted Police
S   Schools   G   Stores
□   Longhouses

(Spatial relationship of houses approximate only)

2. Six Nations Reserve

at present only a few houses remain "back in the bush," as their location is referred to nowadays. Dwelling houses are spread over the entire area of the reserve, but settlement is sparser in the northwest, southwest, and southeast portions. As shown in map 2, concentration is greatest in the central portion in the village of Ohsweken and in the northeast portion of the reserve. It is in this latter area where there is greatest concentration of Longhouse people; however, they are spread in greater or lesser number throughout the reserve.

Population

The first census of the reserve was in 1858 (Reville 1920, 346), and it shows the following number of the various Iroquois and other tribes living there at the time:

Reserve group	Population	Reserve group	Population
Upper Mohawk	458	Upper Cayuga	173
Lower Mohawk	318	Lower Cayuga	333
Walker Mohawk	20	Kanada Senecas	46
Bay of Quinte Mohawk	156	Nikarondasa Senecas	74
Onondaga Clear Sky	230	Delaware	90
Bearfoot Onondaga	68	Oneida	56
Tuscarora	215	Other Indians of adopted tribes	184
		Total	2,421

The population had risen to 2,509 by 1880 (Warner, Beers 1883, 489–90), and according to the census on file in the Indian Office in Brantford it was 6,385 in 1954. Taking into account the fact that a considerable number of members (estimated by the council secretary, Mr. Leslie Smith, to be about 2,500 in 1956) reside away from the reserve for extended periods, there is an approximate density for the reserve of fifty-five persons per square mile. This figure also fluctuates seasonally with the migration of reserve members to jobs outside.

While settlement on the reserve was predominantly by tribal groups, it was not exclusively so. Old band lists kept in the Indian Office indicate that a group of Onondaga, possibly a lineage group, was living with the Cayuga and that a similar group of Seneca had come to Canada with the Onondaga, and so on. This intermixing increased in the years that followed settlement on the reserve, bringing about a diffusion of tribes throughout the reserve.[5]

In addition to the intermixing of tribes, there has been a genetic mixing with Europeans and Africans.[6] It is difficult, if not impossible, to find a single member of the reserve who is genetically of pure Indian stock. This miscegenation manifests itself in an increased variability and modification in the phenotypical characteristics usually thought of as being associated with American Indians. The copper-colored skin has given way in many cases to light, almost Caucasian, skin hues. Straight black head hair and sparse body hair have given way, and it is common to see wavy head hair, mustaches, and moderately heavy facial hair. Brown hair is common, and indeed, carroty and blonde hair are occasionally seen. Baldness, a characteristic not often associated with American Indians, is quite frequent among men on the reserve. The most common eye coloring is for the iris to be brown encircled with a narrow blue fringe. Grey and blue eyes are also frequent.

Government on the Reserve

The members of each tribe migrating to the lands of the Haldimand Grant represented only fragments of original tribes, some larger, some smaller; yet an attempt was made to reconstitute the council of hereditary chiefs. Where necessary, chief titles were assigned to fragments of lineages or to lineages already possessing titles, thus causing them to divide. In this manner the League was reconstituted on the structural model that existed among the tribes when they all resided in their native domain in what is now New York State, even though this meant the existence of duplicate titles in Longhouse communities on both sides of the Canadian–United States border. The council of hereditary chiefs was recognized as a kind of local governing body on the reserve by the Canadian government until 1924, when the government deposed it and set up an elective council system in its place.

The present elective system is similar in structure and in power and jurisdiction to town or local governments of the council type common in Canada and the United States. The reservation is divided into six electoral districts, which elect twelve councilors, two from each district; and a "chief" councilman is elected from the reserve at large to preside over the council thus formed. All are elected by secret ballot for a term of two years. Council meetings, at which the Indian Agent is present, are held on the first Thursday of each month. The activities of the council are related to its capacity to make bylaws (Indian Act, sec. 80), and the most important matters, pertaining to which bylaws may be made, are as follows: providing for health and welfare, including the right to quarantine; regulation of traffic; maintaining law and order; construction of roads and bridges; the survey and allotment of reserve lands; regulation of hawking, peddling, and selling activities; impounding of stray cattle; and the removal of persons trespassing on the reserve. Violations of the bylaws of the council may upon summary conviction be punished by fines up to one hundred dollars or imprisonment for a period of thirty days. Royal Canadian Mounted Police enforce laws on the reserve, and crimes and misdemeanors are handled in Canadian law courts. In order for the council to handle its business in a specialized manner, standing committees are formed composed of three councilors each; and in 1956 there were separate standing committees dealing with roads, welfare, fairgrounds, schools, hospital, and lands and works.

The elective council administered a budget of approximately eighty-five thousand dollars in 1956, over half of which was spent on road construction. The source of these funds is the interest on the money derived from the sale of lands referred to above.

Schools

The first schools among the Six Nations people in their new settlements were mission schools operated by the New England Company and by the Methodist missions, at least one of which was established as early as 1827 (Warner, Beers 1883, 146). About 1875, the Department of Indian Affairs assumed the responsibility for education facilities on the reserve, setting up its own curriculum and undertaking to build a number of one- and two-room schoolhouses. The Ontario public school curriculum was adopted in 1910, and in 1927 the reserve schools were integrated into the provincial system. At the time of fieldwork, their reservation schools were under the immediate direction of a supervising principal and a staff of thirty-two teachers, all of whom were members of the reserve. Teachers were required to obtain an Ontario teacher's certificate.

During the 1956–57 school year, there were eight one-room and five two-room schools teaching grades one through six, and a central school in the village of Ohsweken where grades five through eight were taught. High school students commuted daily to four schools in towns outside the reserve. The grade school curriculum on the reserve consisted of courses in social studies, English grammar, mathematics, music, art, home economics, manual training, and special courses in agricultural science. All teaching was conducted in the English language, although children speaking Iroquoian languages in schools or on school grounds were no longer punished with strappings, as had been the case in the near past. School attendance was mandatory for all children from six to sixteen years of age, and nonattendance could involve fines of five dollars or ten days imprisonment for the parent or guardian of the child (Indian Act, secs. 113–21).

The supervising principal administered a budget of approximately $175,000 for the school year 1956–57, or nearly $1,600 per pupil per year. Salaries ranged from $2,400 to $3,000 for beginning teachers, to $4,800 with seniority. These figures were comparable for those of the Province of Ontario generally.

Church and Longhouse

The greater part of the Mohawk tribe had been Christianized prior to their settling in Canada (Beauchamp 1905, 338–39). On the other hand, the majority of the Cayuga, Onondaga, Seneca, and Oneida who came to the Grand River during the same period had adhered to their aboriginal ritual system; and this cleavage has come down to the present day. It is reflected in the terms in current usage on the reservation of "Church people," or Christians, and "Longhouse people." The census of 1880 (Warner, Beers 1883, 590) shows the number each of Christians and "Pagans" (as the Longhouse people were designated) in the total population. These figures are compared with those for 1944 and 1954 on file in the Indian Office:

Date	Christians	Longhouse people	Total
1880	1,972	537	2,509
1944	4,325	1,195	5,520
1954	5,125	1,260	6,385

This differentiation between the two sectors of the population is popularly conceived of as one of religious affiliation or belief only, which probably arises out of the fact that the difference of ritual behavior between the sectors is the most exotic and patent one. It has also been characterized in terms of the word "faction" by Fenton (1952, 332). However, in light of the observation that the social life of Church and Longhouse people goes on very largely within separate institutions and groups, this characterization seems inadequate. Actually, there are two fundamentally distinct and separate, though not mutually exclusive, structural systems underlying these designations.

Certain institutions and groups characterize the social life of Church people. As is self-evident, they make up the congregations and participate in the activities of various Christian denominations on the reserve (Anglican, Baptist, Methodist, Adventist, Pentecostal), emphasizing these denominational distinctions among themselves. They are also generally recognized as being supporters of the elective system of government described above, are usually ardent supporters of the school system, and are members of the reserve school board. There are also a number of associations connected with rural and agricultural life, such as the Six Nations Agricultural Society, which seeks to promote better farming techniques and which holds an annual agricultural fair; the Six Nations Plowman's Association, which also seeks to promote excellence in farming and holds a plowing competition each autumn; and the 4-H clubs, which sponsor farming and livestock-raising projects among the youth. Three chapters of the Women's Institute, whose activities emphasize improvement of home life as the road to better citizenship, flourish among them. A recreational organization, the Six Nations Young People's Association, provides lectures and sports activities such as softball, volleyball, basketball and table tennis. The only money-lending facility on the reserve, the Credit Union, is managed by Church people. Two groups, known as the Six Nations Benevolent Association and the Six Nations Temperance Union, are primarily associated with the Church sector and concerned themselves initially with the liquor problem but have become principally a form of nonprofit life insurance. Finally, it should be noted that all stores and other businesses on the reserve are operated by Church people. Of these groups, the Christian denominations, the schools, the elective government, the associations having to do with agriculture, the Women's Institute, and the Credit Union are all local subdivisions, or chapters, of their provincial, national, or international counterparts, showing clearly the orientation of Church society on the reserve. For Church people, traditional myths, legends, and tales have largely either been forgotten or have ceased to be relevant to their standardized social activities; and the historical facts outlined above, the provisions of the Indian Act, the teachings of the various Christian sects, and the charters of the above groups and institutions appear to have been substituted for them.

On the other hand, Longhouse people regard these groups and institutions as inimical to their own system of matrilineal descent and are strongly urged by lineage officers and elders to boycott them entirely. "Church people are trying to become white men," they say with contempt; and for a Longhouse person to emulate their conduct is treated with scorn. If a wayward Longhouse person or a former Church member desires to be accepted in full fellowship among the Longhouse people, he must submit to a public confession of his wrongs while holding the strand of shell beads (gadjisdaįtgǫ) that objectifies the corporate unity of the Longhouse group.

Some interaction between Church and Longhouse people occurs, of course, but it is largely confined to that imposed from without by the Canadian government, as that arising out of the bylaw-making powers of the elective council affecting the entire reserve, and to the school system. Many Longhouse people consider the schools to be the insidious device of the white man, with which he seeks to undermine their traditional way of life. Although playgroups of children at school are mixed, these attachments seldom carry over outside school or beyond school age, and Longhouse parents instruct their children to marry within the Longhouse sector.

At the time of fieldwork, voluntary interaction was minimal. One Longhouse man and his son were members of the Credit Union, and a somewhat larger number were members of the Benevolence Association. Although participation in the elective system is regarded as a transgression of their own Creator-ordained ways, some Longhouse people are known to have voted in the elections, and two had run for and won elections to the elective council in the thirty-three years of its existence. Longhouse people patronize the stores operated by Church people but do most of their buying off the reserve. Although the location of dwelling houses is such that Church and Longhouse people are often found living as neighbors to each other (map 2), voluntary contact in the form of visiting or the exchange of services is rare. As one older man put it, "See all my neighbors around here, that's all Church people. They never visit me, and I don't know what they're doin'."

These conditions obtaining at the time of fieldwork on the Six Nations Reserve bear out the observation made by Professor Fortes (1953b, 36) that locality per se does not give rise to social bonds, but that people interact socially when they are a part of the same institutional fabric. Although differences of interest between Church people and Longhouse people were apparent before 1924, the deposition of the council of hereditary chiefs in that year severed the last traditional institutional tie between them. "It became clear then," said one of the chiefs, referring to the deposition, "that we are going one way and they are going another."[7]

The Longhouse People

The rule of matrilineal descent is the foundation of Longhouse social organization. Although this rule has admittedly lost much of its former vigor, as, for example, in the passing of economic activities from the direct control of the lineage system, a considerable amount of corporate politico-jural and ritual activity attaches to it (chapter 5); and lineage chiefs in council have the allegiance of the Longhouse people generally, thus providing a kind of political focus and setting a boundary to what may be called Longhouse society. This underlying matrilineal descent structure brings the various customs and usages of Longhouse culture together in a related, meaningful whole and endows the Longhouse people with a sense of unity separate and distinct from Church people on the reserve and from Canadian society. This sense of unity is reflected in the nomenclature with which they refer to themselves in contrast to others, in the way they regard their genetic make-up, in their use of language, in mythology and in ritual activities. Only a brief consideration of these factors is possible here.

Nomenclature

The designation "Longhouse people" is a translation of the Cayuga Iroquois word Hodinǫsǫni (lit. they, people of the longhouse). The word has its root in the traditional house type of the Iroquois, and it was extended metaphorically to embrace their League or Confederacy. It is used by the Longhouse people to distinguish themselves linguistically from American Indians in general, whom they at present designate as Qgwehǫwe (lit. the original or genuine people), and from Church people (hodiwhiostǫ), whom they regard as trying to become white people (hadihnyǫǫ). Both the vernacular Hodinǫsǫni and its English translation are in daily use by the Longhouse people; however, only the English translation will be used in this work. When "longhouse" (with lowercase l) is used, it designates the edifice in which all public activities of a political and ritual nature take place; and "longhouse ritual group" applies to the group of Longhouse people regarded as being affiliated with a particular longhouse.

Genetic Make-up

As can be seen from the figures given above, the Longhouse people make up about one-fifth of the reserve population, and this proportion has been relatively stable for the past three to four generations. Notwithstanding the genetic mixing noted above, it is common to hear Longhouse persons who possess any, or all, of the lately acquired physical characteristics refer to themselves as "full-blooded Cayuga," Seneca, Onondaga, and so on. Whereas Church people admit or assert quite freely their white ancestry, Longhouse people are very reluctant to do so, and a placatory feast (tadigǫstoais—lit. long whiskers) held for white ancestors is one of the most secret rites held. In addition, to call a fellow Longhouse member a "white man" is a very severe reproach.

Language

Nearly all of the Longhouse people are bilingual; although a few of the older generation speak one or the other of the Iroquois languages only, and a few of the younger generation speak very little Iroquois. Still, on all public occasions, especially those of a politico-jural and ritual nature, one of the Iroquois languages is spoken exclusively. In daily intercourse they use whichever language is most convenient under existing circumstances, whether this is one of the Iroquois languages or English.

Mythology and Ritual

The *Deganawida* myth (Parker 1916), depicting the origin of the lineage system or Confederacy of the Iroquois, continues to differentiate lineage groups and serves as guide in the ceremony for installing chiefs, and it is often cited by Longhouse people in explanation of why they refuse to vote in the elective system. *Deganawida*'s name is avoided in daily speech, and relics from the Tree of Peace (Parker 1916, 100–101), which he was to have planted, are kept by some Longhouse people. Other myths and legends will be discussed below.

For the purpose of this introduction, it is sufficient to note the continuation of traditional ritual institutions among the Longhouse people as an important manifestation of their unity, a topic that will be dealt with in more depth in part 3. There are four longhouse ritual groups on the reservation, each with its ritual center or longhouse (*ganǫses*), although it should be noted that ritual practices on the individual and lineage levels often take place in private homes, as well as the longhouse. Ritual activities involve a number of basic concerns or interests. First is a calendric ceremonial cycle consisting of two principal ceremonies and some eleven appendages. The two principal ceremonies (*wihowanę geiniyiwhage*) conclude with a significant ritual gift exchange between the sides of the dual divisions characteristic of each longhouse ritual group. The appendages (*wiwhawędenyǫ*) are, in most instances, thanksgiving rites performed for the spirit of vegetation (*Dyǫnhegǫ*). Second are placatory rites, which are held biannually for the dead of all the people of a particular longhouse ritual group (*gǫdyogwagwegǫ odyǫhakǫfra*), or by a lineage for its deceased members (*adyęhakǫfrowanę ǫgwadriwhade sęnige'hwhadjiya*) as often as they feel the need, or by individuals (*o'hdyęhakǫfra*) responding to a dream or the advice of a fortuneteller. Third are medicine rites (*ǫdwęnǫgotanǫ*), which are held by individuals and lineages, both as therapy and to enhance general well-being or luck (*ohdraswa*). These rites are at present closely related to those held by some lineages to appease (*ęyetinikowi'h*—lit. to amuse) charms (*otsinnagęda'h*) with which their well-being is believed to be connected. A fourth activity is seen in the conventions held for the preaching of the Code (*Gaiwhio*) of the Seneca prophet Handsome Lake. This is essentially a moral code, a principal part of which enjoins socially acceptable rules to be followed in dealings with the white man and his culture (see Parker 1912). The conventions may be held by individual longhouse groups or by all longhouses, one playing host to the others.

All these aspects of Longhouse society would appear to be sufficient to admit it as a unit for the purpose of this study. However, Longhouse society is not a self-contained unit, and it is therefore essential to see it in the context of its wider environmental setting, in particular the economic and political systems of Canadian society.

Environmental Setting

The Six Nations Reserve is located in the Province of Ontario, and the natural environment imposes no special conditions upon Longhouse social organization. However, important alternatives and limiting factors arise out of the sociological environment.

Economic Environment

The population of the Province of Ontario was 5,046,000 in 1954, more than one-quarter of the whole for Canada; and it is estimated that approximately 90 percent of this total live in the region of southern Ontario, an area of fifty thousand square miles. About 75 percent is further concentrated in the southern thirty thousand square miles of this region, making a density for this latter area, within which the Six Nations Reserve lies, of about 120 persons per square mile (Putnam 1952, 228).

This is Canada's most highly developed economic region, where agriculture, industry, and commerce have grown up together. The region is the most intensively developed agricultural area in Canada, yielding an annual cash income of five hundred million dollars from an occupied area of twenty million acres. The bulk of this activity is carried on within a hundred-mile radius of the reserve in a number of more or less specialized areas. Those areas of most importance for the Longhouse people (map 3) are the fruit belt between the Niagara escarpment and Lake Ontario where peaches, grapes, and other canning fruits and vegetables are grown; the fruit and vegetable belt bordering Lake Ontario between Hamilton and Toronto, where apples, strawberries, and tomato crops provide abundant work in season; and the tobacco and canning fruit and vegetable areas in Kent and Essex Counties in the extreme southwest of the province (243).

As well as being the most intensive farming area of Canada, southern Ontario claims over 60 percent of the country's manufacturing and is the

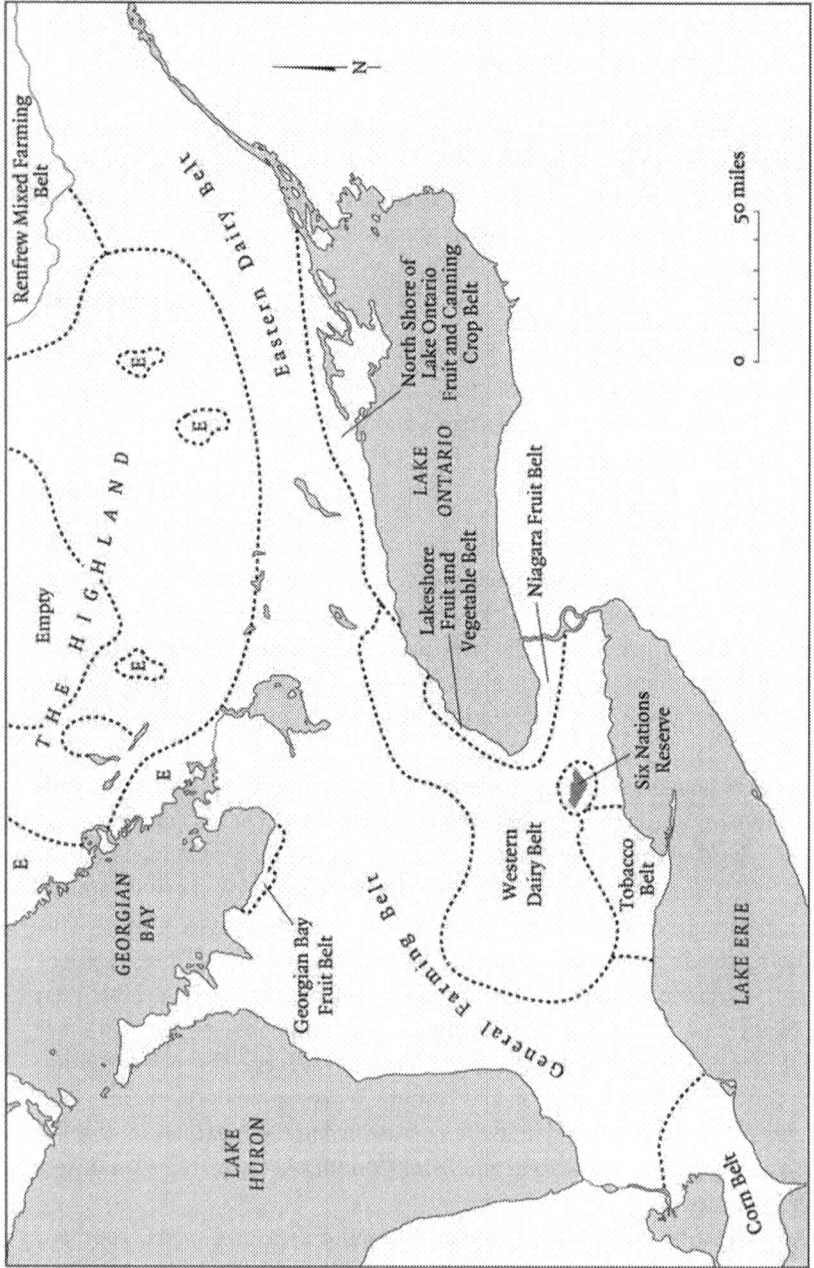

3. Agricultural regions of Southern Ontario (adapted from Putnam 1952, 241)

commercial and banking center of the Dominion. The region was undergoing considerable industrial expansion at the time of fieldwork, and this was drawing heavily on the rural population for the necessary labor force, which was, in turn, bringing about consolidation and greater mechanization in the farming areas (245). As can be seen from map 4, the greatest industrial activity lies within a radius of fifty to one hundred miles of the reserve; and Longhouse people are found in unskilled, semiskilled, and occasionally skilled jobs in many of the industrial centers within this range.

The reservation is thus a kind of pocket in this economically highly developed area; and although reservation lands are ideally suited for farming, very few Longhouse people derive their livelihood from this source, choosing rather the alternative provided in the circumstances just outlined of selling their labor for wages on farms and in industries outside the reserve where, to a very large extent, their earnings are also spent to obtain necessary and desired consumers' goods and services. As the figures given below reveal, the past four decades show a marked trend away from farming for the reserve as a whole; but it appears doubtful that Longhouse men, generally speaking, have ever been zealous farmers:

Date	Farm population	Farm operators	All field crops in acres[8]
1921	3,277	669	22,804
1931	3,083	525	15,843
1941	2,739	268	12,357
1951	2,705	271	10,035

Socio-Political Environment

Canadian government and legal institutions are also an important component in the environment of Longhouse society. Of most direct influence is the Department of Indian Affairs under the Ministry of Citizenship and Immigration. This department maintains an Indian Agent in nearby Brantford whose duty it is under the minister, and with the help of a contingent of Royal Canadian Mounted Police stationed on the reserve, to carry out the policies of the government with respect to the Six Nations people. Governmental policy was summarized by the minister of citizenship and immigration, Mr. Harris, in a speech to the House of Commons in 1950, when he said:

> Indeed, it may be said that ever since confederation, the underlying purpose of Indian Administration has been to prepare the Indian for full citizenship

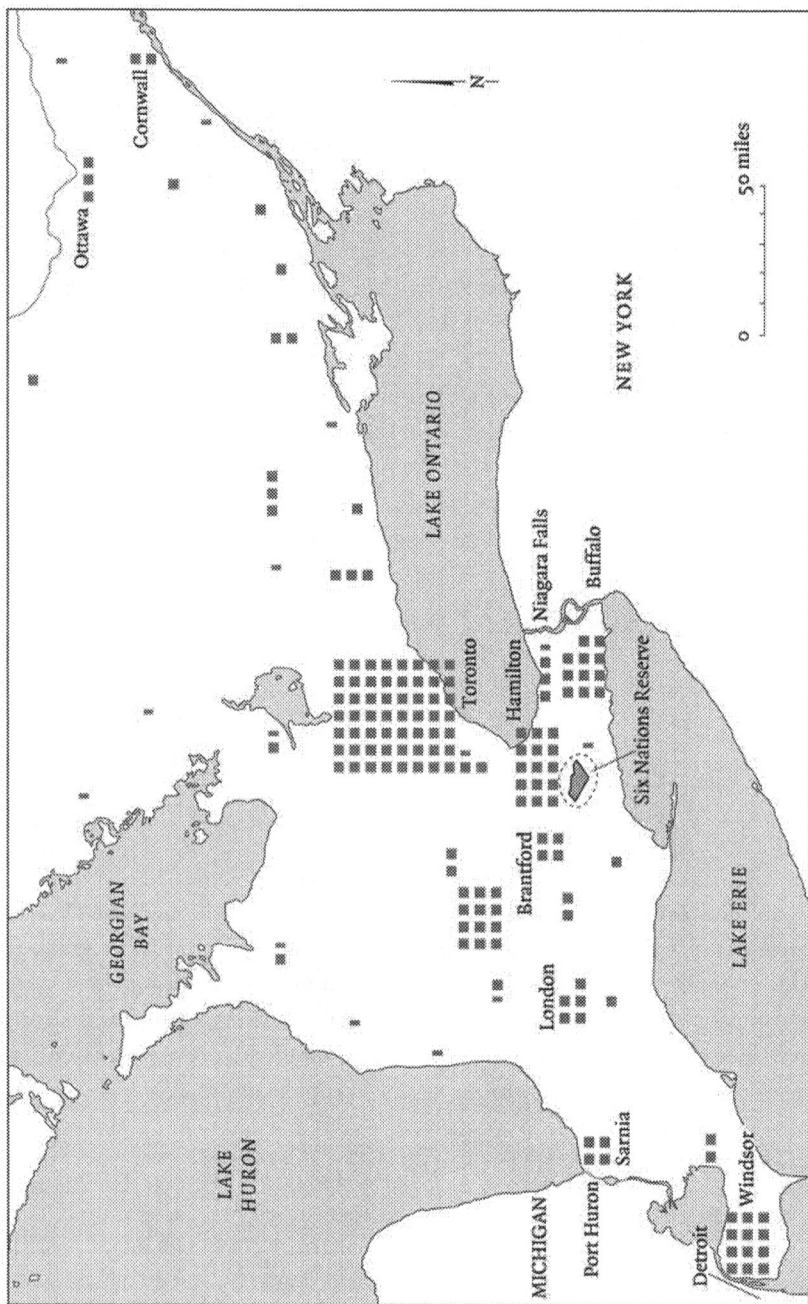

with the same rights and responsibilities as enjoyed and accepted by other members of the community. . . . The ultimate goal of our Indian policy is the integration of the Indian into the general life and economy of the country. It is recognized, however, that during a temporary transition period of varying length, depending upon the circumstances and stage of development of different bands, special treatment and legislation are necessary. (Department of Citizenship and Immigration 1957)

At the time of fieldwork, these had been the guiding principles of governmental policy for eighty or ninety years, and they were reflected in the Indian Act of Canada. The provisions of this body of legislation indicate the de facto political and jural position of the Longhouse people. A summary of some of the important sections of the Indian Act will make this clear:

1. The act establishes the legal status of "Indian," and therefore reserve membership, for children based on paternity and for a woman through her husband. This provision dates from 1868 (secs. 10–11).
2. It establishes ultimate title to reserve lands in the Crown. This reflects the provisions of the Simcoe deed of 1796, referred to above (secs. 18–19).
3. It defines rights of reserve members in the land of the reserve as *possessory rights* and limits the transfer of these rights to members of the reserve (secs. 20–29).
4. It grants the minister of citizenship and immigration jurisdiction and authority in matters relating to the descent of property upon the death of the "owner." It also recognizes wills and establishes a bilateral rule for distribution of property upon intestacy (secs. 42–50).
5. The Indian Act grants the minister authority to provide for the health of reserve members, in keeping with which, a hospital is maintained on the reserve providing medical care without direct cost to members of the reserve (sec. 72).
6. It grants the minister authority to establish an elective system of government. This power was exercised, as referred to above, in the deposition of the council of hereditary chiefs in 1924 (secs. 73–85).
7. It extends the realm of jurisdiction of provincial law to Indians within a given province, except where these laws conflict with special federal legislation for Indians. Public and private delicts are tried in provincial and Dominion courts (sec. 87).
8. The act extends the privilege of enfranchisement to all Indians desiring to give up their Indian status and become full Canadian citizens. This provision dates from 1885 (secs. 108–112).

9. It grants the minister authority to establish schools and enforce attendance of all reserve members between ages six and sixteen years. As seen above, schools were established by the Indian Department in 1875 (secs. 113–122).

In addition to the administration of reservation affairs under the provisions of the Indian Act, both the federal and provincial governments enter into Longhouse society by making subsidies available to Indians under their social security legislation. Prior to January 1952, Old Age Pension payments were restricted to persons seventy years of age and over. Since this date, all Longhouse people upon attaining sixty-five years of age are eligible to receive Old Age Assistance payments from the provincial government, which eligibility continues until they reach the age of seventy, at which time they may receive Old Age Security payments in a like amount from the federal government until death. Family Allowances were made available in 1945. This allowance is paid to either the parents or guardian of children from birth to the age of sixteen years. Veterans' Pensions were received by several men; and since 1952, Disabled Persons' Allowance and Mothers' Allowance have been available to Longhouse people in these categories. Occupations relating to mining, factory, and construction work are insurable under the Canadian Unemployment Insurance Act, and unemployed men in any of these types of employment may receive compensation in proportion to the amount of their weekly wage and the number of weeks worked during the past year (Unemployment Insurance Commission 1959, 8–10).

Despite their dependence on the Canadian economic system as a source of both consumer goods and services and the means for their purchase, and notwithstanding the intrusion of Canadian governmental institutions, the members of Longhouse society still regarded themselves as a separate and distinct unit politically at the time of fieldwork. At least part of the reason that they had been able to maintain this distinction is because what constitutes a governmental function for them does not wholly coincide with what is a governmental function in terms of the Canadian system (chapter 5). Another factor is that the council of lineage chiefs had come to be a focus for opposition to the Canadian government in its effort to carry out this policy of integration.

Opposition to the Canadian Government

Longhouse people maintain that the Six Nations Iroquois have, de jure, a special status among the Indians of Canada (see also Department of Citizenship and Immigration 1957, 4) in that they came to Canada as allies and not subjects of the Crown; but it is clear that the Dominion government, as successor to the Crown, is no longer prepared to admit this status. In discussing their treaties with the Crown in a council in July 1956, the chiefs displayed two "treaty belts" (mnemonic devices made of shell beads, otgǫa'h), which were "read" before the assembly. One of these belts shows two parallel rows of dark beads in a white field, the rows being about an inch wide and running the full length of the belt. The rows were said to represent the Crown and League respectively, both continuing side by side in their own "governments," the one never interfering with the other. So was the agreement, said the chiefs, and so it should continue. On this basis they reject the Indian Act and the policy upon which it is based, saying that the Dominion is acting in bad faith by thus interfering in their system. Whereas the Indian Act prescribes the order for inheritance of real property, personal property continues to be distributed by the traditional lineage rule. During the period of fieldwork, rights extended under provincial law (subsidies excepted) were generally rejected, as was enfranchisement. As noted, the elective system of government was boycotted, and grave suspicions were held about the school system, as well as the government hospital on the reserve, a great many Longhouse people preferring their own medicine to that of the hospital, or preferring to go to white doctors off the reserve when their services were required.

The council of hereditary chiefs was also a factor to be accounted for by the Canadian government in its conduct of affairs on the reserve. The chiefs sent delegations to London in 1930, and to the United Nations in San Francisco in 1945, seeking recognition of their independent status, and delegations to Ottawa were common. In January 1957, the government found it advisable to negotiate with the chiefs in their own council concerning the "legality" of Longhouse marriages; and during the period of fieldwork, the Longhouse people had a court case in process in which they sought to contest the government's right to set up the elective system on the reserve. The uprising of March 1959 was noted above.

In addition, the Longhouse people assert their own peculiar claim to the lands of the reservation in supersedure of the Haldimand Grant, the Simcoe deed, and the Dominion's preemptive right set forth in the Indian Act. Their claim, containing historical and legendary elements, asserts that the area in which the present reserve lies was a part of their ancient hunting territory many years before the breakup that followed the War of Independence. (Mohawk and Seneca warriors dispersed the Neutral tribe living in the area in 1650–51. See

Hunt 1940, 96–100.) In elaborating this claim, an informant, who is himself a chief, said in substance that on one occasion an Iroquois hunting party to the region discovered some Missisaugas who had settled there. (It is a matter of historical record, Stone 1838, 2:240, that Haldimand, acting for the Crown, purchased the Grand River tract of land from the Missisaugas before turning it over to the Six Nations people.) A daughter of one of the Missisauga chiefs was critically ill, and the Iroquois hunters dispatched a runner to their home village for medicine, which when administered, soon cured the girl; whereupon, the Missisauga chief proffered the land in expression of his gratitude, and the Iroquois magnanimously accepted this gift of their own territory. Longhouse chiefs thus maintain that they had no need of the Haldimand Grant in order to settle in the area. They disavow any connection with Joseph Brant as their agent, saying that his insistence on a grant or deed from Haldimand was a part of his own design to establish a basis for future land sales, which he planned to make in his own name, knowing that the chiefs would never give him authority to do so. Longhouse people maintain that the American continent belongs to the Ǫgwehǫwe by birthright from the Creator himself. Each generation is to have use of the land but is to hold it in trust for generations yet unborn. To sell land to the white man is thus both a sin subject to eternal punishment and a delict against society (see also Parker 1912, 68; Snyderman 1951, 15–18).

In all these matters Longhouse society is able to present a rather solid front of opposition to the Canadian government. However, the availability of subsidies presents a much more subtle threat to the integrity of their social order. There is a considerable number who feel that it is wrong to accept subsidies, arguing that to do so is to compromise their position as an "independent government." One man likens the acceptance of Family Allowance to "selling his children to the Canadian government," a step he refuses to take; and there were, in 1957, six or eight elderly people, among them some of the most influential lineage chiefs, who adamantly refused to receive Old Age Pensions, not wanting to jeopardize the claimed independence of their Confederacy. However, most of those eligible for whatever pension accept it, in some instances regarding it as a kind of indemnity for past wrongs suffered at the hands of the white man.

In seeking to establish their claims to independence, the Longhouse people are without ultimate recourse before the Canadian government and find it necessary to submit to its power and authority.[9] Yet, through their sustained opposition to its institutions, laws, and policies, this power and authority remain external to, and have little or no sanction within, their social system. Nevertheless, the conflict between the two societies and the chronic threat to the Longhouse social order posed by Canadian society is one of the most, if not the most, fundamental concerns of the Longhouse people; and in one form or another, it finds its way into their daily conversations and is manifest in ritual practices and in current mythology.

Mythology

In what is likely a recent extension of the *Deganawida* myth already mentioned, the overall conflict and the various tension points in present social life are clearly expressed. It is said that after establishing the League, *Deganawida* foreshadowed its future with the coming of the Europeans. This "prophecy," for so it is called, is given here just as it was written in about the first decade of the present century by the father of a Longhouse friend (Newhouse 1885), and more or less as it was heard from most Longhouse people at the time of fieldwork:

> "He" then said to the Union Lords, look to the East and see what is coming, and the Union Lords and the people did look and saw a thick "Black Cloud" straight edge stretched from North to South. "He" then asked them of what they thought of the sight, which they had seen? And they answered and said they do not know.
>
> And "He" answered and said, a Foreign Nations, and the colour, of this Foreign Nations, are not like your Race. For they are a Pale faces, and they shall come here, from the East. And they shall have a certain class of "Men" with them, and by their appearances, and their movements, and their talks, it seems their "Goodness" is very "great." But they are not, but they are the Reverse of it. And when you shall be beholding them, and conversing with them, you shall be calling them "Ra-ti-heas-ta-jih," literally translated clergymens, or ministers. And it is those clergymen, or ministers, owns the evil schemes. Evil Policies in every shape and forms. That is to say, their governments and their policies, their many religion schemes, their civilization schemes, is of their own inventions. Is the "Black Cloud" symbolizes. They will offer you to accept their religions. "I" will say again, shun it, reject it, refuse it to accept it. For their religions, their Evil schemes, their evil policies, their civilization, their educational schemes and their enlightenment schemes, is all their own inventive schemes, is embodied in the power of their government.
>
> And if you accept any of their offers. "I" will tell you the consequence of it. And the power of your supremacy, or your holding the possession of your empire, shall be crushed by the Pale face's government, besides many of your nations lives shall be destroyed, and of the said government shall turn you out of your homes and you shall become homeless and landless. And you shall individually be absorbed into the laws of their governments, so then, you as a nations shall cease.

> And as "I" said before, when that Black Cloud gets here, shall go by over you, and disappear to the West. "I" shall come again, and this Union Constitution Government of the Great Peace, which "I" have now completed and established, shall be lying down on the ground. "I" shall then re-establish the said Union Constitution Government of the Great Peace, and "I" shall always be with you, and this Union Constitution Government of the Great Peace, shall then reign and cover over your whole birthright empire, as the waters covers the sea.

Myths of origin related by some of the earlier writers on the Iroquois (Clark 1849, 1:34; Zeisberger 1910, 132), which tell of the coming forth of primordial ancestors of the various tribes from holes in the earth at locations in their ancient territories, are no longer known among the Longhouse people; and this is consistent with the greatly reduced importance of tribal and local distinctions in their present social life. A current origin myth recited by some of the preachers (haiwhasaoha), introductory to the recitation of the teachings of the Gaiwhio, is given here as told to me by an Onondaga chief who often preached the Code on the reservation:

> In the beginning the great Creator, Sǫgwayadisǫ, made a body from the clay of North America, which he baked to a nice brown color and endowed with a spirit or life (odǫnhetra). This being was the Indian (Ǫgwehǫwe). Seeing this being, the Evil Minded One (Ha'nikwahetgę) desired to make one for himself; whereupon, he took foam from the water of the lakes, which he made into a body, but he failed to bring it to life. In this interest, he approached Sǫgwayadisǫ, who agreed to quicken the body if he could henceforth claim all its descendants who would follow him. To this Ha'nikwahetgę agreed, and this being was the white man (hahnyǫo). Soon thereafter Sǫgwayadisǫ gave each the Ǫgwehǫwe and the hahnyǫo a bundle of sticks. The Ǫgwehǫwe kept his only, but the hahnyǫo promptly built a fence with his, thus early revealing his avariciousness. Later on Deganawida was sent, first to the Ǫgwehǫwe who accepted him and his plan for peace (Gaiwhio wiwhagowa'h, the Great Law of Peace); and thereafter, to the hadihnyǫo [pl.] [The informant interjected, "Now that must be Jesus Christ, isn't it?"] who refused his teachings and government and murdered him or thought they did. When the hadihnyǫo came to North America, they caused much suffering among the Ǫgwehǫwe because of their religion, their greed for land, their money, their rum and their fiddle dances. Seeing the misery of the Ǫgwehǫwe, Deganawida sent the four messengers (Geiniyǫwedage) to Skanyadaiyo with the Gaiwhio.

These formulations of the contemporary relationships between Longhouse society, on the one hand, and white (Canadian) society, on the other, identify clearly certain factors of differentiation and points of tension between them and reduce the complexity of present circumstances to a simple moral rule in terms of which Longhouse people are able to articulate their thoughts about, and actions toward, the white man and his culture. There are no myths in which white people and Indians ever appear in a complementary relationship, and their concept of heaven (gaǫhyage) is a place eternally forbidden to the white man.

The following case illustrates one way in which the content of these myths and legends is reflected in current Longhouse social life. In the summer of 1958, I was asked by a group of Longhouse young people to narrate a pageant written by one of their number, a twenty-year-old woman. They were offering the pageant to the public in an effort to raise money for the chiefs to carry on court proceedings then in process against the Canadian government. The opening scene of the drama depicted the coming of Europeans to the American continent. Two men coasted in a boat down a small creek that traversed the natural stage, one of whom was dressed in a black robe and carried a black book (the Bible); and the other had a black bottle (of rum) in one hand and a flag in the other. Upon landing, the two men went into ecstatic revelry, kissing the earth and running their hands through the soil while shouting, "Land, land, and it's all ours!" This occurred while a group of Indians stood in the background observing quizzically these strange goings on. The remainder of the plot was concerned with the wanderings of a fragment of the Delaware tribe who, after being divided by the black book and its bearer, demoralized by the black bottle, and dispossessed of their lands by the flag, were taken in by the beneficent Iroquois, only later to betray them by siding generally with the white man in deposing the hereditary chiefs. The concluding sentences of the script read:

> Let it be known that the Delaware have never shown as much resistance to the white man's religions and governments as have the original Six Nations. The proud Iroquois, the real Iroquois, the true Iroquois remains Longhouse, remains under the shelter of the League and accepts neither the white man's government nor the white man's religion. Let those who wish to live as white men leave this land of ours and *go* to live with the white man. Our numbers are increasing. We have room here in this land of Indians only for Indians!

The Reservation As a Factor in the Continuity of Longhouse Society

The division of social space of the Longhouse people and its reflection in their current mythology has a corresponding physical dimension in the reserve itself with its legally demarcated boundaries; and thus delimited, it is an important factor in the continuity of Longhouse society. The Longhouse people obtain a supplementary part of their livelihood from the land of the reserve.[10] However, the greatest importance of the reservation at present is that it serves as a seat for their social order, which supports their claim to title to the land of the reserve and the notion of land tenure precluding the alienation of land to the white man, noted above. In the context of Longhouse mythology and legend, the social order is endowed with a sacred character, which at best can only be profaned by contact with Canadian society or the white man's ways in general. The reserve is a kind of sanctuary, a retreat where they can carry on in their social life and culture to a degree without interference. Also physical aspects of the reserve, such as its plant and animal life, are endowed with special cultural meanings and used as medicines and omens. In addition, the Longhouse people share their reserve with an awesome array of supernatural entities, such as ancestral spirits (ǫgwasotsǫdak), unattended charms (otsinnagęda'h), and mythical monsters like the great serpent (osaistagowah), some of whom have permanent abode in graveyards, vacant houses, swamps, and isolated parts of the bush. Others, like the great false face (Hadoii Gowa'h) and the spirit of death (tęhdegayahdǫt), visit the reserve periodically or occasionally.

Among themselves on the reserve the social life of the Longhouse people is characterized by a general equality manifested in a constant flow of joviality and joking; off the reserve they become cautious, reserved, and in some instances somber. This change of demeanor, as between on and off the reserve, becomes almost automatic and is acquired early in life, as is shown in the following incident. The five-year-old daughter of some Longhouse friends, who were helping me in my effort to learn the rudiments of the Cayuga language, worked out her own scheme to help, in which I was to tell her a Cayuga word each time upon meeting in exchange for a new word from her. On one occasion, my wife and I chanced to meet the child, her mother, and mother's sister in a grocery store in a nearby town outside the reserve. Upon catching sight of me, the child bounded forward enthusiastically to exchange words, when suddenly she stopped short, paused momentarily, then walked quietly to me and whispered, "I can't tell you an Indian word today because these are all white people here."

Each year during the spring and summer months, there is a fairly general migration or dispersion of Longhouse people for wage-earning activities outside the reserve and a subsequent return in the autumn. Often prior to the outflow of people at the beginning of the season, and regularly after their return in the autumn, conventions (Gaiwhio odakhaohasǫ) consisting of preaching the *Gaiwhio* and a session for repentance (*ǫdatrewa'hdǫ*) are held. Some families live away from the reserve on a year-round basis for extended periods; yet they return periodically to attend ceremonies and, like others who are away for shorter periods, to hold their personal medicine and luck rites (*ǫdwęnǫgotanǫ*) whenever they "feel the need to" do so. After longer or shorter periods away, the great majority of these families return to the reserve, as life histories show and as was attested by the return of several families during the period of fieldwork. One man who had spent twelve years away said, "I know what it is like amongst the whites. I went out after the 'big money.' I stood it as long as I could and then came home to die like an Indian." Another woman who had lived in Buffalo, New York, with some of her daughters for fifteen years said, "We never feel completely at ease out there. There is something that always pulls us back; I suppose it's because we're Indians."

A purely descriptive account of the social life and culture on the Six Nations Reserve does not reveal Longhouse society with any degree of precision, and it may be this factor that lies behind the characterization of social life on the reserve in terms of "factionalism" by some writers (Fenton 1952). It is only when the descriptive data are seen within the context of social system and integration that the customs, institutions, and social practices contained within the bounds of the Six Nations Reserve can be seen to be pulling toward separate foci with any degree of clarity and distinctness. At this more analytical level it can also be seen that although, at the time of fieldwork, the balance of power had long since swung heavily in favor of the Canadian government, and the power of the lineage chiefs or Longhouse society had dwindled to mere opposition and a mystical concept, and that many of the rights of Longhouse society had become mere claims, this opposition and these claims were the ramparts behind which Longhouse people carried on their own system.

Prior Research at Six Nations Reserve

During the fifty years prior to this study, a number of anthropologists carried out fieldwork on the Six Nations Reserve, notable among whom are A. A. Goldenweiser, J. N. B. Hewitt, W. N. Fenton, and John A. Noon. In order to indicate how the present study differs from the work of these scholars, it will be sufficient to identify in a general way the theory and methods that appear to have guided the studies of these men.

Goldenweiser spent about nine or ten months at Six Nations Reserve during the years 1911–13. From this work he published only a few short summaries, which are purely descriptive accounts (in the manner of Radcliffe-Brown 1931, and Fortes 1953a) of various units of Iroquois social organization such as "phratiries," "clans," and "maternal families," and other aspects of Iroquois culture such as the "clan sets of individual names," "the role of women," and "puberty customs" (1912, 464–75; 1913, 365–72; 1937, 361–66). He appears never to have made use of his descriptive data either for analytical or ethnohistorical purposes. His particular use of informants (1912, 475; 1913, 365) and his frequent use of the past tense seem to imply that much of what he recorded existed only in the memories of his informants.

Hewitt spent a considerable amount of time among the Six Nations people between 1886 and the time of his death in 1937. His work consisted largely of obtaining and translating texts in Iroquoian of various myths, legends, and ceremonial speeches. The theoretical and methodological orientation of this part of his work is shown in his own account of meeting Seth Newhouse, an Onondaga chief, who for many years previous to their meeting had been writing in broken English a translation of some of the myths and legends of his people. Among his writings was an account of the founding of the Iroquois Confederacy, which Hewitt was pleased to see, but he complained about Newhouse's English and felt that the old man had added a number of spurious ramifications to what he regarded as the genuine legend. He persuaded Newhouse to rewrite the legend in the Mohawk dialect and to leave out the spurious elements, which Hewitt clearly regarded as an obstacle to his work (Hewitt 1929, 201–6). Some of these same spurious extensions continue to be told among the Longhouse people today (one of them has been presented above), showing that the myths of the Longhouse people are a viable part of their daily social life, changing to meet changing social and structural circumstances. Hewitt has also published descriptions of single cultural complexes such as the "White Dog Sacrifice" (Hewitt 1910), the *Requickening Address* (1916; 1944) for the condolence of deceased chiefs, a paper on the Iroquois concept of the soul (1895) and another on the concept of *orenda* in Iroquois religion (1902).[11] Once again, these are purely descriptive accounts, and no attempt is made to relate these various aspects of Iroquois society and culture to each other, to other parts of the social structure, or to the social system as a whole, although his descriptive material often suggests that these relations actually exist. He also used his material to conjecture a probable date for the origin of the Iroquois League (1918).

Fenton spent a considerable amount of time at Six Nations between 1939 and 1945. His first publication in which material from this fieldwork appears is his monograph *The Iroquois Eagle Dance: An Offshoot of the Calumet Dance* (1953).

In this work he describes the eagle dance rite in very considerable detail on four different Iroquois reserves and shows how the rite is a vehicle for individual personality expression, and that this individual expression goes on within the limits of a single "ritual pattern." He then relates origin myths and traditions associated with this rite, discusses its therapeutic use, describes the ritual equipment used, and describes the internal organization of the rite, ending by establishing some twenty-five "traits," which he uses as a guide to establish the historical origin of the rite among the Iroquois from a study of early documents. He thus exemplifies what he calls the process of "historical upstreaming" by using a detailed description of a present "ritual complex" as a guide to reconstituting the past. In another instance he uses essentially the same procedure to describe the former use of, and to establish a date for, a museum piece—a mnemonic cane—from the Six Nations Reserve (1950). He has also given two straightforward descriptive accounts of the various parts, and their sequence, of a condolence ceremony for installing Cayuga chiefs (1946) and of a feast for the dead (O'hgiwe) held at Six Nations Reserve (1951, 139–65).

John A. Noon did fieldwork on the reserve during the summer of 1941. He made what is essentially a historical study of the development of governmental and legal functions by the council of hereditary chiefs during the reservation period (1949). By selecting trouble cases from the council minutes for the period 1860–1921, and filling out the details from informants who remembered the cases, he showed how the council developed appointive, legislative, and judicial powers in an effort to control and coordinate social life in the new circumstances arising out of reservation life.

In terms of Radcliffe-Brown's discussion of the various operations carried on under the general heading of anthropology and the affinities these operations have with disciplines outside anthropology (1931), the work of the above scholars is best characterized as ethnological and historical; and in terms of Fortes's discussion of analysis and description (1953a), they are "descriptive" only. The various units of social organization, social life, and culture are not further resolved into their constituent isolate elements in an effort to assess what significance they have for other units of structure or for the social system as a whole.

The concept of society as a system of interrelated, functioning parts was more central to Morgan's work on the Iroquois, quite aside from his absorption in the climate of theory of his day, than that of his successors (see Morgan n.d.). In most of the essentials, the study of Iroquois social structure remains where Morgan, and Stites (1905), left it at the beginning of the present century. Professor Fred Eggan has noted, as recently as 1960, that "the task of understanding the Iroquois social system and its development still faces anthropologists, and Morgan's critics have added little to our basic knowledge" (Eggan 1960, 196).

The present study began as an effort to see what would be revealed by the application of modern British social anthropological theory and method to a body of North American data on the Iroquois. After a careful study of the literature, it became clear that modern theory and methods built up around the concept of social system, and the descriptive and historical approach characteristic of the literature, are separate and distinct problems and must be dealt with separately. In accordance with this discovery, the fieldwork project upon which this study is based was undertaken in May 1956, lasting until December 1957. After a brief interval, further fieldwork was carried out between June and mid-November 1958.

In the course of fieldwork it became clear that the household is the veritable hub of the entire Longhouse social system, and for this reason it has been selected as the subject of this study. The study of the household is based primarily on a census of 150 households, representing about 75 percent of all Longhouse households on the reserve. Gathering census data was an arduous task, and oftentimes several visits to a single household were necessary before adequate data on all facets of the census could be obtained. However, exactly for this reason, a wealth of additional insight was gained into their social life and culture; and not least in my estimate, some genuine bonds of friendship and understanding were established. I have every reason to believe that the data obtained are of sufficient scope and accuracy to give a true picture of the norms of household life and structure among the Longhouse Iroquois.

In this chapter, an attempt has been made to identify the people to be studied in time and space, and a brief outline has been given of the relationship of Longhouse society to the economic and political system of Canadian society. In part 2 of the study, the household unit will be described as completely as possible, and in part 3 the relationship between household structure and certain factors of the external system will be examined in an effort to explain why household structure takes the form that it does.

2

Samson Miller, Diane Johnson, and Perry Williams play in front of concrete blockhouse. Photo by author.

Family and friends gather on porch of Jack and Sarah (Doxtater) Kick's frame home for wedding of granddaughter, Doris Kick, and LeRoy Smoke. Pictured: Daisy (Key) Warner (?), Myra Kick (?), Edna Clench, Andrew Clench, Emerson Hill (?), Merlin Myers, Jacob Skye, Teenie (Snow) Skye, Ilene Skye, Alice Myers, Mary Green; by tree: Jimmy Skye, Peter Skye. Others unknown. Photo by author.

Elijah Harris with wife's sister's daughter, Diane Johnson, in front of Harris's modern frame home. Photo courtesy of Ariel Harris.

Log home of Jacob and Teenie (Snow) Skye; 54.7 percent of sample are log or modified-log residences. Photo by author.

Household head Susan Johnson in front of her log home. Photo by author.

Alice Myers visiting with Susan Johnson. Photo by author.

2. The Household

The Cayuga Iroquois word ǫngwadǫnǫksǫ refers to the group of people living in one house (ganǫsot), and it is this group that will be designated by the word *household*. A household comes into being when a man and a woman in some form of conjugal union separate themselves from an already existing household and with their children become established in their own house. Childrearing is the social activity of greatest importance occurring within this unit, verified by the fact that children form the largest portion of the membership of most households (tables 12 and 13). It is also within the context of household relationships that all members of Longhouse society fulfill their needs and desires for food and shelter, made possible largely through the cooperative action of the members of the group. Belonging to a household implies that one may take part in customary activities, such as eating meals and sleeping in the house, without special dispensation. It also implies duties and obligations, such as making a contribution to the economy of the group by its adult members. The bonds that unite members of a household are not easily extinguished. This is especially true when these bonds are based on kinship, for in this sense, every existing household has its roots in some household of the recent past.

Household membership is frequently extended to include dead as well as living members. In fact, quantities of Indian tobacco (oyǫ'hgwaowe) are kept on hand in each household as a means of communication between the living and the dead, and offerings of food are set aside for them. The dead most often feasted within the household group are personalized kin of its members. They are predominantly mothers and mothers' mothers of the giver of the feast, although feasts may be held for fathers, siblings, children, and less often for wives and husbands. They are, in the majority of cases, deceased kin with whom the members of the present household have lived in the immediate past and, to this extent, reflect the most important relationships in the structure of the group. Plates of food may be set aside at mealtime or left on the table at night for the dead by a person before retiring, or a proper feast (o'hdyę̣hakǫfra) may be held for them. Houses left vacant over an extended period are invariably regarded as being haunted. Spirits of former inhabitants linger there; and since there is no one to tend them properly, they become irascible. The feasts referred to here are to be distinguished from those held by lineage groups for their dead.

Members of the separate households are integrated into wider groupings for ritual and jural purposes by the principle of matrilineal descent, thus providing continuity between the household and the external system. Consideration of the influence on the household of factors arising in the external system will be reserved for subsequent chapters. The concern here, however, is with some of the material aspects of the household, with house ownership, and with headship of the household group, as these existed at the time of fieldwork.

Houses

The Longhouse people of Six Nations Reserve live in detached houses that line the grid-patterned roads of the reservation on both sides, at an average distance apart of twelve-hundredths of a mile. For descriptive purposes these houses have been placed into three categories largely on the basis of their construction. The first of these is the log or modified-log dwelling, which had come almost completely to replace the pole and bark dwelling of aboriginal times, prior to the turn of the eighteenth century (Morgan 1881, 65). There are two subtypes that follow the log house very closely in layout and design, differing only in the materials from which their exterior walls are constructed, this being studding and planed siding in one instance and formed concrete or stone in the other. A description of the log house will suffice for these as well. The second is a shanty-type frame house usually built of salvage lumber. The third type is of more recent or modern design, is usually built of new materials, and differs from the others in actual layout and number of rooms.

Log houses were the oldest and most prevalent type in use at the time of fieldwork, comprising about 54.7 percent of the sample (table 1). The most recently built house of this kind was said by its builder to be twelve years old in 1958. The diminution of the stand of conifers on the reserve and the fact that log houses are more laborious to build has caused new construction of this type almost to cease. Their prevalence today arises out of their considerable durability. Many of them are nearing, and some have exceeded, the hundred-year mark. An old chief was once heard extolling the merits of the log house to a younger man. They are warmer in the wintertime, cooler during the summer, easier to keep in repair, they last longer and "they are our kind of house," was the gist of his remarks.

These houses are of simple rectangular design built of pine logs from eight to ten inches in diameter, larger ones being used for a sill. The logs are hewn flat on two opposing sides and notched at the corner ends to effect proper seating and to provide a tie at the corners of the building. Each successive course of logs is dowelled or spiked to the previous one, and the walls are built up in this manner, leaving appropriate openings for doors and windows, until the desired height is reached, this being generally high enough to accommodate two stories. Roofs are gabled and are of rather steep pitch. They are built of flat boards over rafters, which in turn are covered with red cedar shingles or with asphalt composition roofing material. The first floor is usually raised a foot or two from the ground. Both floors are built over joists which are fitted into, and bear on, the walls as they are erected, thus providing a tie between opposite walls. The floor joists are covered with planed or grooved flooring, which is often covered with linoleum. The underside of the upper floor, with its exposed joists, provides the ceiling for the ground floor rooms. Interior log walls are seldom left exposed; rather, they are, as a rule, painted, calcimined, or covered with wallpaper. In some instances, they have been lined with pressed paper or gypsum wallboard; and exterior walls, in a number of cases, have been insulated with imitation brick, shingles, or milled lumber siding. Basically, this type of house consists of two large rectangular rooms, one upstairs and one down, with a very steep stairway connecting them. Lean-tos are added to modify the basic structure and are used for kitchens and for storage. In some instances, upstairs rooms have been partitioned to make two or three separate bedrooms where initially there was but one.

While there is some variation in size, variation in design is usually minor. One log house is twenty-two feet wide and thirty feet long in outside dimension. This house has one room upstairs and one on the ground floor, which together have an interior floor area of slightly less than twelve hundred square feet. Another log house has had a lean-to added, which is used for storage and cooking, making the total number of rooms three, the other rooms being a kitchen and a common second-floor bedroom. This house has a total floor area of less than six hundred square feet. All log houses fit this general description to a greater or lesser degree.

It is rather difficult to assign log houses a cash or market value, since they were not often built at the time of fieldwork, and since they did not change hands frequently by purchase. From a few cases noted, their cash value would appear to lie between one hundred and two hundred dollars. In one instance, a man traded his modified-log house and thirteen acres of land for another lot of thirteen acres of approximately equal value and one hundred and fifty dollars. In another case, a woman purchased a log house and a lean-to for one hundred dollars. This house was moved from the seller's land to that of the buyer and required some repair to make it livable.

Shanty-type frame dwellings built of salvage lumber are usually smaller than the log houses and are of a single story. All walls are built of two-by-four lumber studding and planed board siding, which is often covered with tarred building felt as insulation. One such house, the construction of which was witnessed during the period of fieldwork, was eighteen feet wide and twenty feet long, having an interior floor space of near three hundred and thirty square feet. This space was partitioned to make a kitchen and a common bedroom. The cost of building such a house was about three hundred dollars. In the sample there are twenty-one examples of this type, making 14 percent of the total.

Frame houses of more recent design make up 12 percent of the sample. They are in every case built of new materials, have from four to five rooms, all on the ground floor, and have a total floor area of from five hundred to seven hundred and fifty square feet. The rooms are most often used as a kitchen, living room, two to three bedrooms, and a storage room. The cost of construction of this type of house ran from $2,200 to $3,000. Only in three instances were they owned by persons older than forty-two years.

The extensive uniformity of house design reflects the homogeneous nature of the social life of the Longhouse people. Even where this aspect of homogeneity is broken by the intrusion of house types of more recent architectural styling, this diversity in exterior gives way again to interior uniformity.

About 8 percent of the houses in the sample have only a single room, 33 percent have two rooms, 29 percent have three rooms, 22 percent have four rooms, and 8 percent have five rooms or more. There seems to be no direct relationship between the size of a house and the number of its occupants. Seldom is one turned out of a house for lack of room, although a person may take it upon himself to move from overcrowded conditions. Some younger men, without exception household heads whose families are expanding, have added rooms to their houses, when means were available, as the number of

Table 1. House types

House type	Number	Percent
Log and modified-log	82	54.7
a. Frame construction: old type	26	17.3
b. Masonry construction: stone or concrete	3	2.0
Frame construction: salvage lumber	21	14.0
Frame construction: recent design	18	12.0
Total	150	100.0

members has increased. The average number of persons per household for all types of houses is 5.36.

Every house has a kitchen, or kitchen facilities, about which a considerable part of household life is centered. As a general rule, all kitchens have a large wood-burning range that, in most instances, is the sole source of heat both for cooking and for warming the house. For this reason, a good deal of activity other than culinary is drawn to this room. Not only are meals prepared and eaten here, but here also visitors are received. On long winter nights family and friends gather, sit around the warmth of the kitchen stove and talk, tell stories, carry out medicine rites, play a game of cards or, in a few instances, watch television.

Certain items of kitchen furniture are quite standard in all houses. A version of the stove just mentioned is a regular occurrence. These are generally equipped with an oven for baking purposes, and some have a reservoir for a constant supply of hot water. Each kitchen has a table, usually covered with oilcloth, upon which food is prepared and meals are served. Cupboard space is often at a premium; and for this reason, the table may serve as storage space for certain items of cutlery and crockery, as well as for foods such as bread, sugar, salt, and confections. A number of wooden chairs are placed around the table, and others stand at appropriate places throughout the room. Another item of regular occurrence is the water bench, upon which stands a ten- or twelve-quart enameled or galvanized bucket containing the immediate supply of culinary water. A dipper for drinking purposes hangs on the side of the pail and is used in common by the members of the household as well as by visitors. A basin and soap for washing hands and face are kept on the bench beside the bucket. A second bucket usually stands on the floor at one end of the water bench to receive wash water and off-fall from the table and from the preparation of food. Some kitchens have a sideboard or a buffet, which serves as a cupboard for the storage of cutlery, crockery, pots and pans, and food.

Practically placed near the entrance door is a coat rack or hooks, which serve as a wardrobe for keeping items of clothing in current and daily use. Five of the 150 houses of the sample have electric refrigerators in their kitchens.

Thirty-nine percent of the households have separate living rooms. Often, where this is the case, these depend on the kitchen stove for warmth. In a few instances, these rooms are furnished with an upholstered couch and sofa chair; but most often, a cot serves as a kind of divan. Sideboards and buffets are commonly found here, along with small tables and a number of wooden chairs. Nine households, or 6 percent, of the sample possess television sets, and an equal number have radios. These are most often kept in living rooms; otherwise, these rooms are probably the least used of any in the house.

All houses, except those having only one room, have separate spaces for sleeping. Approximately 59 percent of the houses have one bedroom used in common by all household members and overnight visitors, when these are present; 25 percent have two bedrooms; and 8 percent have three.

Beds consisting of metal bedsteads, a set of coil or trestle springs, and kapok-filled mattresses are in general use. Sheet blankets and homemade patchwork quilts are the usual items of bedding. Some bedrooms are equipped with a chest of drawers or a dresser for storing clothing; others have only a large trunk or two for this purpose. Wall hooks are used for hanging clothes. Chamber pots for night use are a common feature.

There is a kind of special regard for, if not sanctity about, bedrooms. Although the whole household may share a bedroom in common, there are a number of ways by which it is differentiated from the other rooms of the house, over and above the fact of its principal use. The most sacred possessions of all members of the family are stored here. Indian costumes, clothing intended for burial use, rattles, false-face medicine masks, lacrosse racquets, and other sacred articles used in connection with various medicine rites for all members of the family are kept in this room. Powerful charms, upon which depends the well-being of individuals, and in some instances whole lineages, may be kept in a bedroom. Money and other valuables may be placed in a bedroom for safekeeping, as was the case with one elderly woman who lamentingly made known that her savings of eight hundred dollars were in a bedroom trunk when her log house burned to the ground.

The concern of the Longhouse people with housing is, by and large, a concern with basic utility; for example, a comfortable shelter from the elements for persons and possessions of the household and a place for eating meals, for sleeping and for receiving one's relatives and friends. Houses are not built or otherwise acquired in the interest of enhancing social status. In fact, a person is quite attentive not to distinguish himself greatly from his fellows by the house in which he lives. One can detect a definite uneasiness in people whose houses are somewhat "nicer" than the average of their fellows, and ritual precautions are taken by these people to protect themselves from the envy and jealousy (ganosęfra) of their neighbors.

The case of an Onondaga Olympic marathon runner illustrates this point. He returned with considerable fame to the reserve where a rather imposing house was built for him. Soon after becoming settled in his new home, he began to drink compulsively, and this was said to be the work of jealous people, that is, through witchcraft or sorcery (gotgǫtra).[1] He moved to Buffalo, New York; but failing to escape the evil powers there, he moved again to Toronto where he had scarcely got settled when his eldest son was struck by a car and instantly killed. From Toronto he went west, spending some time in Winnipeg, Vancouver, and cities in the United States. He later returned to the reserve where he spent the last years of his life, a defeated man. His lineage matron ordered that his Indian name should be forgotten and no longer used by the members of her lineage. This case, as related by the present matron of his lineage, is known in greater or lesser detail by the majority of Longhouse people. Those who seek to acquire outstanding possessions are cautioned, and even taunted, by kin and neighbors concerning the dangers with which they thus surround themselves. Consideration of this point has been extended here because of the weight it carries in maintaining uniformity in the houses and household life of the Longhouse people. When houses enter conversation, they do so in a practical way. No one compares his house to that of another, nor does he boast about the merits of his house.

Houses are generally quite comfortable. Furnishings tend to consist of essentials, which are usually secondhand pieces, though often well kept. Twelve percent of the houses have hydroelectric lighting, while the remaining 88 percent use kerosene lamps for this purpose. The supply of culinary water is obtained from wells, or, in a few instances, from nearby creeks. Not all households have their own wells, and where this is the case, water may be obtained from the well of a kinsman or from wells located on the nearest school grounds. Kinsfolk invariably allow each other the use of their wells, but this is not always the case among neighbors who are not kin. If a well goes dry, as they often do during a dry summer, this is said to be because the owner was "stingy" with his water supply. There is a premium on cleanliness in the preparation of food and in housekeeping, as well as in the care of one's person, the latter being somewhat more in evidence among women than among men. Floors are scrubbed once or twice each week and are kept swept clean of litter. Dishes and utensils are, as a rule, washed up after each meal. Toilets are of the outdoor type and are sometimes shared by adjacent households if they are close kin. There is a residual fire hazard in all houses, since the majority of them are built of wood and other flammable materials and since, in many cases, chimneys are makeshift. Four houses burned during the period of fieldwork. House fires arouse a pervading sentiment among all the people, and contributions of furnishings, utensils, food, clothing, and money are given to the sufferers.

In all households, ritual measures are taken to insure the safety and well-being of members against the machinations of jealous or envious neighbors. When a house is built, it is common for whisky to be added to the concrete as it is being mixed, or bottles of whisky may be cached in the foundation walls at appropriate points, usually at doors and windows as they are formed or laid. Informants said that silver coins are sometimes used in this way as well. Houses are often built with two or more exterior doors, but rarely is more than one of them used, this generally being a rear door; and people frequently lock doors behind them after entering their houses. Where two doors are in use, one is careful to enter and exit by the same door lest he leave his luck (hodraswha'h), good or ill, behind him. In one instance witnessed while in the field, a front door was taken out of use when the illness of a member of the household was thought to have been caused by witchcraft. Roots, such as that of the water lily (ganosanǫn), are often hung above windows to obscure the vision of witches seeking to molest members of the household.

If a person inherits a house in which he was not living at the time, he will likely hold a feast for the ancestral occupants of the house, some of whom he has known previously. In the course of the rite, tobacco (oyę'hgwaowe) is burned and a speech is made, in which the dead are informed of the transfer of occupancy and are asked to look with favor upon the new state of affairs. They are also invited to participate in the feast especially prepared for them to insure their beneficence. These feasts may be delayed until their necessity is communicated by an unpropitious event or by a dream in which a former occupant of the house is featured; yet they may be held to forestall any such event.

A witch or a sorcerer may direct medicine against a house or the ground upon which it stands, necessitating that it be vacated or moved to a new plot. This occurred in two instances during the fieldwork period. There are also a number of houses among the Longhouse people in which apparently no one has lived for some years' time. The reasons given for the avoidance of these houses are either that someone has died unattended in them or that their former owner possessed powerful charms, the custody of which he failed to transfer before his death. Charms and the spirits of people thus neglected become implacable, thus rendering the houses unsafe for occupancy.

Ownership of Houses

Members of the Six Nations Reserve have only possessory rights in real property. A person may transfer property by sale, gift, barter, or will; but when such transfer pertains to real property, it must be to another member of the reserve only. Land may be rented or leased to nonmembers of the reserve with the consent of the minister of citizenship and immigration. Certificates of possession are issued in the name of the minister and registered in the Indian Office at nearby Brantford. These certificates may be held by both men and women, or they may be held jointly by a man and his wife. Real property held by a man solely in his own name may be disposed of without reference to his wife, and vice versa. If a person dies intestate, his or her estate is inherited by the next of kin; namely, his widow, issue, parents, siblings, and siblings' children. Failing these, the property reverts to the band (Indian Act, secs. 20 and 48).

The current concept of ownership among the Longhouse people respecting real property must be seen subject to these limitations. More complete ownership rights are held respecting items of personal property such as automobiles, household furnishings, tools and implements, produce from gardens and farms, livestock and poultry, objects of self-manufacture such as baskets, lacrosse racquets, handles for hand tools, and similar items that may be sold to anyone, in contrast to the inalienability of real property.

Of the 108 male heads of households of the sample (table 2), 71.3 percent own the houses in which they live; 11.1 percent live in houses that are either owned by their wives or have been lent to the latter by their near kin; 3.7 percent have joint house ownership with their wives; 3.7 percent rent houses; and 5.6 percent have borrowed houses, in four instances from their mothers and in one instance each from a maternal grandfather and a father. The data are insufficient for five of the households with male heads.

Table 2. House ownership

Households with male heads	Number	Percent
Head	77	71.3
Wife (8 houses owned and 4 on loan)	12	11.1
Other:		
On loan to head	6	5.6
Renting	4	3.7
Joint ownership	4	3.7
Insufficient information	5	4.6
Total	108	100.0
Households with female heads		
Head	41	97.6
On loan	1	2.4
Total	42	100.0

There is no stigma attached to a man's living in a house owned or otherwise possessed by his wife; although jokes are sometimes made about such a man's returning home to find himself locked out of the house with his belongings on the front porch. As one older man put it, "Getting a house is something they must work out between them. If the woman has a house and he doesn't, it is most logical for them to move into it."

In the forty-two households with female heads (table 2), there is only a single instance where the head does not own the house in which she lives. In this one case, the head is living in a house that her mother has loaned her.

Houses, and the land upon which they are situated, are owned by the same person in all but two of the 150 households. In both of these instances, men have built houses on land owned by their wives. It is clear that there is a close correlation between headship and house ownership, although they are by no means synonymous, as is shown by the fact that a man can be head while living in a house owned by his wife.

Furnishings and equipment for the household are obtained by purchase, gift, loan, or by self-fabrication. Both husband and wife bring various items to the household, usually individually, and neither is obliged by custom to provide particular items. The characteristic statement in this connection is, "We get what we need wherever we can. We get some presents, the old folks give some things, we buy a piece or two at a time, and little by little we have enough to do with." In some instances, near kin lend items of furniture and equipment not required in their own households to a couple starting out. The following list is an inventory of the principal items of furniture and equipment of one house and the sources of each to the household:

> Washing machine, on loan from wife's mother
> Table and chairs, given to wife by her mother and brother
> Stove, on loan from wife's sister
> Wash bench, given to wife by her mother
> Water bucket, purchased by wife
> Twenty-gallon water container, purchased by head
> Crockery, cutlery, pots and pans, purchased by wife and given to wife by mother
> Television set, being purchased on time by head
> Couch, purchased by wife
> Sofa chair, purchased by wife
> Buffet, on loan from wife's mother
> Sewing machine, on loan from wife's mother
> Bed and mattress, purchased by head
> Quilts, made by wife
> Sheets, purchased by wife
> Bed and mattress, on loan from wife's mother
> Other quilts, on loan from wife's mother

Excluding the television set and the sewing machine, both of which were repossessed by the sellers during the winter of 1957–58, the value of all these items was estimated to be not more than $120.

Headship

Household headship among the Longhouse people is rather poorly defined. Present-day Longhouse households are not corporate groups having perpetuity in time, nor does the head direct the work of the members of the household on a corporate estate, or otherwise exercise any stringent rights over the persons and property of the group. However, there is in every household one person who has ultimate say in decisions that relate to the domestic affairs (in the sense of Fortes 1958, 8–9) of the group as a whole. It is recognized that both men and women may be heads of households, and the Native term most often used to designate this person—either a man or a woman—is hanǫsagwęnio (male) or enǫsagwęniyo (female). It often happens that where a man is nominal head of the household, his wife is the practical coordinator of household affairs. Headship may coincide with either paternity or maternity, but involves relationships beyond the proximate generations of parents and their children

Table 3. Age distribution of household heads

Age	Male heads	Female heads
21–25	2	0
26–30	9	1
31–35	6	1
36–40	16	0
41–45	17	3
46–50	12	3
51–55	5	1
56–60	10	4
61–65	5	6
66–70	14	13
71–75	3	4
76–80	7	4
81–85	2	0
86–90	0	1
91–95	0	1
Total	108	42

in approximately 40 percent of the households. In every case, the kinship status of father, mother, or either grandparent is of greatest importance rather than headship per se.

Male Headship

Seventy-two percent of all the households of the sample have male heads, and 63.5 percent of all males twenty-one years of age and over are heads of the households in which they live (tables 5 and 6). Men tend to become heads of households as they approach thirty years of age, and the average age of all male heads is fifty years (table 3). Most men become heads at some time during their lives, but achieving headship is not synonymous with being a head for life. Furthermore, there are ten men living alone, and they have been included in the tables as male heads.

A man in this position is expected to provide the main economic support for his household, especially food and clothing for his minor children. It is also his duty to keep the house in repair, whether it is his own or his wife's. He is responsible for the provision of wood fuel for cooking and heating purposes, and this he usually obtains with the help of his sons when they are old enough. The male head of the household is entitled to the domestic services of his wife, and for this reason, she will usually consult him before taking a job outside

Table 4. Classification of population sample by age and sex

Age	Male	Female	Total male and female
21–25	17	15	32
26–30	19	24	43
31–35	9	18	27
36–40	21	19	40
41–45	25	22	47
46–50	12	11	23
51–55	10	3	13
56–60	10	12	22
61–65	8	14	22
66–70	19	17	36
71–75	7	6	13
76–80	10	7	17
81–85	2	0	2
86–90	1	1	2
91–95	0	1	1
Total	170	170	340

the house that would upset the routine of these services. He will also expect other members of the household to contribute to its economy and to show him respect and deference. If he owns or otherwise holds possessory rights over the house in which the group lives, he likewise has the right to grant or deny house room to whomever he will. He may act as disciplinarian over his children or may take over any earnings they might have; however, in practice he seldom does either of these. A male head may drive his family to Longhouse ceremonies in his car, but once they enter the ceremony, he sits apart from them; and he is seldom identified with other members of his household in recreational activities off the reserve. Individual personality factors play a considerable part in the nature of male headship as it is expressed in the separate households, and the personal qualities of leadership and industry may have a good deal to say as to how long a man will be able to hold his household together.

A word or two should be said about the position of wives in households having male heads. The important point here seems to be the considerable degree of independence and autonomy maintained by a wife in these circumstances. Longhouse women are alert and forceful, and men are aware of the value of a knowledgeable wife in the management of household affairs and seldom take action in important matters, such as whether to purchase a new car or go on a

Table 5. Proportion of male and female heads

Household type	Number	Percent
Male heads	108	72
Female heads	42	28
Total	150	100

specific job, without first consulting their wives. While a man has claim on his wife's domestic services, he does not control her earnings from work outside the household. She may consult him for an opinion in what she does with her money, but it is recognized that it is hers to do with as she desires. Even in the closest of marriage ties, a woman will always have problems and other matters to talk over with her mother, sisters, or other near matrilineal kin, whom she visits often and who often have a good deal of influence over her. In this connection, it should be said that few men may abuse their wives and keep them for long. As one young woman put it, speaking of a ne'er-do-well who notoriously abused his wife, "There are not many women among us Indians like 'So-and-So's' wife, who lets her husband bully her"; and then she added, "This is probably because she's got no folks here," referring to the fact that this man had brought his wife to Six Nations Reserve from a reserve in New York State. A number of male heads work away from the reserve, returning to their households on weekends, or sometimes less frequently. Wives appear to experience little difficulty in managing household affairs under these circumstances.

Female Headship

Twenty-eight percent of the 150 households have female heads, and 24.6 percent of all women twenty-one years of age and over are heads of households (tables 5 and 6). The average age of all female heads is sixty-five years (table 3). Female heads are mostly women who have passed their childbearing years, and sixteen became heads coincident with becoming widows; however, women often become heads by separating themselves from their husbands and setting up their own households, and twenty-three of the forty-two female heads became heads in this way. There are also a few women who have set up households by their own efforts, never entering a permanent conjugal union. Female heads are nearly always mothers and grandmothers to the other members of their households, and this reflects the strength of the mother-child bond. Even where a female head is living in her house alone (of which there are five instances, all included in the tables), her married children often locate

Table 6. Percentage of age groups in
population sample who are household heads

Age	Male	Female
21–25	11.8	0
26–30	47.4	4.7
31–40	73.3	2.7
41–50	78.5	18.3
51–60	75.0	33.3
61–70	70.3	61.4
71–95	60.0	66.6
Total	63.5	24.6

their own houses near her, and the two households overlap with constant visiting and the performance of reciprocal services.

A female head has full right to determine who is to have room in her house and has ultimate say in the regulation of household affairs. She has fewer limitations in this respect than does her male counterpart. The spouses and common-law spouses of her sons and daughters living with her are subordinate to her authority. They control their own earnings but may be censured by her if she feels they are negligent of the needs of their children, or if they are slow to perform certain duties connected with the household such as providing firewood or repairing the house. A common-law husband of the head also has a subservient position in these households.

Once her children are fairly well grown up, a woman is able to keep a household going by her own efforts, although this is seldom necessary, since in most instances some of her children will be living with her. She receives presents of food, clothing, and money from her children either in exchange for services she renders in caring for their children or simply because she is their mother. After she becomes sixty-five years of age, she is eligible for Old Age Pension, and women of this age find little difficulty living on the fifty-five dollars per month received from this source.

The figures show that men become heads of households about two and one-half times more readily than do women, of whom approximately 75.3 percent are living as subordinate members of households: 53.6 percent with their husbands, 17.6 percent with parents or other near kin (spouses present in about 5 percent of the cases), and 4.1 percent with husband's parents or his near kin. On the other hand, about 36 percent of all males twenty-one years of age and over are subordinate members of households; about 24 percent having never achieved headship and about 12 percent having lost headship, either upon entering a common-law union in their later years with a woman in her house or upon becoming a subordinate member of the household of a parent, child, or other near kin subsequent to their being separated or left widowers. These figures reflect the differential social, economic, and jural position of men and women in Longhouse society. These factors, and their bearing on the problem of headship, will be discussed in the chapters to follow.

In this chapter the types and uses of houses have been described, consideration has been given to house ownership and its relation to household headship, and headship has been discussed in terms of the main rights and duties of male and female heads in coordinating the activities of the members of the group. The age at which headship is attained by males and females has also been indicated. Household headship is not a well-defined status apart from the kinship statuses of parenthood or grandparenthood, and this will be readily apparent from consideration of the genealogical composition of the household group and the economic activities of its members given in the following chapters.

Murray Henhawk drying a winter supply of corn (onęhę). Photo by author.

Grant General setting out traps for muskrats (tiyaǫt) near muskrat house at base of trees. Photo by author.

George Green making horn rattles for sale to tourists, as well as for ritual purpoes. Photo by author.

Joseph Skye tapping maple trees to begin syrup-making process. Photo by author.

Wood-cutting bee by members of Six Nations Singing and Mutual Aid Society. Sponsor gives workers a large meal at end of bee rather than cash payment. Photo by author.

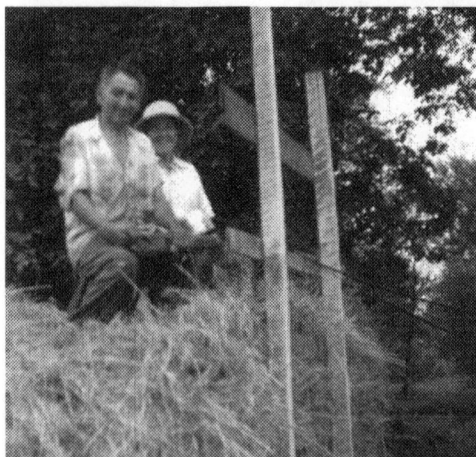

William (Nawǫhais) Johnson and Esther (Henry) Johnson hauling hay for household livestock—two horses, two cows, and a calf. Photo by author.

Alexander (Sęnahse) Jamieson with Nora Hill, who displays her beaded headband and doll in buckskin clothing on a cradleboard made by Sęnahse. Sale of handicrafts supplements income. Photo by author.

3. Some Economic Features of the Household Group

This chapter will address the type of economic activities pursued by the Longhouse people during the period of fieldwork and the degree and nature of the adjustment of interests occurring among the members of the domestic group for economic purposes.

Sources of Economic Income

Cash is of primary importance in all households and is acquired from highly dispersed and individualized wage-labor activities occurring outside the reservation. In some instances, Longhouse people go in groups to fruit farms and canning factories, but their relationship with their employer is always as individuals. Seldom, if ever, are they paid as a group for a task performed and left to allocate the proceeds among themselves. Work is usually performed on a task or piecework basis, and each individual knows exactly what he or she has earned. This applies also where the members of a family go to the same farm as a group, although the earnings of junior members, in cases of this kind, are usually turned over to parents. By its very nature, working for wages off the reserve proscribes the number and kinds of occasions for joint activity either within a single household or between households. Except in the few cases where farming is practiced, woodcutting, house-building, and house-moving are the only activities likely to require joint action. Among the members of the same household, cooperation in these and other matters is taken for granted, and work bees are instrumental in securing interhousehold assistance on these occasions. At the end of such a bee all the participants are given a great meal by the recipient rather than money payment for their services. Occasionally, one Longhouse man will engage another to cut wood for him on the reserve, but this work is not performed under a rigid employer-employee relationship, and wages paid are in every case nominal, consisting of about two dollars per cord of wood cut (a token payment in terms of wages received for work off the reserve) and a meal at the end of the job. By and large then, money flows into the household from extra-reservation work and is little circulated among the Longhouse people themselves.

Work performed for wages is generally of an unspecialized nature. Concomitantly, a person may change from one job to another several times during his lifetime, or even during a single season. The majority of jobs is also seasonal and of short duration. To minimize the uncertainties of this type of work, many people have standing arrangements with employers, whereby they are able to return each season to the same jobs with little or no time lost in quest of employment. In some instances, men or families have worked for the same employer for as many as thirty-five years. Whatever jobs a man may have held during his lifetime, after the age of about fifty he tends to gravitate toward work on fruit farms and in canning factories. Wage income, whether seen from the perspective of a lifetime or year by year, is in most cases of a composite nature.

Government subsidies are also an important, though in most instances supplementary, source of income. They are received monthly by 91.4 percent of all the households in the sample, and will be dealt with in detail later on in this chapter.

Well over half of the households are known to cultivate gardens, which yield an important supply chiefly of potatoes, corn, and beans. Most households rely on the native bush for their supply of domestic fuel. Wild berries, apples, nuts, and maple syrup are also obtained from this source. Some men trap muskrats (tiyaǫt) each spring when the ice flows out of the river and creeks on the reserve. The pelts of this animal are sold off the reserve and the flesh is eaten as a welcomed addition to the usually drab winter diet. During April and May, various fish, especially pike (djigo'hses) and red mullet (o'hwistowęnes), begin their spawning run up the creeks, and schools of smelt appear in the shallows of Lake Erie. Men catch these fish in considerable number, largely for sport, but are always eaten and provide an important supplement in some households each spring. It is also common for members of a household to keep a few chickens, pigs, or a cow or two to augment the domestic food supply in the form of milk, meat, and eggs. These activities are in every case only supplementary to the money earnings of the people.

Division of Labor

In the absence of developed occupational skills and specializations, the division of labor operative among the Longhouse people remains rudimentary and is based primarily on the simple allocation of tasks and responsibilities on the basis of gender. In a library dissertation on Iroquois economics in 1905, Stites notes the division of Iroquois society into what she calls "clans" of men and of women for economic purposes. These corporate gender groups tended formerly to be the units of production and consumption (Stites 1905, 31–32, 74).

This division of economic responsibilities was given ritual expression, a fact that Stites did not note, and here it remains viable today. Each longhouse ritual group is divided on the basis of gender. The groups of men and women thus formed cut across the bounds of individual lineages and are corporate at this more inclusive level. During the first or second week of June each year, the two groups meet to carry out a planting rite (gaoǫtǫwisas—lit. a group of women). In this rite the corporate nature of the groups is graphically manifest in a ritual gift exchange of seeds. After this exchange is completed, the men and women face each other in single file from opposite sides of the longhouse. Each woman sings her personal planting song in turn and petitions either the spirit of vegetation (Dyǫnhegǫ), or the moon (soheka o'hnida) or the thunders (Hadiwęnodages) for blessings on her efforts; after which the men sing women's planting songs and likewise ask for blessings on the women's activities. This is followed by a dance in which the women, reversing the usual order, take the lead, thus emphasizing the paramount role of women in horticultural pursuits. A final dance is performed in which the spatial relationship is side by side. The exclusiveness and the interdependence, the opposition and the complementary nature, of male and female economic roles are dramatized in this ritual.

The pattern of duties and responsibilities dramatized here is operative in the performance of the entire annual ceremonial cycle.[1] The men's group, under the leadership of the lineage chiefs (hodiyanesǫ, pl.) and the male faith-keepers (honadrihǫt, pl.), takes charge of the principal ceremonies (wihowanę geiniyiwhage), setting the date for their performance, making all preparations, and conducting them as they see fit. Meat, the product of men's traditional economic activities, features prominently in these rites only. In former times, it was obtained in a special hunt carried out by the men, but nowadays it is purchased with money obtained from a collection taken up among the men and is cooked by them in a gender-exclusive ceremony. These rites are held twice each year, and at the end of each performance, "control" or "responsibil-ity" (ęsgaiwhįdʌkwęk) is formally transferred to the women, whose duty it is to carry out a service of rites referred to as wiwhawędenyǫ, or appendages. These rites (noted in chapter 1) may be planting, first fruits, or harvest rites, in which vegetable foods only—the products of the traditional horticultural pursuits of women—are featured. These ceremonies are carried out under the leadership principally of the lineage matrons (godiyanesǫ, pl.) who, as a rule, also act in the office of female faithkeepers (gonadrihǫt, pl.).

It follows from the dispersion and individualization of economic activities, referred to above, that the pattern of group activity set forth here has full application in the performance of the ceremonial cycle only. On the other hand, the dual responsibility of the sexes operative in ritual matters provides a model having general validity at present in the economic activities of the Longhouse people. Both the husband and the wife of each household are thought to be responsible for its economic support. The chiefs emphasize in the marriage ceremony and in speeches in the longhouse that a married couple "are a team and should work together in all things." This sense of dual responsibility extends to the obtaining of money with which necessary and desired goods and services are bought. The household serves as a base of operations from which its members can go out to work or in quest of work adequately clothed and nourished, and to which they can return for rest between periods of work; and this is made possible largely through the cooperation of its members, the "teamwork" of the sexes.

Male Economic Activities

It is generally expressed that "a man's work has to do with the out-of-doors." Duties immediately connected with the household consist of the providing of wood fuel from the bush, the building and repair of houses, and well-digging. If the household depends on farming for all or part of its livelihood, this is generally the work of men, although both wives and daughters may assist them. It is interesting to note in this connection that a man may seek to establish a conjugal relationship with an available woman by cutting wood for her, as happened during the fieldwork period when a chief, who had become a widower, spent several days cutting an impressive pile of wood and performing other chores for a young widow, thus winning a place for himself in her household.

In addition to these duties, men are expected to earn money with which to support the household. In the following paragraphs, the main occupations of men are discussed. The quantitative material appearing here and below pertains to the wage-earning activities of males and females twenty years of age and over in the sample of 150 households. The wage rates given for the various types of work were obtained from employers and were the prevailing rates in the region for the period of fieldwork in 1957. Daily, weekly, monthly, and yearly amounts, where given, have been computed based on the established rates and the actual length of time worked, where this is known, or an estimate of the length of time worked where all the details are not known. Estimates have been checked against known figures for most types of work concerned and are known to be representative in each case. The figures are, of course, not offered as a "financial statement" of the economic activities of the Longhouse people and must not be regarded as such. Quantitatively, they are given as expressions of magnitude only.

Fruit Farms

This work may be of a year-round nature, as it is for those who live at the farms in houses provided by their employers. For most people, however, it begins with the ripening of strawberries in June and continues as other fruits ripen, such as raspberries, cherries, early apples, plums, tomatoes, peaches, late apples, pears, and grapes, until mid-October. The work consists largely of picking the ripened fruit and, in some instances, sorting and packing it. Some hoeing and weeding of fields is also done. Work is done on a piecework basis, and earnings vary with the dexterity and propensities of individual workers. In 1957, strawberry and raspberry pickers were paid five cents per cup, or sixty cents per case. A good worker could pick from one hundred to one hundred twenty-five cups per day, averaging from $5 to $6.25 per day. Cherry pickers were paid thirty-five cents per eleven-quart basket and earned on average from $6.30 to $8.75 per day. Grape pickers earned seven cents per eleven-quart basket and could average one hundred baskets per day. Earnings from work in other fruits are comparable.

Tobacco Farms

Tobacco farm work may continue for nearly five full months in a year. It begins with the planting operation in the latter part of May and continues with two hoeings in June and July, topping in July, suckering in July and August, and harvesting, which begins in late August and continues, weather permitting, through October. This work is also done on a piecework basis, and a good worker could earn up to fifteen dollars per day; eight to ten dollars was a more usual daily earnings, however.

Canning Factories

As berries and other fruits begin to ripen during the month of June, the canning factories of the region get well under way. A considerable number of men and women leave the reserve at this time and remain away until November, living in quarters provided by the companies for whom they work. This work is also done on a task basis, and workers averaged between one hundred fifty to two hundred dollars per month.

Work on the farms and in the canning factories of this geographic region has been an important source of income to the Longhouse people for three or four generations. There was some indication in 1957 that young adults of that generation were taking higher paying jobs in mines, in construction work, and in factories; yet farm and canning factory work probably had more significance for a greater number of people than any other single type of employment at the time of fieldwork. During the summer months the reservation is nearly depleted of its active adult Longhouse population by the movement of people to the farms and factories, most of which lie within a seventy-five-mile radius of the reserve. No particular skill is required for these jobs, and individuals may change from farms to factory, and the reverse, once or twice during a single summer. There is a definite social aspect to this work. People often go out in groups, and the atmosphere of a lighthearted joviality that characterizes such groups makes them rather like an outing. Some employers of construction workers express difficulty in keeping their Longhouse employees on the job when these groups leave the reserve for the fruit country. Liaisons may be contracted during these times, which develop into more lasting conjugal relationships, and a number of existing conjugal unions are known to have begun in this way.

Mining

There are two gypsum mining and manufacturing companies located adjacent to the reserve at its northeast and southeast corners, and these companies are an important source of income for the Longhouse people. There is a minimum of job differentiation among the Longhouse employees. Those who work underground are for the most part muckers, whose job it is, after blasting, to load the lumps of gypsum into mine cars to be hauled to the surface. Three men have been trained by the companies in the use of pneumatic drills, and a fourth was being trained as a shuttle car operator. In the manufacturing plant, jobs of Longhouse men are even less differentiated on the basis of skill. These consist of loading wallboard, bagging and loading lime and building insulation materials for shipment, sweeping floors, and general labor in the milling operation. Of the nineteen men in the sample working in these two operations in 1957, most of them had year-round employment. Some, however, were laid off from one to six months during the slack season. Twelve men had worked for these companies from ten to sixteen years, and six had worked from five to seven years. A considerable number of men on the reserve who had formerly worked in these mines had given up their jobs for one reason or another, usually, as they say, because they had no desire to work underground; a more likely reason, however, is that they did not wish to be confined by a steady job. Wage rates extended from $1.62 to $1.76 per hour, the drillers receiving a bonus on a piecework basis, making a gross monthly income of approximately $270 to $310.

General Construction

Other men work at construction jobs, most of which lie within a seventy-five-mile radius of the reserve. Men pursuing these jobs generally work as ordinary laborers in the construction of roads and buildings. A few men drive dump trucks, hauling gravel and earth fill for road building. Such jobs are seasonal, extending from four to ten months' time and lasting only for five to seven months in most cases. In 1957 wages were paid on an hourly basis and averaged from $1 to $1.50 per hour. About nineteen men in the sample were general construction workers and earned approximately $234 to $286 per month.

High Steel Construction

High steel workers are taken much further afield by their work than are men in other jobs, often traveling as far as two to three hundred, or even more, miles away. Married men in these jobs seldom see their families more often than once a week or perhaps once or twice a month. This work is usually of eight to ten months' duration. There are thirteen men in the sample who worked in high steel construction for their primary source of income in 1957. Wages for this type of work ranged from about $2.50 per hour in Ontario to $3.50 per hour in the United States, monthly wages varying from about $495 to $623.

Factories

Seven men in the sample worked in other industrial plants in New York State and Southern Ontario. This work, too, was relatively steady, lasting for six months for one man and from ten to twelve months per year for the other six. The men working in New York State remained away from their families during the week, usually returning to them on weekends. The most specialized of these jobs was that of one man who operated a pipe-dipping machine. Another operated a gasoline-filling pump in a General Motors factory. The others did general labor in an iron and brass foundry, an abrasive factory, a farm machinery factory and a welders' products firm. These men all received a wage of $1.75 per hour or a monthly income of around $352.

Skills and Professions

Although the unspecialized nature of the economic pursuits of the Longhouse people has been emphasized, there were a number of men who had acquired some skills. For example, there were three men who worked as welders in shops, factories, or with construction companies in the region. These men began their trade while working on jobs rather than through systematic vocational training. Two have since passed qualifying practical and written tests to meet vocational standards. Shop work tends to be year-round with temporary layoffs during slack periods. Construction welding is seasonal, usually extending from March through October. These men earned from $1.75 to $2 per hour, or from $308 to $352 per month.

A number of men have acquired skill as carpenters, though only one man used his skill as a principal source of income in 1957. These men have acquired their skill by themselves without serving an apprenticeship or undergoing formal training. Carpenters were paid $1.50 per hour and earned approximately $264 per month.

Auto mechanics, of which there are three or four among the Longhouse people, have also acquired their skill in an informal manner. Three men worked as auto mechanics in garages just outside the reserve during the period of fieldwork. Their jobs tended to be steady and paid about $325 per month.

Although hair-cutting was often done by neighbors for each other among the Longhouse people, one man was a certified barber. He worked in a shop in a nearby town, where he earned an average of about seventy-five dollars per week.

Some men made lacrosse racquets. In one operation these were sold to firms off the reserve for seventy-five dollars per dozen. From two to three dozen racquets were made per month from December to August each year, which produced an income for those months of $150 to $225 per month.

At the time of fieldwork, some Longhouse young people had entered specialized training under the counsel and encouragement of the supervising principal of schools on the reserve, who was himself an Indian, but not of the Longhouse sector. Three young men and one young woman had either entered or completed their training to become school teachers. Another young man had been placed in a vocational school to learn specialized welding techniques;

and two young women were being trained, one in a beautician school and the other as a switchboard operator with the telephone company.

It is, of course, too early to assess the long range impact of this action on the structure of Longhouse society. It is relevant to note, however, that the first young man to complete his training as a teacher left the reserve after his first year and subsequently taught on another reservation in Ontario, where he married an Ojibwa girl. He returned with his wife to Six Nations Reserve in 1958 and was given a school some miles from where he grew up. The mother of the other two young men is often the butt of gossip and ill treatment by other Longhouse women, because, as she said, "I want my boys to get an education." On one occasion, she was scorned as she attempted to assist in the preparation of corn mush for one of the ceremonies at the longhouse, when it was remarked that they must be getting hard pressed for help since this "white woman" (e'hnyǫǫ) was permitted to stir the mush. In discussing this matter with young Longhouse men and women, one young woman said that if ever she should want to be a teacher, she would leave the reserve as the young man referred to above had done. Manual training does not appear to meet this same opposition.

Farming

As stated above, farming is not much in evidence among the Longhouse people, providing the primary income for only five or six households. Where it is carried on, it consists mainly of growing grains such as wheat, oats, and barley as cash crops, which are sold off the reserve immediately after harvest. Quantities of grain may be kept on hand to feed animals or poultry or for seed for the following year. Only two of the farming operations among the Longhouse people were observed where these were the principal source of livelihood for the households concerned. In both these instances the operation was very unspecialized. Soils were weak, having been in long use without systematic fertilization or rotation of crops. Grains are sometimes planted in one half of the field one year and in the opposite half in the succeeding year, thus allowing half of the total acreage to lie fallow in alternate years.

It was not possible to keep a systematic record of the labor and produce of a farming operation. One farmer had a cash income of approximately five hundred dollars from the sale of grain, but also raised cows, chickens, and hogs, as well as potatoes, corn, and other vegetables, which furnished him with the greater portion of his food supply. What seems to be clear is that farming, to make it pay a comparable cash income, requires a good deal more effort and attention than do jobs for wages. In addition, farm income is not immediate, which makes it less desirable.

Supplementary Sources of Income

Because of the seasonal and temporary nature of many of these occupations, and because of the spending habits of the Longhouse people, of which more will be said later on, supplementary sources of income are often required. Mine, factory, and construction work are insurable under the Canadian Unemployment Insurance Act. For the men who qualify, these benefits amount to an average of about nineteen to twenty-three dollars per week for a single man and about twenty-six to thirty dollars per week for a man with dependents, for a number of weeks proportionate to the length of time worked. The maximum duration of such payments was thirty-six weeks in 1957, twelve weeks being a more usual duration for Longhouse men (Canadian Labor Congress 1957, chapters 1 and 6).

Men who work in uninsurable occupations, such as those on fruit and tobacco farms, rely on a variety of supplementary sources to add to their income. One fruit farm worker supplements his income by making walking canes and handles for hand tools, such as axes, hoes, and hammers, which he sells to shops off the reserve. Another keeps about six or eight cows and sells cream to a nearby creamery to augment his income. Gardening, gathering, trapping, and fishing activities, referred to above, are also more in evidence among fruit farm workers. The acquisition of money by working in the occupations listed here is easily the most important economic activity of men, and their role as wage-earners appears to be quite well established.

Female Economic Activities

While the economic activities of men pertain largely to wage earning, those of women lie in two realms, for in addition to their duties immediately connected with the household, they are often important wage earners as well. A woman's primary duties, however, especially when her children are young, lie within the household. It is stated in speeches in the longhouse that a "woman's duty is" to bear children and "to hang the pot" (negodriwhade ayenadjaniyotak), referring to her primary duties within the domestic sphere.

A woman's day begins early, usually at about six to six thirty in the morning, or perhaps earlier in summertime when nearly all adult members of the household are working out. Breakfast is prepared, lunches are made, and workers are sent off. After their departure, or perhaps while they are getting ready to leave, children are awakened, washed, and dressed, given their breakfast and a lunch of sandwiches, and sent off to school. When the woman remains at home, her morning is spent washing up dishes, making beds, and cleaning the house generally. Some women have a set day for the washing of clothes, while others appear to do their washing whenever it is required. When these morning tasks are completed, and if there is time, a woman may do some outside work, such as gardening, or in season gather berries or nuts in the bush.

Lunch is prepared and eaten between noon and one o'clock by members of the household remaining at home and by schoolchildren when their school is near enough to facilitate their return during their noon hour. Afternoons are taken up with ironing, mending, and general repair of clothing or perhaps with further outdoor work. This time of day usually provides opportunities for visiting kin and neighbors as well, and in late afternoon preparations are made for the evening meal and the return of other family members from their work.

After the evening meal and washing up, there is time for further relaxation and visiting. Men often leave the household again and join a group for a game of croquet. Women remain with their children, sometimes taking them, especially the younger ones, for visits with their mothers, sisters (both of whom often live near at hand), or other neighbors. It is common for them to retire by ten to ten thirty at night.

It should not be assumed that women in all households adhere to a rigid routine. Certain of the above details are, of course, a daily necessity, but many of them can be postponed or their order of performance altered as suits personal inclination or the circumstances of each day. If the woman herself is working outside the home, which is most likely during summer and autumn, after the morning details of dressing and eating, the children may be left to themselves, the younger ones in the care of older siblings or perhaps a grandmother. Older girls are capable of performing most household tasks, including the preparation of the evening meal, and other details are just left to the weekend or to convenience. There is close cooperation among all the adult women and girls of the household in the performance of these tasks. As an index of the degree of synonymy between the performance of domestic duties within the household and the role of women, it is interesting to note that a woman may suggest a conjugal partnership to an eligible man by asking who is keeping house for him.

Besides the indoor duties, women cultivate gardens and gather fruit and nuts from the bush. Where cows and poultry are kept, they are often cared for by women. While working on fruit farms, women are given windfall fruit by their employers, which they bottle in considerable quantities during evenings and at night after work; and it is a common thing for them to receive a part of their pay, when working at canning factories, in the form of canned fruits and vegetables. Longhouse women are both industrious and good managers, and it is often their foresight in economic matters that keeps the group going in times of unemployment and scarcity. The fact that the household can serve its members as a base of economic operations is due in no small measure to their industry.

In addition to these duties immediately connected with the household, every able-bodied woman among the Longhouse people either worked for wages for varying periods during the time of fieldwork, or had done so previously. When they did not go out to work, it was usually because they had small children, because of illness, or perhaps because they were caring for their grandchildren while the mother worked. Most often in answer to questions about why they work outside the household, women point to the subsistence needs of their children, or simply reply, "So I can have some money of my own."

Fruit and tobacco farms and canning factories of the region provide the bulk of jobs taken by women. In most instances these jobs are identical with those held by men in these same pursuits, except that tasks involving heavy lifting are restricted to men. The length of time worked varies within the limits of the season for each individual woman and depends usually upon the nature of the demands made on her services in the household. Women work from one to eight months, with the greatest number working from three to four months per year in this unspecialized labor. They are paid on a piecework basis and generally earn slightly more than men doing the same work. They averaged about $170 per month in 1957.

A number of women did housework for white families off the reserve. These women were often in the employ of four or five families simultaneously, working a few hours each day or on alternate days for each. These jobs were quite steady for the women concerned, and they earned $5 to $6 per day, or from $110 to $132 per month.

There were a number of jobs in which only two or three women worked either steadily or seasonally throughout the year. Two women tied trout flies for a firm in Buffalo, New York. They were furnished with the supplies and equipment by their employers and performed this task in their own homes. They were paid thirty cents per dozen flies tied and were able to earn from $100 to $120 per month, the work lasting for five or six months each year. Two women were seamstresses. One of them did reweaving for a tailor shop, and the other sewed small bags of burlap, which she filled with sawdust. These bags were used by the pipe-laying firm for which her husband worked. She earned $408 in 1957 from this employment. Three women did janitorial work in schools near their homes, for which they were paid from twenty to thirty-five dollars per month. Another woman operated a small dairy farm. She milked from four to six head of cows and separated the cream, which she sold to a creamery in a nearby town. She received approximately fifteen to eighteen dollars per week from this activity.

Economic Activities of Children

Children are also expected to make a contribution to the economy of the household, and their first activities of economic consequence begin in and about the house itself under the supervision of their mothers or other adult women. It is generally believed that children should be assigned tasks as soon as they are capable, and in keeping with this belief, young girls from five to eight onward are given tasks to perform, such as sweeping floors, preparing food, and washing dishes, while their brothers from six years and onward do chores, such as carrying water and fetching firewood. Both young boys and girls help in the hoeing of gardens. It is often said that "it is bad when children are not made to work when they are young; they will be lazy and will not know how to provide for their own households when they grow up."

In former times on the reservation, formalized though not elaborate passage rites marked the transition from mere tutelage in economic activities to that of genuine contributors. When their voices began to change, boys were given an axe—some say a dull one—and were shown a pile of logs or a number of trees, which they were expected to cut into usable dimensions. At the first menses, a girl was given a quantity of corn, enough to keep her busy steadily for five or six days, which she was required to pound with pestle (kasiisdʌ) and mortar (ganikdah). It is the general belief that activities performed at times of crisis somehow perpetuate themselves in the lives of those who perform them. In a considerable number of households during fieldwork, pubescent boys (atadwęnadeni) and girls (ęyǫ'hdok) were made to arise early and were kept busy with physical tasks throughout the day. These practices appear to stress the economic value to the household of habitual diligence and industry. From the ages of twelve or fourteen, boys and girls are often taken or sent by their mothers to fruit farms to work. Their earnings are, in nearly all cases, given over to their mothers and used for the entire household, though often a certain amount is returned to the child to be spent on some specific want. The control of the earnings of minor children by parents is general among the Longhouse people, and it is expressed that "it is right for them to do this because the parents have worked hard to raise their children." As one man and his wife explained, "Guidance should be continued until their [the children's] minds are grown up enough to look after their money properly."

As young men and women approach the age of eighteen or twenty, they begin to assert their jural and economic independence. There is no formal rule that fixes the time or age at which they begin to control their own earnings, rather it seems to occur just as it works itself out in individual cases.

The attainment of jural and economic maturity, though informal, often has a spatial correlate in that young people, especially young men, move out of their parental households for longer or shorter periods. I once heard a father instruct his two eldest sons, aged twenty-three and nineteen, prior to their departure for work in a canning factory near Simcoe, Ontario. "Don't leave your money out there," he said. "If you're going to spend it, spend it on something you can bring back with you." The boys had reached the age when further control over their earnings was difficult, and what their father had in mind was for them to use their money to buy clothing and other useful items. He later praised his sons for buying themselves new coats, trousers, and shoes, but complained at the same time that they had not given the remainder of their money to their mother as they used to do. They had gone to stay with their mother's mother after returning from the factory and had presumably given their earnings to her for safekeeping, since neither he nor his wife had met with success in their attempts to find it anywhere in the house. The numerical data do not permit a decisive statement of the facts on this score, but it is clear that departures of this type are a common occurrence, appearing to be more frequent where the father or male head is present and an active supporter of the household.

A complete break with the natal household seldom occurs, however, and once the right to control own earnings has been established, reintegration within the group often takes place. Where this occurs, and in instances where control of earnings has been effected without change of residence, young men and women continue to contribute to the economy of the household; but now their contributions take the form of gifts, including money, and of individual purchases of goods consumed by the entire household group rather than the turning over of money outright to parents. One young man gave both of his parents presents of money and bought clothing for his younger siblings and an electric toaster for his mother. In another case a young man bought his mother a washing machine, costing nearly two hundred dollars; yet another gave ten dollars each month to his mother when he was working, to be used for the whole group.

Most unmarried young men give their money to their mothers for safekeeping, and if the household is in need, they allow this money to be used. The important factor for the point at hand is that it is they who now have the say as to what is done with their earnings. Contributions of this kind usually come to an end upon marriage in order, as they say, "to avoid trouble" with the spouse of the contributor.

Summary Of Wage-Earning Activities

The following tables summarize the data on male and female wage-earning activities. Once again it should be stressed that the figures given are only approximate, that they have only a plus or minus value for individual cases. However, they are helpful in lending a measure of precision to the part of the household economy to which they are related. The information given here relates to the one hundred households in the sample in which there is a conjugal pair, one of whom is head of the household. These households have been used because they afford an appreciation of the empirical division of economic responsibilities within households having the husband-father-wife-mother relationship at the center of the organization.

Table 7 shows that literally all of the one hundred men had access to one of the occupations or sources of income discussed above for at least part of the year. Occupations connected with fruit and tobacco farms and canneries, and with gypsum mine, construction, and factory work, predominate, claiming about 59 percent of the men included. Another 9 percent worked in skilled or semiskilled trades, representing three auto mechanics, three welders, a carpenter, a barber, and a man who manufactured lacrosse racquets. Four percent were farmers, 20 percent received either Old Age or Veterans' Pensions as their main income, 2 percent were incapacitated, and the data are incomplete for 6 percent of these men. As for the length of time worked, 17 percent worked from three to six months, 31 percent from seven to ten months, and 24 percent were employed on a quite steady basis for eleven to twelve months of the year. The level of income for men fluctuated widely, having a range from about $510 to $6,160 per year, with an average estimated wage level, for sixty-nine men for whom the data are most complete, of approximately $2,624.66.

Table 7. Summary of male economic activities

Principal occupation or source of income	Approximate number of months worked during 1957								Total	%	Estimated income (dollars)
	1–2	3–4	5–6	7–8	9–10	11–12	GP*	Other			
Fruit and tobacco farms and canning factories		9							9	9	510–838
			3						3	3	1,020
					7				7	7	1,800–2,000
Gypsum mine and plant				1					1	1	1,996
					1				1	1	2,851
						13			13	13	3,240–3,660
						2			2	2	5,460–5,500
High steel construction				1	7				8	8	3,960–6,160
General construction labor	3								3	3	1,029–1,248
			2						2	2	1,404–1,544
				2	1				3	3	1,802–2,574
Factories				1					1	1	2,352
					2				2	2	3,080–4,095
						4			4	4	3,168–4,548
Auto mechanics						3			3	3	4,032
Welders				1					1	1	2,464
						2			2	2	3,696–4,200
Farmers				4					4	4	500—

Principal occupation or source of income	Approximate number of months worked during 1957										Estimated income (dollars)
	1–2	3–4	5–6	7–8	9–10	11–12	GP*	Other	Total	%	
Handicrafts					1				1	1	1,687
Carpenter				1					1	1	2,112
Barber					1				1	1	2,775
Old-age pension							16		16	16	534
Veterans' pension							4		4	4	1,500
Incapacitated								2	2	2	
Insufficient information								6	6	6	
Total	0	12	5	11	20	24	20	8	100	100	
Percent	0	12	5	11	20	24	20	8	100	100	

* Government Pensions

Table 8. Summary of female economic activities

Principal occupation or source of income	Approximate number of months worked during 1957								Total	%	Estimated income (dollars)
	1–2	3–4	5–6	7–8	9–10	11–12	GS*	Other			
Care of own children and household								20	20	20	
Fruit and tobacco farms and canning factories	19								19	19	170–340
		19							19	19	510–704
			8						8	8	850–1,020
				1					1	1	1,232
Domestic help					2	1			3	3	1,100–1,210
Tying fishing lures			2						2	2	600–720
Janitor work					1	1			2	2	350–600
Dairy farm						1			1	1	
Seamstress			1						1	1	408
Old-age pension							10		10	10	534
Mothers' allowance							1		1	1	948
Incapacitated								3	3	3	
Insufficient information								10	10	10	
Total	19	19	11	1	3	3	11	33	100	100	
Percent	19	19	11	1	3	3	11	33	100		

* Government Subsidies

Table 8 summarizes the data on wage-earning activities of the wives in these same one hundred households. Twenty percent of these women did not work out (that is, outside the home) during 1957, and in every case they were mothers in expanding families. All had worked off the reserve previously, and all expected to do so again when it should become convenient. It is clear, however, that a considerable number (56 percent) worked outside the home for wages despite the demands made on their time and energies within the household itself, 47 percent working on farms and in canning factories and 9 percent working in various jobs. Eleven percent received government subsidies as their main source of income, but most of these women worked for a time on fruit farms or in canneries as well. Three percent were incapacitated, and the data are incomplete for 10 percent. Forty-nine percent, most of whom worked either on farms or in the canneries, worked from one to six months, and the other 7 percent worked for seven to twelve months. Those receiving government subsidies received them monthly throughout the year. The level of income for these women ranged from approximately $170 to $1,232 per year, with an average estimated wage level, for fifty-eight women for whom the data are most complete, of $612.53 per year.

Correlated with the extensive role of women in economic activities is the strong desire on the part of most women to keep mobile. Although Longhouse women love their children and are faithful to them when they arrive, they do not appear zealously to desire them in advance, and their confinement at childbirth is often very brief.[2] These circumstances also stress the value of the mother-daughter bond and of having a mother close at hand to take care of children once they are born, thus freeing the young mother for outside work.[3]

By comparison with men, the range of occupations worked in by women is considerably limited. They also worked for shorter periods of time, as a rule, because of their household duties; and their income was likewise, in most instances, less.

The numerical data have lent a measure of precision to the stated rule that the economic support of the household is to be a matter of teamwork between the sexes. The nature of the contributions made by junior members of the household will become clearer from a consideration of the household budgets presented below. The data given here also suffice to show the nature of income in households having male heads, since 91 percent of those considered are of this type.

As for the forty-two households with female heads, each head has her own personal income in about 85 percent of the cases, 50 percent being in the form of government subsidies and 35 percent being in the form of wages derived from work on fruit farms and in canning factories, as domestic help, and on her own farm. Income from these sources is usually sufficient for the head to meet her own immediate economic responsibilities. As stated above, women who receive government subsidies, such as Old Age Pensions, often supplement these by work outside the reserve whenever they are not too old or otherwise incapacitated. A few female heads, about 7.5 percent, rely almost completely on their sons and daughters for their sustenance. The data are incomplete for the remaining 7.5 percent of the female heads.

Where the household is composed of two, three, or four generations, the income of the head is often overshadowed by that of sons, daughters, or their spouses. This is so for both male and female headship, though more especially for the latter, and this indicates that household headship is not definable simply in economic terms.

Where households with female heads are of a single generation, the head is more immediately dependent upon her own resources, although in most households of this type, the house itself is situated in close proximity to that of married sons or daughters, and there are frequent exchanges of goods and services between them. Where a female head has a separated daughter and her children living with her, there develops a close partnership between them, in which presents of money, food, and clothing are exchanged for childcare. The daughter, as a rule, bears the main economic burden of feeding and clothing her own children under these circumstances, although there is a general sharing of food within the group irrespective of the purchaser. It sometimes happens that a female head will keep a grandchild in her household while its mother resides elsewhere. This is done by the woman in the interest of having some help and company in her approaching old age, and she may assume full economic responsibility for such a child or children. One of the adult women, usually the daughter, will be free to work outside the household. The two women cooperate also in work about the house. The spouse of the daughter in these households usually has the largest income, and he is expected to use a good deal of it in support of the household, since his children are there. If he is shiftless or wayward in his responsibilities, he may be censured by the head, which he takes usually in complete silence.

Where a female head of the household takes in a common-law husband, each has his or her independent income, and the relationship appears to turn on cooperation in specifically domestic tasks, with the man perhaps contributing the larger portion of food in exchange for having his daily needs looked after by his common-law wife. Men in this relationship are always on a precarious footing, since their contribution to the household economy is dispensable.

Government Subsidies

Money paid to individuals by both the Canadian federal government and the Ontario provincial government in the form of Old Age Pensions, Family Allowance, Unemployment Insurance, Veterans' Pensions, Mothers' Allowance, and Disabled Persons' Allowance is an important source of income in most households among the Longhouse people. The amount of the Old Age Pension was twenty-five dollars per month prior to January 1952, when it was increased to forty dollars. In July 1957, a federal election year, it was increased to forty-six dollars per month; and in November of this same year it rose to fifty-five dollars. Fifty-six men and women in the census of 150 households received Old Age Pensions in 1957, amounting to $534 per person per year.

The amount of Family Allowance paid for each child varies from five to eight dollars with the age of the child. One hundred and two households of the census received these payments in 1957, ranging in amount from $60 to $672 per year, making a total of $29,076 or an average of $285.06 per receiving household per year.

Six persons in the census received Veterans' Disability Pensions amounting to $1,500 per year for each. Other Disability Allowances amounting to $534 per year were received by two people, and two women received Mothers' Allowance payments of $948 each per year.

The data are incomplete with regard to the amount of Unemployment Insurance paid to Longhouse workers. However, based on the length of time worked in insurable occupations during 1957, about twenty men in the sample of 150 households were eligible for these payments. The majority of these men had dependents and would have received about thirty dollars per week for twelve weeks, amounting to approximately $360 per man, or $7,200 total.

The approximate total of all government subsidies received in 1957 by members of the 150 households, not including Unemployment Insurance, was $72,024; and this is an average of $480.16 per household. The actual range in amounts covered by the households is from nil to $1,788. Nineteen households received no subsidies; however, they constituted the principal source of income to thirty-one households. In most cases where subsidies were not the main source, they were the chief supplementary income to the household. These data are summarized in table 9.

Table 9. Types and amounts of government subsidies (dollars)

Type of subsidy	Amount per household	Number of households	Total amount
Family allowance	60–672	102	29,076
Old-age pension	534–1,068	46	30,984
Veterans' pension	1,500	6	9,000
Disability allowance	534	2	1,068
Mothers' allowance	948	2	1,896
Total			72,024
Unemployment insurance	360	20	7,200
Total			79,224

Interhousehold Exchanges of Goods

Any consideration of economic activities among the Longhouse people would be incomplete without some mention of the redistribution of goods effected by certain aspects of the ritual system. It was said earlier in this chapter that the circulation of money among the Longhouse people themselves is very limited. On the other hand, goods such as food and cloth are transferred; and though the amounts involved are not vast, they have some economic and a good deal of social significance. The aggregate of ceremonies held annually at each of the four ritual centers called longhouses (ganǫses), lineage rites, and the personal luck or medicine rites of individuals are the media through which this redistribution is accomplished.

In the course of a year's time, the officials of each longhouse ritual group collect about four hundred fifty to five hundred dollars among their own members, which they redistribute within the group, largely in the form of meat and cloth. In addition, participants in the various ceremonies of the annual cycle bring quantities of food, which are placed in a common lot and redistributed among all present at the end of each ceremony. The amount of food thus contributed and redistributed probably exceeds in value the cash referred to above. Both the money and the contributions in kind come from the households that make up each longhouse group and are subsequently reallocated to them.

During the winter months from mid-October through February, the pace of ceremonial life is greatly intensified. Individual or lineage rites, most of which are nocturnal, are almost a nightly occurrence. A Longhouse friend, who was forty-five years of age at the time of the census, told of how as teenagers he and his friends would spend the wintertime attending lineage O'hgiwe and individual medicine rite feasts. "We would eat all night and sleep all day," he said. During the winter of 1956–57, I found it very difficult, indeed, to keep up with the pace of these activities, partly due to their frequency (more than one sometimes being held on the same night) and partly due to their nocturnality. This intensification of ritual activity during the winter months is taken for granted by the Longhouse people. When called upon to explain it, they refer to the fact that many of the rituals performed relate to the dead who are believed to be present, and that their presence always causes severe frost; hence, it would be ruinous to hold the ceremonies before crops are harvested and the vegetation ceases to grow.[4] There is the occasional agnostic among them, but the rites are never questioned generally; and it appears quite logical in the eyes of the Longhouse people that since these are medicine rites, and since the incidence of illness is greater in winter, this naturally calls for an intensification of therapy during this period. This whole complex is projected onto the earth itself, which must be nurtured back to life and health through the appropriate rites after each winter.

Of greater significance for our present concern is the correlation between wintertime and the intensification of ritual activity on the one hand, and the incidence of leisure and unemployment on the other. Winter unemployment is the cause, in many households, of a considerable reduction in the amount of food and clothing available. This reduction is no longer severe, and has been mitigated considerably by the receipt of Old Age Pensions since 1950, Family Allowance since 1945, and to a lesser degree by Unemployment Insurance. Yet one can detect a loss of body weight among the members of some households for this reason. Since nearly every ritual culminates in the redistribution of food and cloth, at least one very important function of this intensification of ritual activities is that it insures a distribution of available resources at a time when this is important. This was, no doubt, a significant factor in past times (Stites 1905, 74–76)—a kind of Indigenous welfare system. The system continues to be relevant today, though supervened to a degree by the payment of subsidies by the Canadian government, as noted. On one occasion during the fieldwork period, a lineage matron joked with her husband, saying that he made his living in wintertime by "talking to stoves," alluding to the tobacco-burning rite that is a part of most ceremonies, and for which the performer is usually given a shirt and an extra portion of food at the feast. He countered with the idea that if he could find some way to trade shirts for trousers, he would be "well fixed up." This exchange between the couple arose because my wife and I were present in their household at mealtime when much of the fare was "feast food." It is not unusual during winter months to accumulate considerable quantities of food in this way, as was experienced during the winter of 1956–57, when on several occasions my wife and I accumulated (and shared our excess with needy families) twenty-five or thirty pounds of food consisting of bread, corn bread, pies, cakes, cookies, doughnuts, crackers, baked beans, mashed potatoes, rice pudding, corn soup, salt pork, and apples. The following are lists of kinds and amounts of food appearing in four of the numerous feasts attended during the winter 1956–57.

Feast 1

On this occasion an Eagle Dance rite (*Ganregwae*) and a Bear Dance rite (*O'hhnyagwii'kya'h*) were performed for two men who are "ceremonial friends" (*honatsi*). Each man had the responsibility to carry out the rites on alternate years, which includes the bearing of the expense involved. Twenty-one adults from twelve different households were in attendance for this performance, which began at 8:30 p.m., December 10, 1956. The goods distributed were as follows:

> One chicken, weighing approximately seven to eight pounds
> Eight to ten dozen cookies
> One plug of chewing tobacco
> Forty cigarettes
> One and one-half gallons cooked rice with dried currants and sugar added
> Four gallons corn soup with salt pork added
> One pound peanuts (consumed in connection with ceremony)
> One gallon thimbleberry juice (consumed in connection with ceremony)

Feast 2

Three separate rites were performed on this occasion: a "word-shaking" rite (*gaihǫdadǫ*) for one man, and a Dark Dance or Blow-out-the-lights rite (*Deyotsǫdaigǫ*) and a Bear Dance rite (*O'hhnyagwii'kya'h*) for another. Each of the men furnished the food necessary for his own rite or rites and had enlisted the help of a woman, who was the mother of one of the men and a sister's daughter of the other, to prepare the food for the rites, which were held beginning about 9:00 p.m., December 11, 1956. There were twenty adults and one child present from nine separate households. The singers, the speakers, and the lead dancer all received special portions of food. All others present shared equally.

One gallon thimbleberry juice (consumed in connection with rite)
One boiled pig's head (partially consumed in connection with ceremony)
Three gallons corn soup with salt pork added
One and one-half gallons sweetened corn mush

Feast 3

This was the occasion of an *O'hgiwe* feast for the dead of a small lineage group held December 23, 1956, with thirty-six people present who were members of twenty-five different households. The goods distributed were:

Ten pies	Four dozen apples
Four cakes	Two pounds candy
Five pounds crackers	Six plugs chewing tobacco
Ten dozen cookies	Eight loaves corn bread
Eight dozen scones	Two gallons rice pudding
One dozen oranges	Five gallons corn soup
Three men's work shirts	One large towel
Sixteen yards cotton print cloth	Eight silk handkerchiefs
Eighteen white handkerchiefs	

The bulk of these items were furnished by the members of the lineage, although it is common for friends and others present to bring contributions of food.

Feast 4

The following items of food were distributed in connection with a feast, *o'hdyẹhakọfra*, held to placate the deceased maternal grandmother of the young woman for whom the feast was held on March 6, 1957. Twenty-one adults and six children were present, representing twelve households.

Twelve pies	One gallon baked beans
Twelve dozen doughnuts	One gallon rice pudding
Five cakes	Seven half-pound loaves of bread
Ten pounds salt pork	Four loaves corn bread
One gallon mashed potatoes	Four gallons corn soup

The goods distributed on each of the above occasions were seen both in aggregate and after they had been distributed. Some of them were consumed on the spot, but much was carried home. Every household has a special basket and a soup pail used to carry food to and from the longhouse and such feasts held in homes as the ones mentioned here. Some feasts are simpler than feast

2 above, yet some are more elaborate than feast 3. The actual number of such feasts held varies somewhat from one year to the next; however it would be a conservative estimate to say that there are between fifty and sixty ceremonies held each winter involving distribution similar to those given above. The well-being of literally every man, woman, and child is believed to be associated with one or the other, sometimes several, of a long list of supernatural forces, all of which require to be placated or "amused" (ɛyetinikowi'h) in this manner; and it is unusual for a person to allow more than two years to elapse without finding some reason to have his or his children's rites performed. Because it is less expensive, many people have their personal rites performed at the great Midwinter Festival, in which two days are set aside for this purpose.

Circulation of goods in the manner just described overshadows in importance any circulation of cash among the Longhouse people, and this fact affords a good deal of insight into the way in which the current economic system is adapted to, or joined onto, other aspects of the social system. This feature of the system will be discussed in more detail in the final chapter.

The level of income of the members of the households, noted above, may appear to preclude the activities under discussion here from any virtual economic relevance. It is true that their significance has been reduced in some instances by year-round employment and by the receipt of government subsidies within the last ten to fifteen years; yet the spending and consumption habits of the Longhouse people ensure them of at least a minimum of economic relevance, and it is the problem of expenditure within the household which must now be considered.

Expenditure and Consumption in the Household

The highly dispersed wage-earning activities characteristic of the Longhouse economy appears to narrow greatly the range within which a person is willing regularly to share his earnings; and this factor has considerable influence in initiating early fissioning within the household group, therefore inhibiting the development of a more extended household structure. This inference is strengthened by the departure, referred to earlier, of young adults from their natal households in order to gain control over their earnings and by the fact that their reintegration into the group, when this occurs, is accompanied by the use of money in the group's interest. It is also significant that there are very few instances where two or more married male siblings or married males of the same generation live in the same household. The following case is pertinent here.

During the winter of 1955–56 and the following spring, John and Tom, who had married sisters, were living with their wives in the household of their mother-in-law. John, who had been doing construction work, was laid off at the onset of winter. He had no savings and no income except a few dollars now and again, which he earned cutting wood. In his extremity he managed to open a credit account at a nearby grocery store. Tom, on the other hand, was doing maintenance work in a farm machinery factory and kept his job throughout the winter. He was the only member of the entire household to have any significant income during the period concerned. Upon arriving home on payday, he was given a grocery list, which his wife had made up in collaboration with her mother and sister, and was sent off to make the purchases. Tom knew about John's credit account; and when he had gotten all the items on his list together, he instructed the storekeeper to charge John's account with half of the total amount, which seemed only fair. Tom said nothing about his handling of the grocery account to the other members of the household, however. This procedure occurred several times during the winter and spring. In due course, John obtained employment and upon receiving his first paycheck, went off to settle his account with the grocer. The shock that followed his discovery of Tom's action precipitated an alienation between the two men, which eventuated in the setting up of a separate household by John and his wife a short distance from that of his mother-in-law.

We have noted that at least a portion of the earnings of some adults flows into households other than their own, as in the instances where elderly men and women rely on their sons and daughters for at least part of their sustenance and where daughters give their mothers gifts of money and other desirables in return for childcare. It also happens among a woman and her daughters that they will share a portion of their earnings with one of their number who was unable to work outside the home for one reason or another. This applies *a fortiori* where the one remaining at home performs a service such as childcare for those who go out to work, as was the case with one woman who was unable to work out during the summer of 1956 because of illness. She looked after her mother's house and took her sister's child into her own, thus freeing them to spend the summer working in a nearby cannery. For this she received a blouse from her sister and a set of beverage glasses from her mother, as well as a few dollars over and above the cost of food for her sister's child. Gift-giving on birthdays and exchanges at Christmas time are common among a woman and her daughters and sometimes between neighbors who are not kin.

Sons may continue to give their mothers money after marriage, but this is often a source of complaint by wives, which may lead to accusations of witchcraft between the wife and her mother-in-law or between the mothers-in-law on both sides. Glen was censured severely by his mother-in-law, in whose household he was residing, when she discovered through her daughter, Glen's wife, that he had given his sister, Myra, fifteen dollars from his paycheck on several occasions with which to buy clothes. Myra was a single mother residing with her father and stepmother. Upon being told by a neighbor that a witch light had been seen moving about near her home, the stepmother commented that it was probably Glen's wife out looking for him. Because of such events women often lament the marriage of sons or grandsons upon whom they have built hopes for assistance in their old age, and most people agree that a person's first duty economically is to his or her own household. The flow of earnings into households other than that of the earner, then, is both limited and irregular, and the availability of government subsidies at present to both the aged and incapacitated obviates a good deal of necessity for this.

On the other hand, it is necessary to guard against the impression that all the wages of the various members of the household flow into a unitary fund from which the daily wants and exigencies of the household as a whole are met, for such is seldom if ever the case. A concomitant of the high degree of individuality in wage-earning activities is seen in the fact that the earnings of adults are managed and spent by those who earn them. A man seldom turns money over to his wife for her to disburse, except for a predetermined purchase or perhaps to pay a bill. He may receive a grocery list from her, but generally it is he who makes the purchase with his money; and this is so for all the adult members of the household. The fact that spouses may contract debts with each other by the lending of money, as may siblings, is indicative of the degree of autonomy in financial matters maintained by individual adult members of the group. There is general agreement, however, that it is difficult, especially in the case of sisters, "to ask them to pay back." People also expressed the idea that adult children should repay money borrowed from their parents, but parents should not be expected to repay money received from their children, believing that children are eternally indebted to parents for having been nurtured and raised by them.

It is clear that there must be a degree of coordination between the spending of individuals and the interests of the household group as a whole, especially if the task of childrearing is to be fulfilled successfully. In nearly every household it is a woman acting in the role of wife-mother who stands as coordinator between the individual wage earners and the needs and desires of the group, especially those of her minor children. A woman in this position has a sustained and intimate contact with the economic interests of the group, whereas the husband-father, upon whose earnings initially the group is primarily dependent, is detached from the household group in wage-earning activities and to a considerable extent in his spending as well. There is a general exodus from the reserve on Friday and Saturday evenings, regular paydays for most types of employment. Groups of men form for drinking parties and gaming activities such as billiards, bowling, and bingo, which take place largely in the nearby town of Caledonia. Men are rarely seen in company with either their wives or children on these occasions. It was not possible to obtain detailed information on the amounts of money spent in this manner, however it appears likely that it is considerable in many instances.[5]

Without the aid of a central household fund of some sort to establish a priority of general household interests over individual spending of this type, the task of coordination can be a difficult one. While reflecting on her personal experience, one young woman said, "When I was a child, most of my clothing came from the places where my mother worked [were given by her mother's employers]. I don't remember my father ever buying me a pair of shoes or a stitch of clothing. I believe my mother is in heaven, but I hope my father is in hell!" While this is, no doubt, an extreme case in some respects, it fits a context within which all people are familiar, though perhaps in milder form, either from their own experience or that of kin or neighbors. It is not uncommon for a woman to leave her husband under such circumstances and assume the burden of caring for her children by herself, and Budget Case 1 (below) provides an example of how a household economy is ordered when this happens.

As discussed earlier, women frequently supplement the income to their households from other sources by going out to work themselves. Whatever lessens the value of the husband-father's earnings for the group is likely to enhance the value of those of the wife-mother, and the importance of a woman's earnings for the household must be seen in this context. Older children may also be sent out to work to help with household expenses, and women importune their adult, unmarried sons to buy groceries and other needed items for the group. It appears oftentimes that it is easier for them to do this than to approach their husbands. It is commonly said that "a woman will always find some way to provide for her children," and these are some of the means by which she does so, if it becomes necessary. Since 1945, Family

Allowance subsidies from the government have made her task of coordinating the domestic economy somewhat easier.

While the factors set forth here have a fairly general application, only in extreme cases do they eliminate the support of the husband-father altogether, for he provides a major portion of the economic support in most households having a conjugal pair, although the nature and amount of his contribution in nearly every case is limited to a greater or lesser extent by these factors. In structural terms (Fortes 1958, 8–9; Radcliffe-Brown 1950, 81), this whole problem of coordinating the domestic economy can be seen as an interaction between the cell of mother and children in each household and persons within the more inclusive domestic order (sometimes coterminous with the nuclear family) in a society that has remained matrilineal in the institutions of its external system, while the matricentral cell of the internal system has, to a large extent, become economically dependent upon the husband-father rather than upon the cooperative action of the members of other like cells of a more inclusive matrilineage group. The high degree of independence in the domestic economy maintained by the husband-father is in keeping with his attenuated and ambiguous jural position within the group.

Among the Longhouse people, a person appears to share his economic substance regularly only with others with whom he has first- or second-degree ties of kinship or affinity. It can be inferred from this general practice that when either money or consumer goods are brought into the household, this is done in response to a desire or sense of duty felt in connection with kin or affinal ties; and further, that the allocation of goods within the group occurs on this same basis. Kin of remote degree expect to be given food and lodging even when their visits are unannounced, although a prolonged relationship of this type would be untenable without a contribution being made.[6]

Although a woman may be given money by her adult sons and daughters, or occasionally by her husband, to be used in the group's interest, the unification of the cash income of the various members of the group generally does not occur until money has been exchanged for consumer goods. These are either turned over to the wife-mother or put into a common store under her supervision and thus become the common property of the group. In this position a woman becomes a kind of focus for the unity of the group. She assigns articles of clothing to junior members and prepares or directs the preparation of food. At mealtime the food is placed on the table in large serving bowls, pitchers, or on platters. The entire household gathers round, each in his own place, with younger children near their mother, to share the meal together. Each member of the group is, for the most part, allowed to serve himself under the supervision primarily of the mother.

The earnings of Longhouse men and women flow into retail markets outside their system and generally outside the reserve. There is little deliberate budgeting of expenditures against income, and the flow of earnings out of the household tends to be immediate. There is little saving except to a degree among older people, especially older women. Ostentation in spending is strongly disapproved, and money is spent on items of immediate consumption rather than on objects or items having display value. It is held in very poor taste to discuss amounts of earnings, prices paid for objects, wage rates, and financial affairs generally, although it is common to hear comments about the elusiveness of money. "We just live from one paycheck to the next," said one young woman. "It's no use [to try to do anything about it]! Some people say you can really make good money in the States, but you can't save it there either. Everything is open on Sunday; there are too many things to do with it. You can't save money over there even if you do make a lot!"

Theoretically the entire range of the Canadian-U.S. market is open to Longhouse purchases, but in practice their consumption of goods and services is confined to a limited sector of the overall market, even though incomes in many instances would permit a wider range of participation.[7] It is usual for household furnishings and equipment, automobiles, and, to a lesser extent, clothing to be purchased from secondhand shops. In the nearby town of Hagersville, there is held each week a "barn sale" to which white people in the surrounding area bring poultry and livestock as well as various used furnishings and equipment for resale. This has been an important retail market for the Longhouse people for over two generations; and there is scarcely a household among them in which there are not found articles such as crockery, cutlery, pots and pans, chairs, tables, sofas, stoves, clothing, or other items purchased there. If a household is in need of some item, it is likely to be sought first at this "barn sale." After a period of working outside the home, at canneries and farms, women also visit this sale to purchase required household items.

Main Items of Expenditure and Consumption

Goods and services consumed by the Longhouse people are of two general types: those obtained from gardens, small-scale animal husbandry, and from the natural environment, and those purchased with cash in the retail markets of Canada and the United States. This latter type may be further subdivided into items purchased regularly from day to day and those purchased only occasionally. Goods of the first type are usually only supplementary to those of the second type, although it is common for many households to have a winter supply of potatoes, corn, bottled fruit, and tomatoes, as well as a year-round supply of eggs and milk from these sources. Because of their primary importance in nearly all households, the main concern here lies with the goods and services bought for cash.

Regular Purchases

FOOD

Food requires a steady outlay of money in all households and is the item of greatest expenditure in most. The actual amount of food purchased varies with the amount available from gardens and other sources and with the amount of money available. Three meals per day are the rule, although this may be reduced to two, or even less, in times of shortage. There is a remarkable uniformity in diet from one household to another of potatoes, fresh or salted pork, and large quantities of bread (either bakery or homemade pan bread), and tea or coffee. Homemade fruit pies or bottled fruit is often added to this basic fare. Potatoes are probably the most important single item of food and often appear with a minimum of variation in mode of preparation in each meal of the day. Indian corn (onę̨hę̨) may rival potatoes in importance in some households, especially during winter and spring months. There is very great interest in food, and most people eat heartily whenever possible. One of the first questions asked about an event in which a meal or feast is featured, such as a marriage or a wood-cutting bee, is, "What did they have to eat?" Food offerings are of first importance in all ceremonies held for the dead, in fact in those held for all supernatural entities.

A more precise picture of the daily diet can be had from the menu of a household consisting of three adults and one child for the day Wednesday, March 15, 1957. The members of this household estimated that it cost them from ten to twelve dollars per week for food.

    Breakfast: 7:30–8:00 a.m.
        Fried eggs
        Warmed-over potatoes
        Bread and butter
        Tea

Noon meal: 12:00–1:00 p.m.
   Boiled potatoes with melted pork fat
   Fried strips of salt pork
   Bread and butter
   Imitation fruit drink

Evening meal: 6:00–7:00 p.m.
   Dried sweet corn soup
   Roasted fresh pork
   Boiled potatoes
   Bread and butter
   Tea

Amount and cost of food:

5 eggs	0.21
2 lbs. potatoes	0.08
$\frac{1}{4}$ lb. salt pork	0.10
1 lb. fresh pork	0.25
1$\frac{1}{2}$ lb. loaf bread	0.22
6 oz. butter	0.24
1$\frac{1}{2}$ oz. tea	0.06
1 oz. imitation fruit drink powder	0.05
5 oz. sugar	0.03
dried sweet corn	0.00 (given by kin)
Total:	$1.24

This menu does not take into account a number of items used in the preparation of the food such as flour, salt, and condiments; nor does it include milk, fresh or condensed, sometimes used with tea and coffee. Variations occur in that cereals and porridges are common in many households at breakfast time, especially in those having their own supply of milk; or breakfast may consist only of tea and toast. Bologna, popularly referred to as "Indian round steak," is often substituted for pork. Beef is eaten less regularly among the Longhouse people. This same fare might well have cost only ninety-five cents in a household having its own supply of potatoes and eggs, which is common.

CLOTHING

In late summer and autumn, people appear in various articles of new clothing, such as shoes, trousers, dresses, shirts, and hats. Although clothing may be purchased at any time when desired, a number of factors, such as the possession of sufficient money from summer work, the beginning of school, and the forthcoming winter, coincide to make this a time for the purchase of new clothing. Trousers, dresses, shirts, and other apparel are usually ready-made articles, although some women are clever seamstresses and sew dresses for themselves and their daughters. Almost everyone has clothing for everyday use and also for use on special occasions, probably averaging from two or three sets for each purpose, for women, and slightly less for men. Native costumes are possessed by the majority of men and women and by some children. These are worn on special ceremonial occasions and are often obtained at considerable expense. Older people usually keep sufficient material on hand from which their burial clothes are eventually made. Clothing is generally kept in use by one means or another until it is quite worn out. Women whose children were nearly grown have been seen to give bags of clothing to sisters with young expanding families. Expenditures for clothing are considerable in all households.

RECREATION

Money for recreation is spent largely off the reserve. The regular exodus to nearby towns on Friday and Saturday evenings, mentioned above, is a great attraction to most people. Men participate in drinking parties, bingo games, billiards, and bowling, while women attend movies or bingo games. The sexes rarely appear together on these occasions, and men spend considerably more money, as a rule, than do women. Automobiles are an important recreational device, especially for men, and trips covering distances of three or four hundred miles on a single weekend are common.

Once or twice each year the four longhouse ritual groups, referred to earlier, hold field days in an effort to raise money for conventions (*Gaiwhio odakhaohasǫ*). A general holiday air pervades these occasions, and money is spent rather freely on admission to ball games, raffle tickets, and on refreshments, such as soft drinks, "hot dogs," candy, popcorn and like items. "Suppers" are sometimes sold as well.

During the long summer evenings men foregather to play croquet. To heighten interest in the game, each player puts up ten cents at the beginning of each round, which goes to the winning player.

TOBACCO

Most men use tobacco for both smoking and chewing, but women use it much less. Some older women chew tobacco and smoke short-stemmed pipes in their leisure, while young women smokers use cigarettes. The average man smoker probably spends from three to five dollars per month on tobacco, and most women smokers considerably less. Their own tobacco (oyę'hgwaowe), grown by many households, is used only ceremonially or medicinally.

FUEL

Most households have their own bush or access to that of a kinsman for their supply of fuel for heating and cooking purposes. Wood could be purchased for six dollars per cord in 1957 from Christian Iroquois men on the reserve, and about six to eight cords are required for a winter's supply. Few Longhouse people are required to spend money on wood, however. Five percent of the households in the sample used natural gas for heating and cooking and paid an average of about $3.75 per month for this fuel.

LIGHTING

Eighty-eight percent of the households used kerosene lamps for lighting at an average cost of sixty-two cents per month. The other 12 percent of households used hydroelectric power at a cost per month of two to eight dollars.

DRY-CLEANING SERVICE

Many households spend a few dollars off and on throughout the year on dry cleaning. Outside firms extend their pickup and delivery services to the reserve.

DONATIONS TO LONGHOUSE CEREMONIES

Nearly all households make contributions (in kind, as a rule) to longhouse ceremonies regularly throughout the year. These contributions probably average in cash value about ten dollars per year per household. One exception to this general amount was noted in the case of Sidney, a young family man who made a number of very generous contributions to the longhouse ritual group to which he belonged. Although this was apparently done without ulterior motive, it set off a wave of gossip. It was said that he was trying "to buy an 'office' in the longhouse." Later on, when a faithkeeper (hodrihǫt) was required on his side of the dual division, his maternal grandmother, who wielded considerable influence as head female faithkeeper on this side, put up her grandson, Sidney, for the position and got him approved on her own side. When the proposal went to the opposite side for approval, they rejected him and refused to perform the installation rite. Gossip again had it that it was the way he had used his money that was the cause of the deadlock. On the third day of the festival in which such installations are made, a number of leaders of the opposite side were absent, and when Sidney's maternal grandmother became aware of this, she seized upon the occasion to get him installed. A storm of protest broke out when the absent leaders of the opposite side were informed, and one of them declared that the appointment should be null and void. However, nothing was done about it, and Sidney was allowed to continue in this position, although his irregular appointment continued to be a subject for gossip.

The whole affair emphasized the egalitarian nature of Longhouse society. Those in favor of his appointment supported it not on the grounds of his money contributions, but rather because of the fact that he was a good worker and was always on hand to perform duties even before his appointment—a manifestation, they said, of his foreordination to the position. Sidney, himself, who was innocent enough in the whole matter, refused to look upon his position as that of an officer. "We have no officers," he said. "In the longhouse we are all equal."

CREDIT PURCHASES AND LOANS

With the exception of the purchase of automobiles, discussed above, credit purchases occur in only about 4 percent of the households. Purchases of this type, linked with seasonal employment and immediate spending, often lead to repossession by the seller. From the summer of 1956 to that of 1958, the repossession of four automobiles, two television sets, one refrigerator, and one sewing machine was recorded, involving four separate households. Repossession is always an occasion for bitterness between Longhouse buyers and white sellers.

Borrowing or lending money occurs most frequently in the form of small amounts between kinsfolk, sometimes within the same household. Banks and lending firms off the reserve are reluctant to extend their services to Indians on the reserve, since the latter are unable to pledge real property as collateral. However, five instances of borrowing on credit were recorded, and there are undoubtedly a few cases not recorded. In two of these cases a father and his son made minimal deposits in a branch of an outside credit union organized and managed by Christian Iroquois in order to be able to borrow money. Each was lent one thousand dollars at a moderate 3 percent per annum interest rate, and both men were badly in arrears with repayment in 1958. Another man negotiated a four-hundred-and-fifty-dollar loan with an outside finance company, which he was repaying in twelve monthly payments of forty-five dollars each. The other two cases were that of a man and a woman who each borrowed one hundred dollars from a woman on the reserve at the rate of 25 percent per annum simple interest. Credit purchases and the borrowing of money do not occur frequently or on a widespread basis, but where they do occur, repayment is made more or less regularly.

Nonrecurring Expenses

HOUSES

It is unusual for a person to build or purchase more than one house during his lifetime, although he may inherit a second house. The building or purchasing of houses is usually done by men and may require from about one hundred to three thousand dollars. Houses are usually built or expanded in stages, and once the outer walls and roof have been erected, years may pass before the interior is completed. This is attributable, at least partially, to the difficulty in accumulating sufficient cash for the entire project. Loans for building houses were not available at the time of fieldwork.

HOUSEHOLD FURNISHINGS AND EQUIPMENT

The initial cost of furnishing a house is moderate, and subsequent expenditures for this purpose are very limited. As noted in chapter 2, there is general uniformity in the furnishings and equipment of the various households, and most items, except perhaps crockery, tend to be secondhand. Once a household has obtained the requisite furnishings and equipment, they are seldom replaced until completely worn out. About 6 percent of the households (those having hydroelectric power) possess refrigerators, radios, and television sets, and about twice this number possess washing and sewing machines. These items also tend to be secondhand.

MEDICAL SERVICES

The duality of the social space of the Longhouse people is brought into sharp relief in their expenditures for medical services. While on a visit at our house, a young mother asked my wife if she really believed "that germs cause sickness." Desirous of leaving scope for the woman's own view, my wife answered somewhat haltingly that she rather believed they did, whereupon the woman quickly replied, "Perhaps this is so for white men's diseases like chicken pox and measles, but Indians [i.e., Longhouse Iroquois] have sicknesses that the white man's medicine won't help." It is deemed all right, or even wise, to go to white doctors in some cases, but there is clearly a whole category of diseases of which they are not cognizant, and for which their medicines prove ineffective. It is commonly held that if a sick person resorts to white doctors while Indian medicine (ǫgwehǫwe onǫ'hgwatra'h) or medicine rites (ǫdwęnǫgotanǫ) are being used, their curative power will be nullified. Treatment in their own society often involves considerable expense; and except for the fifty cents usually given a diviner when his or her services are required, these expenses are incurred for food and cloth used for medicine feasts. The cost of these feasts varies from only a few dollars to perhaps fifty, and prolonged illness, requiring a variety of feasts, may even involve financial assistance of kin. As indicated above, these expenditures occur largely in wintertime. The amount of food and cloth required for these feasts is also given above.

There is a hospital on the reserve where medical services may be obtained free of charge. Most women have their babies in this hospital, although the Longhouse people generally express a lack of confidence in its staff. When the services of white doctors are desired, Longhouse people often go to doctors in the nearby towns off the reserve, even though they must pay cash for such services. The amount of money spent for this type of service is considerably less than that spent on goods for the medicine feasts above.

FUNERALS

Funerals vary in cost, with the price of the casket primarily determining the total expense. One funeral, the details of which were observed very intimately, cost $275.90. Others observed appeared to have cost somewhat less than this, perhaps approximately $225. This amount includes the cost of the feast held ten days after death. Ideally this expense is borne by the members of the lineage, and therefore several households; but the children or the siblings of the deceased seem to be bearing a progressively increasing portion of it.

MARRIAGES

At the time of fieldwork, marriages were usually quite simple and cost no more than was required to feed the chiefs, the kin of the bride and groom, and friends who attended. Such a feast would cost from ten to thirty dollars.

Household Budgets

At this point it will be helpful to look at some budgets from actual households in an effort to add a degree of specificity to the material on income, expenditure, and consumption given above. The four budgets presented here were kept by members of each of the households concerned on forms I had prepared beforehand. Three of the budgets were kept for the month of August 1957, and one was kept for November of the same year. Regular visits were paid to these households during the period of the budgets, and though each separate expenditure was not actually confirmed, they are believed to be reasonably accurate. It was my hope to obtain budgets from households in various phases of development and from ones being supported by various types of work, and although the members of a number of households agreed by word to keep a record of income and expenses, they tacitly refused by failing to produce a result. In each case where a budget was obtained, there was manifest a good deal of apprehension in handing over such intimate financial data, and it was necessary repeatedly to give assurances that the information would be treated with confidence. All this is understandable in the light of the general attitude of caution concerning financial matters. For this reason, randomly selected pseudonyms are used in the cases recorded below and some economic activities are not specified, so that the cases do not appear to relate to any specific or identifiable households. The period covered by the budgets falls within the season of the year when there is maximum opportunity for employment, when almost everyone who desires to work may do so, and for this reason, it is necessary to recall the seasonal nature of income for many of the households. Despite the strictures mentioned here, the general unspecialized nature of jobs and the uniformity of spending habits among the Longhouse people lend an element of generality to the budgets.

Budget Case 1

This budget for the month of August 1957 was kept by the members of a four-generation household, who shared the facilities of a two-room log house situated on a sixty-seven-acre plot of land. The household consisted of a sixty-nine-year-old widower, Simeon, who owned both land and house; his thirty-five-year-old, separated daughter, Cloris, and her seven children, ranging from two to fourteen years of age; and a twenty-one-year-old granddaughter (the child of another of Simeon's daughters), Janeen, with her two children, ages eighteen months and two months; making twelve members in all.

Simeon had earned his living in past years by a combination of activities such as farming, keeping small numbers of livestock and poultry, gardening, and working off the reserve on fruit farms. He had also earned part of his livelihood as a well digger, since he had a "gift" for divining the presence of underground water. At the time of the budget, he received forty-six dollars per month of Old Age Assistance, "which is," as he says, "enough for me to live on." He felt that he was too old then to work outside the home for wages, although a number of men his age and older continued to do so. The bulk of his farm lay idle, although he did plant a garden plot of about a quarter of an acre, in which he grew corn, potatoes, beans, tomatoes, and other vegetables.

He kept a flock of about forty chickens, which supplied eggs and some meat to the household. With his older grandsons he brought firewood from his own bush, a distance of approximately five hundred yards. In addition to Simeon's Old Age Pension, the household also received a further government subsidy of forty-nine dollars per month in the form of Family Allowance.

The income of most significance to the household was that of Simeon's daughter, Cloris, who worked seasonally on fruit and tobacco farms and in canning factories. Her work began in May and continued more or less steadily until the last of October. She also took her fourteen-year-old son with her to work and controlled the greater portion of his earnings. As shown in the budget, this woman was able to earn $280 for the month of August, and her son earned $59.99. Though she was an exceptionally diligent worker, her earnings for this month correspond with the busiest part of the tobacco season and represent an amount somewhat higher than her average for the season.

The total income for the household for the month was $434.99. Since job opportunities diminish rapidly during and after October, the household would not have been able to continue to operate at the level indicated in the budget; and as savings were used up, its members became increasingly dependent upon government subsidies.

The $434.99 did not constitute a unitary fund from which money was drawn to meet the needs of the household. Each of the adults commanded a portion of the income. The head bought his own clothes and a considerable amount of bread and cakes from the bakery truck that came to the house on alternate days. He sometimes made a purchase of groceries and kerosene for lighting from a nearby store and also provided an occasional treat for his grandchildren. This he contributed in addition to produce from his garden and eggs and meat from his chickens.

Cloris controlled the largest amount of income and, at the same time, had the great responsibility of providing for her seven children. After her marriage she lived alternately with her husband and at home with her father, her mother having died when she was quite young. Each time she became pregnant, her husband would stay away from home for long periods and would spend most of his money drinking, whereupon she would return to her natal household. When she became pregnant in 1955, the same pattern ensued, and she decided not to return to her husband after the baby was born. Her oldest daughter and son were then thirteen and eleven respectively, and the help they could give in tending the children would free her to work out herself. She hoped to build her own house soon on land given to her by her father. Cloris exemplifies the saying that "a woman will always find some way to provide for her children."

She bought the bulk of the provisions for the household, as well as clothing for herself and her children. She also made monthly payments on an automobile she was buying on time and paid the expenses connected with its operation and maintenance.

Simeon's granddaughter, Janeen, had only five dollars income per month, which was her portion of the Family Allowance at the time the budget was kept. She received an additional five dollars per month when the record of the birth of her second child was completed. She used this money in the care of her two children. Her presence in the household at the time answered the need of her mother's sister, Cloris, to have someone to assist in the care of her young children. Cloris's own eldest daughter had become pregnant, married, and had gone to live with her husband earlier in the year, and Cloris's small children required more attention than their grandfather, Simeon, could give them.

Of the $279.66 expended for the month, the greater portion was spent on food, payment and operation of the automobile, and for clothing. Smaller amounts were spent for recreation, fuel and lighting, tobacco, and for gifts, which, in this case, were for members of the household. The loan repaid was an intrahousehold affair between Cloris and her father and did not represent money leaving the household. The amount extra after expenses belonged, for the most part, to Cloris, who was trying to save to build the house mentioned above. It is doubtful, however, that much of the surplus would have remained after winter.

Budget 1
Income (in dollars):

1. Daughter of head

From work on tobacco farms	280.00

2. Son of daughter of head

From work on tobacco farms	59.99

3. Government subsidies

a. Old Age Assistance to head	46.00
b. Family Allowance to head's daughter	44.00
c. Family Allowance to head's daughter's daughter	5.00
Total Income:	434.99

Expenditures (in dollars):

1. Food

a. Groceries	103.99
b. Bread and cakes	29.93
Total Food:	(133.92)

2. Clothing	32.61
3. Operation of automobile	40.00
4. Time payments (automobile)	20.00
5. Gifts (within household)	12.75
6. Recreation (cinema)	8.90
7. Tobacco	1.60
8. Fuel and lighting	3.82
9. Hire of ride	0.30
10. Repayment of loan (within household)	4.00
11. Dry-cleaning services	1.55
12. Other	20.21*
Total Expenditures:	279.66
Surplus for Month (in dollars):	155.33

* The items in this category were noted, but the
notation has been lost.

Budget Case 2

This budget is for the month of November 1957 and was kept by the members of a two-generation household, consisting of the head, Marvin, who was forty-seven years of age; his wife, Ramona, who was forty-four; Ramona's twenty-five-year-old son, whom she had as a single mother; and Marvin and Ramona's own children, a twenty-three-year-old son, an eighteen-year-old daughter, two sons aged fourteen and twelve, and an adopted girl age four. They lived together in a three-room log dwelling that has a lean-to built on for a kitchen. The house was situated on a six-acre plot, and both house and land belonged to the head's wife.

The household was supported in the main by the income of the head, which he derived from his work in a nearby gypsum plant, a job that he had held for the past seven years. His hourly wage rate was $1.62, and his income for the month of November was $260. However, his work for the past few years had been seasonal due to a cutback in the level of production at the gypsum works; during 1957, he worked only from the first week in June until mid-December and for approximately the same period in 1956. He was able to draw Unemployment Insurance of thirty dollars per week after his layoff for a period of approximately twelve weeks and also had some income from pruning fruit trees during February and March of 1957.

Ramona's eldest son also worked seasonally at the gypsum plant. In fact, his work terminated for the year at the end of the third week in November. He had the same hourly wage as his stepfather and was paid $195 for his work during this month.

The next eldest son, who had been unemployed for most of the summer, got a job this month with a road construction firm. He remained away from home during the week, returning on weekends. He gave his mother $117 of his earnings for safekeeping.

In addition to managing the internal affairs of the household, Ramona cultivated a small garden, in which she grew tomatoes, green beans, radishes, carrots, and a few other vegetables. She also kept twenty-five or thirty hens for a supply of eggs and an occasional chicken dinner. During the year 1957, she worked for about a month on a fruit farm and for a slightly longer period in a canning factory during late summer and autumn. Besides owning the house and the plot upon which it stands, she owned an additional fifty-eight acres of land, which she rented to a Christian Iroquois man for twenty-five dollars per season. She received this payment in November and also another twenty-five dollars at the beginning of the month from canning factory work.

Unemployment Insurance was received during the first part of the year; however, twenty-two dollars Family Allowance was the amount of government subsidy reaching the household for the period of the budget.

There was a total of $644 income to all the members of the household. Again, this amount does not represent a central fund from which the household was operated. Each wage-earner controlled his or her own earnings, and Ramona, the wife-mother, controlled the Family Allowance in addition to her personal earnings. While the $195 of the oldest son represents his entire earnings, the $117 of the next eldest son represents only that portion of his earnings that he turned over to his mother for safekeeping during the period of the budget. Both sons were buying automobiles on time, bought their own clothes, and had recreational and other extra-household interests upon which their money was spent; and these expenditures were not recorded in the budget. The total expenditure of $352.15 shown for the period represents, by and large, only the amount spent on group interests.

The exact portion of this amount spent by each member of the group is not known, but it is certain that Marvin controlled the greatest amount of income and spent most of it in support of his family. His wife had about seventy-two dollars at her disposal, consisting of her own earnings and the Family Allowance payments. As a rule, she bought her own clothes and spent the Family Allowance on clothing for the children and on supplementary purchases of food. It is known, however, that she did not spend her entire sum during this month. The difference between the total expenditure of $352.15 and the combined total of the earnings of the head and the amount of the Family Allowance received (this difference being $70.15) provides a rough index of the amount contributed by the sons to the economy of the household during this period. The eldest son gave ten dollars to his mother for the group, but the principal amount came from the next oldest son, who put a large portion of the $117 given to his mother for safekeeping at the disposal of the group. Marvin explained the contributions of his sons to the household in these words, "I have told the boys that I will help them if they will help us when I am in a pinch. If they don't want to help out when we are in need, they don't need to expect any help when they want it." This is in keeping with the general rule, almost a sine qua non, that within the household group, assistance is freely asked and freely given. It is worth noting, however, that both sons made their money available to the group through their mother.

Of the $352.15 expended for the month, the largest amounts were spent on food, gasoline and maintenance of the automobile, clothing, repayment of a loan, and payments for a washing machine and a portable radio bought on time. The relatively large amount spent on clothing represents coats, gloves, and underwear purchased against the onset of winter. Sometime prior to the budget, the head was able to negotiate a loan of four hundred fifty dollars from a commercial credit firm off the reserve largely on the basis of his job at the gypsum works, the proceeds of which were used to buy a car. He was repaying the loan in monthly payments of forty-five dollars each. Other expenditures involving lesser amounts were made for fuel and lighting, medical service, tobacco, recreation (cinema), a gift for a married daughter's child, purchase of a flashlight, donations to the longhouse for the Handsome Lake Code Convention (the donation was made partly in cash and partly in kind), and for dry-cleaning services.

Because of seasonal and temporary employment, this household also was not able to maintain its economy at the level indicated in the budget throughout the year. There was manifest little tendency toward saving against the period of unemployment, except to a degree by Ramona, the wife-mother. During the first five months of 1957, the period when the head was not working for the gypsum company, the group depended largely on government subsidies (Unemployment Insurance and Family Allowance) and on income from odd jobs and work on fruit farms for its sustenance. Income to the household was reduced to $144 per month during part of this period, and possibly less than this amount after the head's twelve-week period of eligibility for Unemployment Insurance expired. The economy of this household resembles closely that of other households that depend on seasonal employment, with the exception that the kind of jobs held by the majority of seasonal workers among the Longhouse people do not qualify them for Unemployment Insurance.

Budget 2

Income (in dollars):

1. Head
   From work in gypsum plant — 260.00
2. Head's wife
   a. From rental of land — 25.00
   b. From work in canning factory — 25.00
3. Government subsidy
   Family Allowance — 22.00
   Total of Head and Wife only: — (332.00)*
4. Son of wife only
   From work in gypsum plant (3 weeks) — 195.00
5. Son of head and wife
   From construction work — 117.00
   Total Income: — 644.00

Expenditures (in dollars):

1. Food — 96.00
2. Operation of automobile — 69.50
3. Clothing — 68.97
4. Time payments (washing machine and radio) — 25.00
5. Repayment of loan — 45.00
6. Fuel and lighting — 12.80
7. Medical service (treatment of cut) — 11.00
8. Recreation (cinema) — 6.00
9. Tobacco — 5.00
10. Gift (to married daughter's child) — 5.00
11. Dry-cleaning service — 2.25
12. Donations to longhouse ceremonies — 2.13
13. Other (flashlight) — 3.50
    Total Expenditures: — 352.15

* This figure represents the basic amount with which the household operated, since only a portion of the income shown for the sons was used for the group.

This budget was kept for the month of August 1957 by a forty-two-year-old man, Harry, who was the head of his household, and his thirty-two-year-old wife, Dora. Besides themselves, their household consisted of a nineteen-year-old daughter of the head only, who was a single mother; a son and daughter of the present marriage, who were twelve and ten years of age respectively; and a two-year-old girl, child of the single mother. They lived in a seven-room, two-story frame house, the construction of which had not been entirely completed. The house was situated on a two-acre plot of land, the title to which was held by the head and his wife.

Harry had graduated from a trade school and had worked at his trade somewhat periodically for the past two and one-half years. He was the only household head among the Longhouse people, at the time of fieldwork, who had learned a trade in this way and the only one who did not earn his living by some sort of strenuous manual labor. To this extent he is somewhat unrepresentative. The income from his trade for the month shown in the budget was $394.75. In addition to this, he received twenty dollars from passengers who rode with him to the town where he worked. During 1957 he worked from nine to ten months, losing time because of a job change and time spent in hospital. His work was not covered by Unemployment Insurance.

The head's wife, Dora, had a steady job on the reserve, for which she was paid twenty dollars per month for nine months of the year. She received only six dollars from her usual work in the month of August; but also in June and July she had taken her two children with her to fruit farms, where they worked together picking berries and cherries. The household received nineteen dollars from Family Allowance, and it was she who managed this amount.

Harry's daughter by his former marriage sometimes gave fifteen dollars per month to her stepmother for the care of her child. However, because she was not working at the time of the budget, she made no contribution.

The household had a combined income of $439.75 for the month of August, $414.75 of which was controlled by Harry, and $25 by Dora. The precise amounts spent by each the head and his wife are not known, although it is clear that the great bulk of the money spent was that earned by Harry. About fifteen dollars was spent by Dora, from the money she controlled, on clothing for her son and daughter, with which they were to begin school.

Expenses for the month totaled $415.94. The items on which the greatest amounts were spent were food, payments on time purchases, operation of automobile, recreation, repayment of a loan, and school clothing for the children. Lesser amounts were spent on a bicycle given as a gift to the ten-year-old daughter, tobacco and beer, necessary tools for Harry's work, laundry and dry-cleaning service, and for medicine. This household had a very large amount to pay on time purchases, and the reason was probably that the head was able to obtain credit on the basis of his relatively steady and well-paying job. His monthly payments were $55 for a car, the total cost of which was approximately $2,700; $10 per month for eye glasses; $11.70 per month on a life insurance policy;[8] and $14.07 per month for a natural gas space heater for his house. He was also in debt over one thousand dollars to a credit union, a branch of which has been established on the reserve, and was paying this money back at the rate of thirty-seven dollars per month. Expense for tools represents a purchase of capital equipment, a kind of expense seldom incurred by Longhouse people. Money paid out for laundry service is equally unusual, and in this case, it was needed for the specialized clothing required for his work.

It should be noted that the head had five paydays during the month for which the budget was kept, and that the last one fell on the last day of the budget period. The larger part of the surplus of $23.84 shown on the budget represents the remainder of the head's wages after bills and weekend grocery shopping and recreation were paid for. This is the amount of money the household has with which to carry on through the following week until Harry's next payday. It is clear that money in this household tends to be quickly spent; and judging from the amount of the head's indebtedness, income and expense balance each other out only over a very long period.

In both his job and in his use of money, Harry evidenced considerable waywardness from the accepted norms and standards of his society. He had a flair for ostentation in dress and automobiles, and all this prompted warnings from kin and neighbors, who often told him of seeing witch lights and witch animals about his place by night. Harry, himself, sought confirmation from me on several occasions concerning the inefficacy of witchcraft. In all this, he brings into light the restraints his society places on the economic activities of its members, especially on the kind of occupation pursued and the manner in which money is spent by its members in the interest of preserving social and economic homogeneity among the households of Longhouse society.

Budget 3
Income (in dollars):
1. Head

a. From work at his trade		394.75
b. From passengers to work		20.00

2. Wife

From work on reserve		6.00

3. Government subsidy

Family Allowance		19.00
Total Income:		439.75

Expenditures (in dollars):
1. Food

a. Groceries		82.07
b. Café lunches		12.00
c. Bread		6.69
Total Food:		(100.76)
2. Clothing		17.98

3. Time Payments

a. Automobile		55.00
b. Space heater		14.07
c. Life insurance		11.70
d. Eye glasses		20.00*
Total Time Payments:		(100.77)
4. Operation of automobile		69.15

5. Recreation

a. Bingo		13.00
b. Cinema		12.85
c. Field day		6.00
d. Other		5.80
Total Recreation:		(37.65)
6. Repayment of loan		37.00
7. Bicycle for daughter		12.00
8. Tools for work		10.00
9. Beer		15.66**
10. Tobacco		4.92
11. Laundry and dry-cleaning service (incidental to work)		5.05
12. Medicine (doctor's prescription)		5.00
Total Expenditures:		415.94

Surplus for Month (in dollars):		23.84

* This amount represents two installments.
** I added ten dollars of this amount on the basis of information
given by the head's wife. Harry received a ten-dollar bonus on
the last payday of the month, which, according to Dora, he spent
on beer, but he did not record this in his expenditures.

Budget Case 4

This budget pertains to a household group consisting of the head, Ralph, who
was twenty-nine years of age; his twenty-five-year-old wife, Sally; and their
three children, who ranged in age from two to five years. Ralph bought his
present house soon after his marriage and had it moved to its present location
on a half-acre plot, which he purchased from his mother's brother. The house
itself is of a modified-log type, having the exterior walls covered with imitation
brick siding and having the ground floor partitioned into three and the upstairs
partitioned into two rooms.

During his boyhood, Ralph was sent out by his maternal grandmother,
who raised him, to sell cornhusk mats (ǫhsidagewata) to motorists along the
highway and to work in a canning factory. However, for the past three or
four years he had worked year-round in a nearby gypsum mine. He was paid
on a piecework basis, and his earnings for the month of August were $600;
however, this amount corresponds with the busiest time of the year at the
gypsum works and includes considerable overtime pay. Ralph stated that $450–
$500 was a more usual wage.

Sally, the wife-mother in the household, did not work outside the reserve
during the time covered by the fieldwork, although she had done so previously.
Since the coming of her children, she had been closely bound to their care
and to her household tasks generally. Her husband did not drink and had few
outside interests upon which to spend his money, so there was no real pressure
for her to leave her household to work. In addition, the household received
fifteen dollars per month from Family Allowance.

The total income for the period of the budget was $615. Of this amount,
Ralph managed his own earnings and his wife managed the Family Allowance
payment. He was frequently given a grocery list by her, but he did most of the
actual buying for the household himself. He also made the payments on his
installment purchases.

The total expenditure for the month was $257.81. The largest single amount
was expended for payments on time purchases, including an electric refrigerator, an electric range, a television set, and an electric fan, amounting to

ninety-four dollars per month. The next largest amount, $67.67, was spent for food. Ralph continued to give money to his maternal grandmother and gave her thirty dollars during the period of the budget. He also paid a three months' bill of twenty-six dollars for electrical service. Lesser amounts were spent for recreation, donations to his longhouse ritual group, transportation to work, tobacco, and clothing. He had no automobile at the time of the budget and paid a fellow workman twenty-five cents per day for transportation to and from his work.

This household had an excess of income over expenditure of $357.19, and although this amount corresponded to the busiest period at the gypsum works, it was a regular occurrence for him to have a substantial part of each weekly paycheck left over after the expenses of his household were met. It will be recalled from table 7 above that a fairly large number of men had a relatively high level of income, comparable in some instances to many middle-class Canadian households. Yet it can be safely stated that there were only two, or perhaps three, men among the Longhouse people who had any but a very temporary surplus. The general practice of immediate spending on immediately consumable goods and services absorbed any potential surplus. The Friday and Saturday evening recreational activities, referred to above, which meant largely drinking and gaming for men, were particularly effective as a means of absorbing money in a manner having a minimum of display value.

The possession of a surplus is clearly exceptional, and it is this feature of Ralph's budget that raises the problem of what one does with a surplus in a society that rigidly opposes social differentiation on the basis of wealth. Something of the nature of his problem is seen by the way in which he sought to use his money. He began to lend money to his fellow Longhouse members on an interest basis, but soon stopped this upon being told that witch lights had been seen at his place. He commented to me that "it might be the very ones you've tried to help out" who were behind this.

Ralph's own house differs little from that of his neighbors, although he had had hydroelectric power installed and was buying a number of electrical appliances, as noted above. That the possession of these appliances was cause for some apprehension on his part is seen in the fact that he allowed practically his whole neighborhood access to his television set, and it was a very common thing to call on him in the evening and find a dozen or so viewers gathered in his front room around the TV.

By opposing the use of money to create social differences, as in this case, or by opposing occupational specialization referred to earlier, Longhouse society prevents the husband-father from consolidating his position in the household by imparting social status to the other members of the group on these bases. Although the influence this opposition has on the position of the husband-father in the household is somewhat incidental, it is nonetheless effective.

Budget 4

Income (in dollars):

1. Head
    From work in gypsum mine — 600.00
2. Government subsidy
    Family Allowance — 15.00

Total Income: — 615.00

Expenditures (in dollars):

1. Food
    a. Groceries — 62.47
    b. Bread — 5.20

Total Food: — (67.67)

2. Time Payments (refrigerator, electric range, television, and electric fan) — 94.00
3. Gifts (to maternal grandmother who raised head) — 30.00
4. Lighting (includes three months' service) — 26.00
5. Recreation
    a. Bingo — 5.20
    b. Ball games — 2.05
    c. Cinema — 8.00
    d. Baby sitter — 3.00

Total Recreation: — (18.25)

6. Donation to longhouse — 10.00
7. Transportation to work — 5.75
8. Tobacco — 5.74
9. Clothing — 0.40

Total Expenditures: — 257.81

Surplus for Month (in dollars): — 357.19

Albert Thomas family—an expanding family. George, Albert holding
Betty, Norman, Inez, Norma, Mary holding granddaughter Joanne, cousin
standing right, (Leo absent). Photo by author.

Teenie (Snow) Skye and adopted daughter, Diane.
Photo by author.

An enduring marriage union in the early phase of household and family development: Samuel Jamieson, with wife Esther (Jacobs) Jamieson, and son, Lorne, ca. 1916. Photo courtesy of Lorna Hill.

Final phase three-generation family, 1970. Back row: Brenda, Lorna (Jamieson) Thomas. Middle row: Gilbert, Beverly, Samuel. Front row: Esther (Jacobs) Jamieson holding Bryan, Patrick. Photo by author.

4. Composition of the Household Group

This chapter provides an account of household structure among the Longhouse people of Six Nations Reserve, as it appeared to me during the year 1957, and gives a description of the development of this structure in time.

In the material that follows it has been necessary to classify persons according to their conjugal status. The Longhouse people themselves use terms that are quite unambiguous, and most of the terms used here are a part of their daily parlance. Only the following are likely to require clarification:

1. *Married* pertains to persons whose conjugal relationship has been solemnized by Longhouse chiefs or by a judge or justice of the peace in a provincial court.

2. *Common-law married* refers to persons who cohabit without having their relationship solemnized. People refer to their own common-law union, or that of other couples, as "getting together" (*adyǫdranegę*) or "keeping house," thus emphasizing the element of cohabitation. The terms "his woman" or "her man," rather than husband or wife, are frequently used in referring to the common-law spouse of a third person.

3. *Single mother* is used to designate a woman who has given birth to a child without ever having entered into a marriage or common-law union. There are single fathers in the biological sense, but such fatherhood receives very little social recognition, and for this reason, this category has been omitted.

4. *Single* denotes a person who has never had a relationship with another person of the opposite sex involving cohabitation. Since single fatherhood is not recognized socially, men who have sired offspring without being married or common-law married are classed as single males.

5. The meaning of the terms *widow, widower, common-law widow, common-law widower, separated,* and *common-law separated* is clear from the above. When the term "spouse" is used, it refers to the mate in either a marriage or common-law marriage.

Table 10. Average number of members per household

Number	1	2	3	4	5	6	7
Frequency	15	26	11	13	20	17	10
Percent	10.0	17.4	7.3	8.7	13.4	11.3	6.7

It is important at this point to recall that there are between thirty and forty Longhouse household groups living off the reserve. The heads of these households are usually between thirty and sixty-five years of age. Many of these people own land, houses, and other property on the reservation and maintain rather close ties with relatives and friends, returning often to visit, to attend principal ceremonies, and to carry out their own personal rites. The majority of them eventually return to the reserve and take their place in its social life. Forty-nine percent of the men of the sample over sixty-five years of age have spent from four to thirty-five years living off the reserve. The return of these people in their later years and the absence of younger families causes some disproportion in the age structure of the population. A firsthand acquaintance with many of these households reveals them to be comparable in structure to those on the reserve in the corresponding phases of development.

Numerical Composition of Household Groups

The average number of members of household groups among the Longhouse people is 5.36. There is a mean deviation from this average of 2.7. The modal number per household is 2, and there are twenty-six households having this number of members. There are also fifteen households having only one member; and together, the one- and two-member households comprise about one-fourth of the sample. Households with two members do not represent conjugal pairs recently married, nor are they cases of enduring conjugality after all children have dispersed. Their main genealogical composition will appear below (table 11) where one- and two-generation households are considered. Over and above these cases of one- and two-member households, which reflect to a degree the absence of younger household groups noted above, the average number of members is consistent with the fact that they develop, for the most part, around a single conjugal pair. These data are summarized in table 10.

Generation Depth and Genealogical Composition

Longhouse households vary in generation depth from one to four generations. Thirty-two, or 21.3 percent, are households whose members belong to a single generation. These households are, in every instance, those referred to above having one and two members only. Among them are six childless couples; ten

8	9	10	11	12	13	14	15	Total
10	8	8	4	3	2	2	1	150
6.7	5.3	5.3	2.6	2.0	1.3	1.3	0.7	100

single, separated, or widowed males living alone; five separated or widowed females living alone; five couples having no children of their own, but one of whom has children by a previous union; four couples living alone with married children living in separate houses on the same plot; and two households having a brother and sister sharing the same house. The greater part of all these people are over sixty-five years of age.

There are sixty-five two-generation households, which comprise 43.4 percent of the total. Fifty-two of these consist of a conjugal pair and their single children; eight are widowed or separated women with a single or separated son or daughter; two are elderly widowers, each having a single son living with him; two are conjugal pairs with a sister's child of either; and one is a childless couple with the wife's mother present.

Households with three generations make up 32 percent of the total. The basic two-generational structure has been augmented in the following ways to create a three-generational structure: fourteen households have married daughters or sister's daughters; eight have single mothers with their children; seven are married sons with spouses and children; one has the child only of a married son; eight are separated or widowed daughters and their children; two are separated sons and their children; and there are two with adopted children of the second descending generation, making forty-eight in all.

There are five households having a depth of four generations, which make up only 3.3 percent of the total. These resemble the three-generation households, with the addition, in one instance each, of the father, spouse's father, mother's brother, son's daughter's child, and daughter's daughter's children of the head.

Basic to the structure of almost all of these households, except those of one generation, is the nuclear relationship of parents and children. Table 11 summarizes this information.

Genealogical Relationship of Members to the Household Head

Household headship has been defined above, and either a man or a woman has been identified as head in each household. The tables given here enumerate household membership in terms of genealogical relationship to the household

Table 11. Generation depth of households

Generation	Frequency	Percent	Genealogical composition
1	32	21.3	a. Six childless couples. b. Ten single, separated, widowed males living alone. c. Five females as in "b." d. Five couples having no children by present union, but one of whom has children by a previous union. e. Four couples living alone with children living separately. f. Two siblings.
2	65	43.4	a. Fifty-two conjugal pairs and their single children. b. Eight widowed, separated, or single women with their single or separated son or daughter. c. Two widowed men with single sons. d. Two conjugal pairs with sister's child of either. e. One childless pair with wife's mother.
3	48	32.0	Basic two-generation structure with the following additions: a. Fourteen married daughters' or sisters' daughters' children. b. Six children only of married daughters. c. Eight single mothers' children. d. Seven married sons' children. e. One child only of a married son. f. Eight separated or widowed daughters' children. g. Two separated sons' children. h. Two adopted children in second descending generation.
4	5	3.3	a. One man and his daughter's and daughter's daughter's children. b. One mother's brother of head of three-generation household with separated daughter and children. c. One son's daughter's child. d. One common-law spouse's father added to three-generation household with separated son's children. e. One head's father added to three-generation household with the single mother's children.
Total	150	100.0	

Table 12. Relationship of household members to ninety-eight male heads

Kinship category	#	%	Lineage kin	Non-lineage kin
Spouses	91	17.4		91
Children	332	63.4		332
Grandchildren and great-grandchildren	73	14.0		73
Spouses of children and grandchildren	9	1.7		9
Kin of head	11	2.1	8	3
Kin of head's spouse	3	0.5		3
Adopted	5	0.9		5
Totals	524	100.0	8	516

Table 13. Relationship of household members to thirty-seven female heads

Kinship category	#	%	Lineage kin	Non-lineage kin
Spouses	9	6.9		9
Children	44	33.6	44	
Grandchildren	49	37.4	34	15
Spouses of children, sisters, and sister's children	13	9.9		13
Siblings	6	4.6	6	
Children and grandchildren of siblings	8	6.1	8	
Other	2	1.5		2
Totals	131	100.0	92	39

head. A more detailed account of the categories shown in tables 12 and 13 is given in tables 14 and 15.

Relationship to Head of Members of Households Having Male Heads

Referring to table 14, we see from categories one and two that about 93 percent of all male heads have their wives living with them, 16.6 percent of these being common-law wives. Domestic activities are said to be the domain of women, and there is, in nearly every case, a woman who is the organizer and manager around whom domestic life is centered. Men experience great difficulty in trying to manage the domestic order by themselves, and it is exceptional for a man to be living with his young children where their mother is not present also. "A woman," they say, "can raise her children alone, but that a man

Table 14. Relationship of household members to ninety-eight male heads

Kinship category	#	%	Lineage kin	Non-lineage kin
1. Wife	76	14.6		76
2. Common-law wife	15	2.8		15
3. Sons				
a. Under 18	128	24.4		128
b. 18 and over (single)	15	2.8		15
c. Married	3	0.5		3
d. Separated	1	0.2		1
e. Son of spouse only	6	1.2		6
4. Daughters				
a. Under 18	136	26.0		136
b. 18 and over (single)	10	1.9		10
c. Single mother	16	3.0		16
d. Married	4	0.8		4
e. Common-law married	1	0.2		1
f. Separated	4	0.8		4
g. Widowed	1	0.2		1
h. Daughter of spouse only	7	1.3		7
5. Son's children	10	1.9		10
6. Daughter's children				
a. Single daughter's child	13	2.4		13
b. Married daughter's child	12	2.3		12
c. Child of daughter of head only	1	0.2		1
d. Child of daughter of spouse only	5	0.9		5
e. Common-law married daughter's child	6	1.2		6
f. Separated daughter's child	22	4.2		22
g. Widowed daughter's child	1	0.2		1
7. Daughter's daughter's child	2	0.4		2
8. Son's daughter's child	1	0.2		1
9. Son's wife	3	0.5		3
10. Daughter's spouse				
a. Husband	4	0.8		4
b. Common-law husband	1	0.2		1
11. Son's daughter's husband	1	0.2		1
12. Brother	3	0.5	3	
13. Brother's child	1	0.2		1

Kinship category	#	%	Lineage kin	Non-lineage kin
14. Sister's child	2	0.4	2	
15. Sister's daughter's child	2	0.4	2	
16. Mother's brother	1	0.2	1	
17. Wife's sister's child	1	0.2		1
18. Wife's brother	1	0.2		1
19. Father	2	0.4		2
20. Wife's mother	1	0.2		1
21. Adopted boy	4	0.8		4
22. Adopted girl	1	0.2		1
Total living in households with male heads	524	100.0	8	516
Percent of lineage and non-lineage kin			1.5	98.5

can never do." The position of common-law wife has certain disadvantages arising out of involvement in Canadian economy and government in that a common-law widow is not eligible for insurance benefits from the company for which her husband worked, nor can she qualify for Widows' Allowance or benefits from her common-law husband's Veterans' Pension. Since women qualify for such benefits only in isolated instances anyway, the influence of these factors remains limited. Within Longhouse society itself, very little, if any, social disability attaches to common-law marriage. It is said that the most important aspect of marriage is "the getting and raising of children together."

The children of the head and (or) his spouse are shown in categories three and four. They represent 63.4 percent of all the members (excluding the heads) and are the largest single category of members in the households. Of these children, 79.6 percent are sons and daughters under eighteen years of age; 7.5 percent are single sons and daughters eighteen years of age and over; 4.8 percent are single mothers; 2.4 percent are married sons and married and common-law married daughters; 1.8 percent are separated sons and separated and widowed daughters; and 3.9 percent are sons and daughters of the head's spouse only. The number of single sons over eighteen years of age in the households is small, and this is in keeping with the practice of young men leaving their natal households to establish their jural and economic independence. A number of these young men remain away from the reserve entirely, working in the larger surrounding towns. That young women leave less frequently in

Table 15. Relationship of household members to thirty-seven female heads

Kinship category	#	%	Lineage kin	Non-lineage kin
1. Common-law husband	9	6.9		9
2. Sons				
a. Under 18	6	4.6	6	
b. 18 and over (single)	5	3.8	5	
c. Married	2	1.5	2	
d. Common-law married	2	1.5	2	
e. Separated	4	3.1	4	
3. Daughters				
a. Under 18	12	9.2	12	
b. Single mother	2	1.5	2	
c. Married	4	3.1	4	
d. Common-law married	3	2.2	3	
e. Separated	4	3.1	4	
4. Son's children	15	11.4		15
5. Daughter's children				
a. Single daughter's child	5	3.8	5	
b. Married daughter's child	11	8.4	11	
c. Common-law married daughter's child	14	10.7	14	
d. Separated daughter's child	4	3.1	4	
6. Son's spouse				
a. Wife	2	1.5		2
b. Common-law wife	2	1.5		2
7. Daughter's spouse				
a. Husband	4	3.1		4
b. Common-law husband	3	2.2		3
8. Sister's husband	1	0.8		1
9. Sister's daughter's common-law husband	1	0.8		1
10. Brother	2	1.5	2	
11. Sister	4	3.1	4	
12. Sister's child	3	2.2	3	
13. Sister's daughter's child	5	3.8	5	
14. Common-law husband's father	1	0.8		1
15. Adopted girl	1	0.8		1
Total living in households with female heads	131	100.0	92	39
Percent of lineage and non-lineage kin			70.3	29.7

this way can be seen in that the number of single daughters eighteen years of age and over, plus the number of single mothers, is nearly twice that of the single adult sons present. The presence of children of the head's spouse only indicates that a woman is able to bring her children by other men into her marriage with her. There is an adage in common use that says a man who takes in such a child and treats it as his own will be rewarded for doing so: "The child will be grateful when it grows up and will treat him better than his own." Where a husband refuses these children, as occasionally happens, they remain, as a rule, with their mother's mother. Nearly 40 percent of the women of the sample aged fifteen years and over are, or have been, single mothers, and the number of children women bear while single ranges from one to several. The absence of children of the head only emphasizes the fact that there is very little social recognition of fatherhood of children sired in these casual liaisons. This would appear to be consistent with the matrilineal institutions of Longhouse society and emphasizes the identification of children with their mother and the precedence of the ties of maternity over the paternal bond.

Categories five through eight represent grandchildren and great grandchildren of the heads, comprising 14 percent of the total. There are over seven times as many daughters' children as sons' children, and the number of great-grandchildren is almost negligible, representing only two instances.

Affines, in the form of son's wives and daughter's husbands and common-law husbands, are shown in categories nine through eleven. The ideal is for a young couple to have their own house; however, it is the exception for them to achieve this coincident with marriage, and most young couples spend a period of time as subordinate members in an already established household. More will be said on this topic further on.

Categories twelve through eighteen indicate collateral kin of the head and his spouse present in the households. The numbers are small in every case, but show that members of the household beyond the nuclear family are more often related to the head than to his spouse. The number of parents of the head and his spouse shown in categories nineteen and twenty show that it is rare for a man to be head with either of his parents as members of the same household.

Categories twenty-one and twenty-two are adopted boys and girls and make up 1 percent of the total. These children have full filial status in the household into which they are adopted.

A fact readily apparent from the tables is that households with male heads are kinship units, and the relationships of greatest importance are those of

Table 16. Generation depth and headship

Percentage of households with	Generation Depth				
	1	2	3	4	Total
Male heads	19.4	51.9	25	3.7	100
Female heads	26.2	21.5	50	2.3	100

conjugality, parenthood, and grandparenthood. As indicated in table 16, these households are, for the most part, two-generation units consisting of expanding nuclear families. The presence of grandchildren, principally in the form of daughters' children, though small in number compared to own children, represents an important feature of the system in that they are in the potential focus of new household groups. This matter will be considered presently. Since the matriline is emphasized for certain jural and ritual purposes among the Longhouse people, it is important to note the absence of the avuncular factor in particular, and of lineage kin in general, in the composition of households with male heads.

Relationship to Head of Members
of Households Having Female Heads

Referring to the categories in tables 13 and 15, it is readily apparent that households with female heads are also kinship units. Table 16 above shows that these same households are predominately of three generations or more in depth, whereas two-generation households predominate where males are heads. This fact seems to indicate that a woman is able to keep her children around her for a longer period of time than is a man. Almost all of the nine two-generation households with female heads are composed of a woman and her sons or daughters who have stayed on with her. These facts appear to permit the inference that it is largely the mother-child bond that is the basis for the presence of married children, especially daughters, in households with male heads. Indeed it could be argued from the fact that upon separation children almost without exception go with their mothers (there were only three cases contrary at the time of fieldwork) that all children are present in their fathers' households by virtue of their mothers' presence there.

The presence of nine common-law husbands in households with female heads is a point of importance. While it is exceedingly rare for a woman to be head while living with the husband or common-law husband with whom she has raised children, she may, after separating herself from the father of her children or after becoming a widow, take in a common-law man. These women, without exception, own the houses in which they reside, and there is little doubt with whom ultimate authority actually lies. This feature will be taken up more fully further on where the development of the household in time is considered.

That sons and daughters of the head are an important feature of these households can be seen from categories two and three in table 15. They make up 33.6 percent of the entire membership, exclusive of the heads. Most of them are adult married, common-law married, separated, or single daughters and sons, in contrast to households with male heads where the heads' minor children greatly outnumber the adult children present.

In households with female heads, grandchildren are present in greater number than own children and make up 37.4 percent of the total. If sister's daughter's children are added, the figure becomes 41.2 percent. The ratio of son's children to daughter's children is fifteen to thirty-four. There are no great-grandchildren present in these households.

Categories six to nine are affines of the head. There are seven daughters' spouses, four sons' spouses, and one instance each of a sister's and sister's daughter's spouse, comprising 9.9 percent of all members. It will be seen that this percentage is considerably larger than that for the corresponding categories in households with male heads.

Categories ten to thirteen are siblings, or kin where the primary link is through a sibling, of the head and comprise 10.7 percent of all members. They are, in every case, no more remote than second order kin of the head. Their total number is small by comparison with own children and children of own sons and daughters, and this reflects the fact that it is the maternal bond that is of primary influence in bringing people together in these households rather than the wider ties of matrilineal descent.

Category fourteen represents the old father of the head's common-law husband and is clearly an exceptional case. There is one case of adoption by a separated woman who was not able to have children of her own.

The relationships of greatest importance in households having female heads are those between a woman and her own children and the children of her daughters. Even where a woman lives alone, the houses of married sons and daughters are likely situated on the same plot. Conjugal relationships are largely limited to the sons and daughters of the head, but do appear in a some-what modified form among some of the female heads. Where common-law husbands of the female head are present, this is largely because the conjugal ties of her children work against her or that she has no offspring.

The foregoing material gives a fairly clear picture of the number of members, generation depth, and the arrangement of members in relationship to the heads in the households as they appeared at the time of fieldwork. It is a part of the argument to be advanced here that there is a systematic relationship between the various "types" of households implicit in the descriptions given and that the variations in form really represent household groups at various points in a developmental cycle. The soundness of this argument will be tested by noting the changes occurring in the structure of the households of the sample through time.

Because it was not actually possible to observe a given collection of households over a period of time, the method applied here is that first used by Professor Fortes for the Tallensi (1949a) and for the Ashanti (1949b) and since then by a number of other anthropologists (Smith 1956; Goody 1958). This method considers the ages of the various household heads as points on a time coordinate. In a relatively stable situation, the age of the household head may serve as an index to the particular phase of development of his or her household at a given time. Morgan noted that matrilineal extended family groupings among the New York State Iroquois had disappeared by the turn of the eighteenth century (Morgan 1881, 122–23, 65, 99–100). This change probably came about somewhat later among the Canadian Iroquois, but there is little indication that any important changes in household life have occurred among the Longhouse people during the last three generations. In noting then the characteristics of the collection of households, whose heads are of differing ages, spread through the various generations in Longhouse society at the present time, a reasonably accurate account of the phases all households of the society pass through during the span of their existence can be described. In noting this process, some insight into the principles upon which it is based should also be gained.

Phase Specific Characteristics of the Development of Household Groups

It is the birth and impending birth of children to daughters in existing households that determine the lines of cleavage that eventuate in the setting up of new households. The fact was mentioned earlier that the accepted ideal is for a young couple to have their own household upon marriage. The ideal is seldom readily achieved, and this fact is recognized by the people themselves,

Table 17. Residence of couples after marriage

Household	Relationship				
	Mother	Father	Both parents	Other kin	Total
Wife's kin	7	1	4	2	14
Husband's kin	4	1	2	0	7
Totals	11	2	6	2	21

who, in stating the ideal, invariably add, "If they can't be to themselves, it is better for them to stay with the girl's parents." They feel that this arrangement requires less of an adjustment, since the husband's activities lie for the most part outside the house. Table 17 gives residence data on the twenty-one married couples living as subordinate members of households.

The period of time during which a newly married couple resides with the parents of either spouse averages about three years. The average first marriage age of males is about twenty-four years, and the age at which male headship comes into prominence is thirty years, which indicates a living-in period of from nil to six years, or an average of about three years. Carrying this computation further on the basis of the number of marriages occurring each year, which was an average of five for the three summers (marriages tend to occur in summer) covered by fieldwork, we might expect approximately fifteen recently married couples to be residing with the parents of either in a given year. Actually, as has been shown in table 17 above, there were twenty-one married couples living with their parents at the time of fieldwork, and the difference can be explained by the fact that some couples do not leave their natal households, but stay on to take over from their parents when they pass on.

A crucial factor in becoming a differentiated household unit is the acquisition of a house. Neither the husband, nor the wife, nor the kin of either are at present obligated by custom or jural rule to provide a house upon marriage. Getting a house is an individual concern, and there are no regularized means of involving other persons or groups in activities related to acquiring a house. Kinsfolk sometimes help with construction, or they may lend money or may even lend the house itself, but this is a matter of personal inclination rather than of duty. These circumstances have a correlate in the rules of inheritance imposed by the Canadian government entitling both sons and daughters to inherit equally both the real and the personal property of their parents, and in the individualization of economic activities considered in the previous chapters. A small number of people expressed the idea that the husband should

Table 18. Acquisition of houses in fifty-one two-generation households

Means of acquisition	Source to household		Male heads		Female heads	
	Husband	Wife	#	%	#	%
Inheritance	3	2	5	10.0	3	5.8
Construction	19	1	20	39.2	–	–
Purchase	4	–	4	7.8	–	–
On loan from near kin	6	4	10	19.6	1	2.0
Renting	4	–	4	7.8	–	–
Insufficient information	–	–	4	7.8	–	–
Total	36	7	47	92.2	4	7.8

provide a house, and in a few instances, parents had actually given over land upon which to build a house to their sons, to the exclusion of their daughters. Where this has happened, it would seem to reflect a sense of responsibility in keeping with the fact that the economic activities of men are the primary source of economic support to the household.

Of the sixty-five two-generation households, fifty-one are households that have mostly individuated during the past fifteen years and have not yet begun to disperse. Forty-seven of these fifty-one are households with male heads, and only four have female heads. Men have provided houses in thirty-six of these instances, women in eleven, and the data are incomplete for four.

A woman may purchase a house or have one built for her with money obtained from her own efforts as a wage earner. One woman of the eleven had had a house built on land inherited from her father. The other ten have acquired houses either by inheritance, in five instances, or by borrowing from near kin in five.

The thirty-six men have acquired houses by the whole range of means. The means occurring most frequently is construction, which occurs in nineteen instances. Six men have borrowed houses to become established, three have inherited houses, and there are four cases each of purchase and renting. These data are summarized in table 18.

The value of houses purchased or constructed ranges from about one hundred to three thousand dollars, and rental charged is usually from about five to ten dollars per month. There are no special means by which money is acquired for the purchase or building of houses, although four houses in the construction category have been obtained as veterans' grants from the Canadian government. These costs can be compared with the estimated average earnings of adult men and women shown in chapter 3.

The point to emphasize is that the main initiative, capital, and labor for acquiring houses, incident to becoming independently established, is supplied by men, the majority of whom are upwards of thirty years of age.

Households begin their existence as two-generational units; that is, they are already expanding households by the time they become differentiated. As has been seen, fifty-one of the households are of this type, and they are headed in 89 percent of the cases by males. The average age of the heads of these households is 40.2 years, ranging from twenty-seven to fifty-seven years. This is important because it indicates that all households pass through a period where their composition is that of a man, his wife, and their children.

During this period of expansion, the dependence of a woman and her children on the husband-father for their sustenance is at a maximum. This dependence arises out of the duties of motherhood and the limitations these duties place upon the economic activities of women outside the household. A woman may become free for periods between the birth of her children to leave the reserve for work, but as the number of small children increases, she finds this very difficult to manage unless she has her mother near at hand. This is often a period of trial and privation for a woman, and it is made more difficult, as pointed out in the previous chapter, by the fact that many men spend a considerable portion of their earnings outside the household group. Drinking, a favorite pastime of a number of men, often places a severe limitation on the value of their earnings for their households. Women, on the other hand, seldom drink. These circumstances appear to reflect the attenuated and ambiguous position of the husband-father in his household, as this is related to the total system, and by contrast, the position of the wife-mother who is firmly integrated within the domestic group socially, economically, and jurally.

It would be wrong to say that all men critically neglect the needs of their wives and children, and it is interesting to note that where men do not drink or have ceased drinking, they have usually acceded to certain positions of leadership within their own lineage group or within a longhouse ritual group. One elderly man put it this way, "I used to drink quite a lot when I was younger, but my grandchildren have never seen me drunk." He had, meanwhile, become chief (hoyane'h) of his lineage. Drinking by men is given as the principal reason for separation, and this is largely because of the privation it entails for the woman and her children. It is said of a woman thus deprived that she leaves her husband because she "grows up on him." The Longhouse people are here comparing the position of a woman in these circumstances with that of minor sons and daughters who leave their natal households to establish their jural and economic independence.

As the children begin to mature, dependence upon the husband-father is lessened. With older children able to take care of domestic tasks and tend their younger siblings, a woman may begin again to leave the household to work. She may take some of her older children with her who work by her side, or she may send her young sons and daughters after the age of about twelve or fourteen years out to work. Government subsidies in the form of Family Allowance also alleviate some of the stress on the wife-mother role during this period, since she usually manages this money. There is a general feeling that a woman should be allowed to control the earnings of her minor children. In explanation of this, people say that "she has given birth to them, and it is she who looks after them and knows their needs." A woman at this time begins to join the groups of women between the ages of about forty to sixty-five who leave the reserve during summer and autumn to work on fruit farms and in canning factories, and this reflects the fact that the burdens of child-rearing are becoming lightened.

It has been said that young men at about twenty years of age—perhaps younger for subsequent sons—begin to leave their natal households to establish their economic and jural independence. This is one of the phenomena that signals the dispersion phase in household development. Some of these young men leave the reserve for jobs outside, as the differential in the population figures for both sexes between the ages of sixteen and thirty indicates (tables 19 and 21), and a few others move in with relatives who are principally matrilineal kin on the reserve. This latter is not done, however, as in claiming a jural right. These young men usually maintain connections with their natal households, especially with their mothers, to whom they often give money for safekeeping. They may also give her presents of money, clothing, and luxury items and may buy clothing and other necessities for younger siblings. These factors reflect the strength of the mother-child bond and the growing marginality of the position of the husband-father.

It is at this point in its development that the household begins to become a three-generational unit. This occurs first, as a rule, with the appearance of single mothers' children and continues with the accretion of married daughters and their children and the return to their natal homes of separated daughters and their children. During this process the household may move alternately between two and three generations. Fifty-three, or 35.3 percent, of the households are of either three or four generations in depth, and the average age of the heads is 60.3, ranging between thirty-eight and seventy-seven years.

It is an important feature of the development of the household that from about the age of forty-five years and onward, the number of female heads begins to increase; and from the age of sixty, they appear as frequently as do male heads. Table 21, showing the distribution of the females of the population sample by age and conjugal status, sheds some light on these facts. It can be seen from the data on "previous unions" that there occurs a kind of reshuffling of the members of conjugal unions from about the age of forty years and onward, and twenty-three of the forty-two female heads set up households of their own concurrent with these changes. In one instance of this type that occurred during fieldwork, a forty-one-year-old woman left her husband and moved into her own house, taking her children, who ranged in age from three to fifteen years, with her. She adamantly refused to go back to her husband or to accept boxes of groceries that he sent as a truce. She later brought a married son and his wife and child into her household, a son who only a few years before had moved out to gain control over the fruits of his own economic efforts.

The percentage of common-law unions also increases, and when a woman enters a common-law union from this age and onward, she is head of the household in about 47 percent of the instances. When a woman takes in a common-law man in this phase, she invariably owns the house in which they live. Even when the common-law husband owns a house of his own, she refuses to live with him there. He is not apt to be taken in at all if the woman has sons and daughters with whom she can surround herself. Widowed and separated men often come to women living alone and, in all subservience, perform odd chores such as chopping firewood, husking corn, spading gardens, or running errands in a car, if they own one, in an effort to make a place for themselves. They are, in every case, on a very precarious footing and there is little doubt about headship in these cases.

The tables also show that widows begin to appear at about forty-five years of age. Sixteen of the forty-two female heads have attained headship coincident with becoming widows.

When a household becomes one of three generations with the accretion of members as referred to above, there is no reallocation of authority within the group. Spouses of sons and daughters are subordinate to the established authority, and a young husband in such circumstances may be chided or in-

Table 19. Age and conjugal status of male population[a]

Age	S	Mar	CLM	W	CLW	Sep	CLS	Total	(16–30)	%	PU	%
0–1	18	0	0	0	0	0	0	18		4.6	0	0
2–5	66	0	0	0	0	0	0	66		17.0	0	0
6–10	65	0	0	0	0	0	0	65		16.7	0	0
11–15	45	0	0	0	0	0	0	45		11.6	0	0
16–20	24	2	0	0	0	0	0	26		6.6	0	0
21–25	9	6	2	0	0	0	0	17	62	4.3	1	5.9
26–30	2	14	2	0	0	0	1	19		4.9	2	10.5
31–35	2	5	2	0	0	0	0	9		2.3	3	33.3
36–40	2	17	2	0	0	0	0	21		5.4	2	9.5
41–45	1	12	10	0	0	2	0	25		6.4	14	56.0
46–50	1	10	1	0	0	0	0	12		3.1	1	8.3
51–55	4	2	2	0	0	1	1	10		2.6	4	40.0
56–60	1	6	1	1	0	1	0	10		2.6	3	30.0
61–65	0	4	2	2	0	0	0	8		2.0	3	37.5
66–70	1	5	4	3	1	3	2	19		4.9	11	57.9
71–80	2	6	4	4	1	0	0	17		4.3	9	53.1
81–90	0	1	0	2	0	0	0	3		0.7	0	0
Total	243	90	32	12	2	7	4	390		100.0	53	13.6
%	62.3	23.1	8.2	3.1	0.5	1.8	1.0	100.0				

[a] Key to Abbreviations: s, single; sm, single mother; Mar, legally married; CLM, common-law married; w, widow or widower; CLW, common-law widow or widower; Sep, separated from legal spouse; CLS, separated from common-law spouse; PU, previous unions. These refer to the number of persons who have had one or more previous unions rather than to the number of separate unions.

structed as a filial member of the group. In some instances, grandchildren, especially single mothers' children, are assimilated to the filial generation and address and refer to their grandparents with parental terms, while their own mother and her siblings are called by their own given names. In some cases, the grandfather, who in these instances was over sixty-five years of age, was called "grandpa," "gramps," or other terms for grandfather, while the term "ma" was used for his wife, this usage probably reflecting the marginality of his authority in the household at this phase. Where the grandfather is younger, as is often the case with single mothers' children, he is less likely to be placed in the second ascending generation category. In some instances, the siblings of the grandparents were also referred to as "aunt" and "uncle." The explanation most often given for this usage was that "they hear what their parents call us and do the same." The fact that grandchildren are assimilated in this way

Table 20. Age and conjugal status of male population[a]

Age	S	Mar	CLM	W	CLW	Sep	CLS	Total	%	PU	%
20 and under	218	2	0	0	0	0	0	220	56.4	0	0
21–40	15	42	8	0	0	0	1	66	17.0	8	12.2
41–60	7	30	14	1	0	4	1	57	14.6	22	38.6
61–100	3	16	10	11	2	3	2	47	12.0	23	49.0
Total	243	90	32	12	2	7	4	390	100	53	13.6
Total over 20	25	88	32	12	2	7	4	170	43.6	53	31.3
Percent over 20	14.8	51.9	18.8	7	1.1	4.1	2.3	100			

[a] Key to Abbreviations: s, single; SM, single mother; Mar, legally married; CLM, common-law married; W, widow or widower; CLW, common-law widow or widower; Sep, separated from legal spouse; CLS, separated from common-law spouse; PU, previous unions. These refer to the number of persons who have had one or more previous unions rather than to the number of separate unions.

extends the period of effective motherhood for a woman, and it sometimes happens that a married daughter's child or the child of a single mother will be left behind to be raised by its maternal grandmother as her own child.

Initially, the coming of daughters' children may extend the limitation on a woman's freedom. Usually, however, there develops a kind of partnership between the mother and her daughter, in which the mother looks after the children while the daughter goes out to work. In return, the daughter gives presents of clothing, money, and other desirables. On the other hand, if a woman has younger children of her own, she may leave these in charge of this daughter and go out to work herself. This system of reciprocity or partnership becomes well developed as daughters bring spouses into the household, or as separated daughters return with their children.

There may also develop very close ties between a woman and her son, whom she sometimes attempts to keep with her as a source of support in her old age. Women often lament the marriage of sons, and the giving of presents to mothers by newly married men can be a source of complaint by their wives, sometimes leading to witchcraft accusations between the wife and her mother-in-law. Some women actually succeed in keeping their sons with them at the expense of marriage.

Even in households where the founding pair remain together in their original conjugal union, the position of the male head often undergoes considerable modification. Equality between spouses tends to develop at this age. Each provides his or her own support, and the tensions of premenopausal conjugality are gone. With the presence of adult single, separated, or married

Table 21. Age and conjugal status of female population[a]

Age	S	SM	Mar	CLM	W	CLW	Sep	CLS	Total	(16–30)	%	PU	%
0–1	33	0	0	0	0	0	0	0	33		7.9	0	0
2–5	60	0	0	0	0	0	0	0	60		14.5	0	0
6–10	67	0	0	0	0	0	0	0	67		16.2	0	0
11–15	51	1	0	0	0	0	0	0	52		12.6	0	0
16–20	16	12	4	0	1	0	0	0	33		7.9	0	0
21–25	2	4	6	2	0	0	1	0	15	72	3.6	1	6.7
26–30	0	0	16	6	0	0	1	1	24		5.8	5	20.9
31–35	0	1	14	2	0	0	1	0	18		4.3	2	11.2
36–40	1	0	11	5	0	0	2	0	19		4.6	9	47.5
41–45	0	1	15	4	1	0	1	0	22		5.3	5	22.7
46–50	0	0	6	2	0	0	3	0	11		2.7	7	63.2
51–55	1	0	1	0	0	0	1	0	3		0.7	1	33.3
56–60	0	0	4	3	3	0	2	0	12		2.9	6	50.0
61–65	0	0	7	2	3	0	1	1	14		3.4	7	50.0
66–70	0	0	2	4	4	1	2	4	17		4.1	11	64.8
71–80	0	0	4	2	3	3	0	1	13		3.1	7	54.0
81–90	0	0	0	0	0	1	0	0	1		0.2	1	100.0
91–100	0	0	0	0	1	0	0	0	1		0.2	0	0
Total	231	19	90	32	16	5	15	7	415		100.0	62	15.0
%	55.7	4.6	21.7	7.7	3.8	1.2	3.6	1.7	100				

[a] Key to Abbreviations: s, single; sm, single mother; Mar, legally married; clm, common-law married; w, widow or widower; clw, common-law widow or widower; Sep, separated from legal spouse; cls, separated from common-law spouse; pu, previous unions. These refer to the number of persons who have had one or more previous unions rather than to the number of separate unions.

children and grandchildren, the male head is definitely overshadowed, and about 30 percent of the three-generation households with male heads fit these circumstances. It is a common thing in fieldwork to visit a house and find a group of women assembled, the core of which is a woman and her daughters. The male head on such an occasion is often found in a detached location teasing and joking with his grandchildren who have come with their mothers, or he may be found, if present at all, sitting outside or in a corner smoking his pipe. In one of the above instances, the male head had taken up residence in a small secondary log house some yards behind the main house where his wife, a married daughter with her husband and children, and a separated daughter and her children dwelt. Men in this position often remain away for extended periods.

Table 22. Age and conjugal status of female population[a]

Age	S	SM	Mar	CLM	W	CLW	Sep	CLS	Total	%	PU	%
20 and under	227	13	4	0	1	0	0	0	245	59.0	0	0
21–40	3	5	47	15	0	0	5	1	76	18.4	17	22.3
41–60	1	1	26	9	4	0	7	0	48	11.6	19	39.7
61–100	0	0	13	8	11	5	3	6	46	11.0	26	56.0
Total	231	19	90	32	16	5	15	7	415	100.0	62	15.0
Total over 20	4	6	86	32	15	5	15	7	170	41.0	62	36.6
Percent over 20	2.3	3.5	50.8	18.8	8.8	2.9	8.8	4.1	100			

[a] Key to Abbreviations: s, single; SM, single mother; Mar, legally married; CLM, common-law married; W, widow or widower; CLW, common-law widow or widower; Sep, separated from legal spouse; CLS, separated from common-law spouse; PU, previous unions. These refer to the number of persons who have had one or more previous unions rather than to the number of separate unions.

A household reaches its full measure of expansion with the presence of the grandchildren of the founding couple, there being only a few instances where collaterals of either have joined the household. It is useful to note again that one of the children of the founding couple replaces them in their household when they die, although no formal rule operates here. The recent history of fifty-one two-generation households shows that about eleven, or 21 percent, of them became independent units upon replacing their parents in the houses of the latter, while the other 79 percent moved out to build, purchase, or borrow their houses. Generally speaking, when there are younger siblings present in a household where a conjugal pair are living with the parents of either, the couple tends to move out. Where there are no other siblings, they tend to stay on, taking over from the old folks. There seems to be a kind of tacit acceptance of the idea that the one who has cared for the parents in their old age deserves to get the house, and transfer of the house and at least part of the property may actually be made to this son or daughter prior to the death of the parents. Parents, especially mothers, are seldom left to live completely alone in their old age, and there are sanctions against this happening. The house may be rendered useless by the uncontrollable presence of their spirits thus maligned, or the spirit of an abused parent may "get after" the neglectful son or daughter.

If the departure of grown sons and the presence of single daughters' children signal the onset of dispersion, the presence of only one child, either married with spouse and children, separated, or single, signals the final dissolution of the household. We have come full cycle through the process. Two- and three-generation households are thus seen to be the matrix for each other. This is not a mechanical process, however, and there are at any time households that do not fit this model. When this is so, it is in every case for some disqualifying reason such as death or infertility of the members of the group concerned. These are principally households among those having one and two members, mentioned at the beginning of this chapter. This leaves approximately 80 percent of all households for which the generalization is relevant.

That the developmental process described here is not just an artificial construct can be seen by examining the practical circumstances of specific households in various phases of their development. Pseudonyms are used in each of the following cases.

Case 1

Richard and Mattie, aged thirty-three and twenty-five years respectively, lived together in a common-law union. Besides themselves, their household included Mattie's six-year-old daughter by another man and a two-year-old son and two-month-old daughter of the present union.

Richard had had a legal wife who left him for another man about a year after their marriage, but he had no children by this woman. Mattie had a casual affair with a young man when she was seventeen, which resulted in the birth of her daughter. Mattie's mother chastised her severely when the pregnancy was discovered but, as she said, "When the baby came, I forgot my anger." At first, Mattie's mother looked upon her daughter's child as "another daughter for me to raise up," but after Mattie entered her present union, the mother encouraged Richard to take the child in as his own. Indeed, the little girl was considered a full member of her stepfather's household although she spent many hours, and sometimes days, with her mother's sister and her grandmother.

When this couple first got together, Richard came to live with Mattie in her mother's house. A son was born in the same year; and two years later, when their second child was to be born, Richard borrowed five hundred dollars each from his parents and his mother's sister with which to purchase fifty acres of land and a two-room house only a few hundred yards from that of Mattie's mother.

From his occupation as a welder, Richard earned about $2,352 in 1957, and he provided the main source of income for the support of the household. Until the birth of their youngest child, Mattie was able to leave the older children with a married sister while she went out to work in a nearby canning factory, and she earned about $680 per season. At the time of fieldwork—except for $192 per year Family Allowance, which she controlled—she and the children were primarily dependent upon Richard for support.

This case illustrates how, after a period of living in, a couple are able to set up their own household, and how a woman is able to bring her children by other men with her during this phase when the husband-father is in a predominant position.

Case 2

Milton, a thirty-eight-year-old man, returned to the reserve after having served in World War II and having traveled about "on the outside" quite extensively thereafter. Upon his return, he began living with thirty-seven-year-old Grace who, along with her two sons by another man, was then living in the household of her parents. When Grace became pregnant, they were married in a Long-house ceremony; and for a year or so afterward, when not living in the fruit country where they worked, they continued to share the facilities of Grace's two-room log house with her mother, an unmarried sister, and an older sister who was living there with her common-law husband and their five children. Grace's father had moved into a one-room log house some yards behind the main house.

Milton had a serious drinking problem (which he sought to attribute to witchcraft), and in the spring of 1956, because he neglected his family, his wife left the fruit farm, where they were then living, and again took up residence with her mother and sisters. Milton attempted to entreat her to return to him, but her parents turned him away. However, later on in the summer, on the occasion of a longhouse ceremony, they got together and were reconciled.

During the summer of 1957, Milton was able to earn about $1,800 from his work as a steady hand on a fruit farm; but because of his drinking problem, the value of his earnings for his wife and children was greatly reduced. For this reason, Grace's own earnings and the $120 Family Allowance, which she managed, were of considerable importance for the household. In the autumn of the same year, Milton rented a small house on the reserve, to which he brought his wife, their one-year-old daughter, their two-month-old son, and Grace's four-year-old son by another man. Grace's eldest son, who was six years of age, was left with her mother to be raised by her.

Here is seen a nuclear family, the stability of which was weakened by the drinking problem of the husband-father, which also hindered the group in becoming established as an independent unit. This case also offers an example of how the mother-daughter bond and sister bond offer a source of security to a woman outside her own conjugal relationship.

Case 3

James began living with Nelda at the home of her mother and stepfather. The following year, when she became pregnant, they were married in a traditional Longhouse ceremony. Subsequent to the birth of their first child, they moved to New York State, but after a few months, they again went to live with Nelda's parents in Ontario, where they were working on a fruit farm. In 1944, they returned with her parents to the reserve, where they continued to live until James was finally able to build a house on twenty-five acres of land given his wife by her stepfather.

At the time of fieldwork, their household consisted of forty-two-year-old James, thirty-nine-year-old Nelda, their eight single children, ranging in age from seventeen years to six months, and their married nineteen-year-old daughter, with her twenty-four-year-old husband. An eighteen-year-old son, Charlie, asserting his independence from his natal household, had gone to live with his maternal grandparents.

James worked as a construction laborer from June to September 1957, and earned about $1,248 for this work. A considerable part of his earnings, however, was spent on liquor, and he sometimes beat his wife and children while drunk. His wife controlled $516 per year Family Allowance, but she was unable to work outside the home because of ill health connected with her last pregnancy and because of the responsibility of caring for her young children, and she often importuned her eldest son for economic assistance. Her married daughter, Tricia, who worked on the reserve, contributed to the economy of the household during a part of the year, but because of her pregnancy, these contributions ceased. Tricia's husband, who had no steady job, contributed only sporadically.

Although this household had begun to disperse, it was clearly still in need of a great deal of support from the husband-father, which it did not always receive. The wife-mother's position had begun to be lightened with the help afforded by her eldest son and daughter, although this was somewhat short-lived because of the marriage and subsequent pregnancy of this daughter. Therefore, the problems characteristic of the expansion phase will likely continue paramount until the cessation of childbearing occurs and the burden of childrearing lightens.

Case 4

Dan was forty-five years old, and his wife, Lottie, was forty-two. They lived in a four-room, modified-log house faced with imitation brick siding, which Dan inherited from his mother, along with eighteen acres of land and two storage sheds. The other members of the household included Lottie's twenty-five-year-old son, Andy, whom she had as a single mother; their sixteen-year-old daughter, Liz, who was a single mother; a fourteen-year-old son; seven-year-old twins; a five-year-old daughter; and Liz's two daughters, aged eighteen months and two months respectively.

Prior to the present marriage, Dan had lived in a common-law union with another woman. Soon after she gave birth to their son, both mother and child died. Thereafter, Dan sired a daughter in a casual liaison with another woman, but he gave no support to either the child or its mother. Finally he brought Lottie into his parents' home, where they were married in a traditional Longhouse ceremony. Through the years, some of Dan's younger siblings brought their spouses and children into their parents' home to live for short periods, but eventually each of these established separate households. Dan and Lottie stayed on to care for the old folks, and Dan inherited the old homestead.

The couple also had had a third child who died, and shortly after this, Dan left his wife, whereupon a delegation of hereditary chiefs came to "preach" to them to remind them of the responsibilities and obligations entailed in marriage. As a result of this effort, the two were reconciled and have since managed to work out a quite compatible relationship.

Dan received very little cash income from his farming enterprise, but the supply of eggs, meat, milk, and garden vegetables produced was an important economic feature of this household. He also supplemented his farm income by working occasionally on fruit farms and for nearby white farmers at harvest time, and by trapping muskrats in the spring of 1957, the pelts of which brought him twenty-five or thirty dollars.

Lottie's son, Andy, worked as a high steel painter in cities thirty to forty miles distant from the reserve, and although he managed his own income, he bought gifts for his mother, clothing for his younger siblings, and made cash contributions to the household through his mother.

Lottie, by leaving their eldest daughter, Liz, in charge of the younger children, was again beginning to work out on fruit farms and in canning factories and earned about $235 in 1957. She also managed $384 per year Family Allowance. Her period of effective motherhood was being extended with the birth of Liz's children, who were being assimilated into a filial relationship within the household.

Case 5

Dave and his wife, Nadine, were sixty-four and sixty-one years of age, respectively. Their household consisted of themselves, their eighteen-year-old son, Bill, their thirty-four-year-old separated daughter, Reba, and her four children, ranging in age from four to twelve years.

They also had a thirty-five-year-old married daughter, who lived nearby with her husband and four children, and a thirty-year-old separated daughter, who was rearing her two children in her own household on the reserve. One other son had died when a child, and four other sons had been stillborn.

When Dave and Nadine were married by the hereditary chiefs, they began living with his widowed mother, and upon her death about fourteen years later, they stayed on to inherit the family homestead of thirteen acres and a sturdy, four-room log house. Later, when Nadine was convalescing from an illness, Dave, under the influence of alcohol, traded his inheritance for another thirteen acres of land, on which stood a small shanty, plus $150 with which he could buy more liquor. When his wife came home from the hospital, however, he built a four-room frame house in which they lived at the time of fieldwork, although the interior had never been completed.

Dave, the household head, received a Veterans' Disability Pension of $1,500 per year and also worked periodically on fruit farms, but little of his income was directed to the support of the household. Nadine was unable to work, but she cared for Reba's children, thus freeing her to go out to work on fruit farms and in canning factories. Between the contributions made by this daughter and those made by the son, Bill, who worked on fruit farms, together with the $288 per year Family Allowance and the irregular contributions of the husband-father, the household was able to maintain itself adequately.

In this household the husband-father was completely overshadowed by his wife. It was she whom their daughters and grandchildren came to visit almost daily and with whom reciprocal services and gifts were exchanged. Oftentimes on these occasions, Dave would retire outside the house or to a corner to smoke his pipe or playfully tease his grandchildren, and he was periodically away from home altogether. It is their mother also to whom the daughters came for advice and for aid in carrying out the individual medicine rites so vital to their welfare and the welfare of their children.

Case 6

Madge, aged seventy-one, was head of her household. Living with her were her sixty-five-year-old common-law husband, Orville, and her separated son's twelve-year-old son, whom she was raising as her own child.

Orville had been married previously and had five children by his former wife. Madge was married to her first husband by the hereditary chiefs and raised four sons and one daughter to maturity, of whom two sons and the daughter had left the reserve with their spouses to work. After thirty years of marriage, she left her first husband and set up her own household in the three-room log house that she had inherited, along with twenty-five acres of land, from her mother. Her husband managed to make a place for himself later in the household of another woman, with whom he has continued to live in a common-law relationship. Madge, in turn, took Orville into her household.

In the early years of their union, they worked together seasonally on fruit farms, but for the past fifteen years, Orville had been employed at a nearby gypsum plant, and he earned about $3,240 in 1957. Madge received $520 Old Age Pension in 1957, and $84 per year Family Allowance. They each managed their own money; and although Madge owned all the household equipment and furniture, Orville had built kitchen cupboards for her (an unusual feature for Longhouse kitchens) and had kept the house in repair generally. They seemed to have worked out a fairly harmonious relationship through the years based on reciprocal services, but Madge was clearly the authority in the household. This case is included to illustrate how common-law husbands will often be taken in by women at this stage, especially if the women are unable to keep their daughters or a son near at hand. Near the end of fieldwork, however, Madge's next youngest son moved his house next door to hers, which added to her security.

Case 7

This case concerns Lavina, a sixty-seven-year-old widow, who was head of her own household. When she had married Les about forty-six years previously, she said, "My mother and others tried to break up the marriage by telling me all that Les was doing wrong," but she turned a deaf ear and managed to work out an enduring relationship with her husband. Upon Les's recent death, he left Lavina just over thirteen acres of land and a small two-room log house, the title to which continued to be disputed by his sister.

Lavina and Les had a son who died in his early teens, and they later adopted a ten-month-old girl, Darla, whom they reared as their own child. When Darla married, she and her husband took up residence with Lavina, and in 1957 the household had expanded to include their infant daughter. As members of her household, the twenty-one-year-old, Darla, and her husband, Gary, submitted themselves fully to Lavina's authority and advice, and when they left the reserve periodically to work, their daughter was left with its grandmother to be reared by her.

Besides receiving $520 Old Age Pension, Lavina earned about $340 in 1957 for work on a fruit farm. Her son-in-law averaged about $80 per week during January and February of 1957, but his work was sporadic and he was about $3,100 in debt at the time of fieldwork. As a result, he had often borrowed money from Lavina, and she had signed as surety on his purchase of a new car; however, she often reprimanded him and her daughter for their frivolous spending habits. Both before and after the birth of her baby, Darla also worked, and with her earnings bought clothing for herself and her child, gifts for her mother, and food for general household consumption.

This household has entered the final phase of its existence, and its dissolution will be complete upon the death of the head. Then, with Darla at the center of the remaining domestic unit, the cycle, already reborn, will be relived again.

It would be possible to go on to place each of the households of the census (except those disqualified by reason of the accidents of death and infertility) in its position in the developmental cycle described, however this would not seem to be warranted here. It is clear that what might otherwise appear to be separate types of household structure by other criteria, reduce to a single form when seen under the aspect of the time dimension. It is central to the argument of this study that the particular arrangement of the various parts that make up the whole of any one household at a given point in time is the result of the differential incidence through time of the underlying principles involved. An analysis of these principles is undertaken in the following chapters.

3

After a meal provided by the host lineage of the *keyadawę* (lit. brother's daughter, [f.s.]) side of the Confederacy, chiefs of the *agadǫni* (lit. father's sister) side embark for Sour Springs Longhouse to raise up chief *Deyotowe'hgǫ*. Chief Joseph Logan Jr. (center with back to camera) chants the "roll call" of chiefs as they proceed. Photo by author.

Groups of chiefs and visitors converse during lunch recess of Confederacy council meeting at Onondaga Longhouse. Photo by author.

Longhouse marriage at home of bride, 15 September 1956. Mothers, Verna Logan and Daisy Thomas, sit beside their children, Garnet Logan and Ivan Thomas, symbolizing the rights of the matrilineage over its members. Officiating chiefs pictured: Joseph Logan Sr., David Thomas, *hoyoan'h* of groom's lineage (standing). Photo by author.

Great grandparents of Esther (Jacobs) Jamieson—Esther *Ęhędawass* (Big Bear, Oneida) and John *Nadjagehdę* General (Bear, Cayuga). *Ęhędawass*, through whom the chiefly title of *Hǫwatsadęhǫ* was perpetuated, migrated to Six Nations from Green Bay, Wisconsin. (See fig. 1.) Photo courtesy of Lorna Hill.

5. Some Politico-Jural and Ritual Aspects of Matrilineal Descent

In part 2, the principal features of the domestic domain and the structure of the household group were examined. In this part of the study the objective is to relate household structure to the external domain in an effort to shed some light on the question of why household structure takes the form that it does. The concern here is principally with the systems of descent and of kinship and marriage. The economic system was accounted for in chapter 3, and an outline of relations with the Canadian government as a factor in the external domain was given in chapter 1. It is referred to in this part of the study only as it affects the jural content of specific relationships within the household.

The social organization of Longhouse society is founded upon the rule of matrilineal descent, and it will be necessary, therefore, to examine this feature of the society if the principles at work in structuring the household are to be understood. Since the central issue of the present study is the household, or the internal system, the consideration given here to the politico-jural and ritual aspects of matrilineal descent will necessarily be paradigmatic, giving attention mainly to those features that bear on the problem at hand.

Among the Longhouse people, the whole range of cognatic kinship is recognized. Kinship is traced through females only, through males only, and by alternate steps, through males and females. The term used to designate kinship in this broad sense is kenǫksǫ (my kinsfolk). Within this inclusive range, the various types or kinds of kinship ties are differentiated based on the ways in which they are used for social purposes. Uterine kinship, or kinship through females only, is used as a basis for forming corporate groups for political, jural, and ritual purposes. Males form the genealogical boundaries of these groups and mediate ties between them through marriage. Agnatic kinship is also recognized (as Morgan's tables also show, 1870, 293–382; 1878, 447–52); but in contrast to matrilineal descent, it does not serve as a basis for the formation of corporate descent groups. Agnatic kinship establishes interpersonal bonds only, and these are given institutional expression, as will be shown in the following chapter.

Although the Longhouse people regard a person as being genealogically related to both of his parents, he is thought to be related in a rather special way to each. It was stated by a number of older informants that in the generative process the "mother supplies the blood" (ganohage gwii gatgwęsagwęniyo) or "lineage follows the mother's side" (ganohage gwii gayadagwęnio), while the father furnishes the substance from which the body (oya'hda'h) is formed (ganifrage gwii gayadagwęnio). Hence a person is related to his father through the body and to his mother through the blood.[1] It is further said that the spirit or "life is in the blood" (odǫnhetrot gotgwęsage), and for this reason a person is deemed to be more closely related to his mother. This provides a rationale for establishing the priority of matrifiliation and the blood line (otgwęsadagyeh) as a basis for the formation of descent groups, and a person is by birth a member of his mother's matrilineage (o'hwhadjiʌ).[2] This lineage includes all the male and female descendants in the matriline of a known ancestress by a known pedigree.

A better appreciation of the nature of Longhouse Iroquois lineages can be had if it is recalled that the forbears of the present members of Longhouse society came to the area in which they now live after the dispersion of the Iroquois, in 1783, that followed the American War of Independence. Their settlements then consisted of fragmented lineage groups of mixed tribal affiliation, in some instances of non-Iroquois origin. Migrations continued for a time even after the establishment of the present reservation (see population figures in chapter 1). Iroquois migrants fit into the existing social system, and non-Iroquois groups were given place by adoption (agaǫdǫgwedaǫgoh).

An attempt was made to reconstitute the system of fifty hereditary chiefs, and this necessitated, as it were, the stretching of the existing human personnel to fill this objective ideal structure. Where original lineages were not represented, titles to chiefly office (hoyaneda'h) were reassigned to the women of individual families or to women who were already members of existing chiefly lineages, and this brought about a further division of lineages and the establishment of new segments.[3]

The overall numerical strength of Longhouse society has increased over time. However, that of particular lineages has waxed and waned with the accidents of birth and death and, in some instances, by the fact that some lineage women became Christians, although this latter factor appears to have been fairly well arrested for the forty to fifty years prior to fieldwork. In some instances, lineage groups of three or four generations' depth from present adult members have grown from these groups or from individual migrant women. In other instances, they have remained fragmentary and participate in group activities on the basis of matrifiliation only.[4]

Longhouse society is segmentary in form, however the irregular way in which new segments have been formed, as just noted, has upset the order of the "feeding-in process" to the more inclusive segments above the basic lineage unit (see the discussion of the sides of the dual organization later in this chapter). Looking at Longhouse society as a whole, the following four orders of segmentation are discernable above the level of the household: (a) a matrilineal sublineage; (b) a corporate matrilineage serving as the basic politico-jural and ritual unit of Longhouse society, which shall hereafter be referred to as the lineage; (c) the "sides" of the dual organization of each longhouse ritual group, each of which includes several of the above lineages and families and individuals; and (d) the longhouse ritual group, of which there are four in the total society: Lower Cayuga, Onondaga, Seneca, and Sour Springs (also called Upper Cayuga).[5]

The Matrilineal Sublineage

The group referred to by this designation is, as a rule, a tightly knit corps of women, usually consisting of a woman, her daughters and sisters' daughters, and their children, or of several sisters and their daughters and daughters' children. The term *sublineage* is used for this group because it is not an effective corporation, although one of the older women serves as a focus of the unity of each group, which is nearly always a segment of a more inclusive matrilineage. It appears as a kind of domestic subdivision of the lineage. Figures 1 and 2 below show the genealogical composition of such units. Some, or all, of the members of these groups live in separate households, frequently within easy access of each other. It would appear that a woman oftentimes lives in her husband's household on the condition that she is still able to visit her mother or other near matrilineal kinswomen often. The relative ease of transportation may facilitate frequent association even where households are separated by considerable distance.

Individual members refer to their group as "my family" or *agewhadjiya*, the same word used for lineage. The members share a high degree of solidarity and confidence, and the influence of the group on the separate households of its members may be considerable. The women cooperate in numerous ways, such as in childcare, quilting bees, lending of staples, and the performance of rituals. They frequently go off the reserve to work together, and at least one such group cooperated in gardening activities at the time of fieldwork. Women share a common lot, and whatever the occasion for getting together, there is usually a sharing of personal problems. Older women frequently advise the younger women in their domestic problems, instruct both young men and women at puberty, and act as overseers of the moral conduct of both young girls and boys. Adult male members are less frequently associated with these groups, although they do return to hold personal rites, since the efficacy of these often requires the assistance of one's matrilineal kin. Members of a sublineage are the first to help out with funeral expenses and with preparations for a wedding feast. They also support each other in differences with outsiders. Although infrequent, quarrels between two individuals on public occasions are known to deteriorate into free-for-alls, in which the members of the respective sublineages, or even of whole lineages, line up solidly behind the opponents.

The Lineage

This group is the unit in which are vested the key political and ritual offices of Longhouse society, and it is, therefore, a corporate group politically, jurally, and ritually.[6] Because all do not possess hereditary chiefships, however, they vary somewhat in degree of corporateness. Birth to a female member of this group carries with it the rights and duties of citizenship in the total society. It is a true lineage, tracing descent to an ancestress through three or four generations from present living adults, this depth corresponding, in some instances, to the arrival of the Iroquois in Canada. In a few instances, the descent lines of two of these lineages converge in a known ancestress, and where this is so, it has come about by the placing of a vacant chiefship (hoyaneda'h) with a woman member of a lineage already possessing chiefship, as noted above. These lineage groups are each designated by their individual eponyms at present, but are included under a different eponym at the level of the "sides" of the dual division of the longhouse ritual groups. Thus, the lineage of chief, Dyǫhyǫgo, is designated by the eponym Skanyadiga (usually translated "Heron" in the literature), but call themselves "Wolves" (Honatahyǫni) at the more inclusive level. It is not appropriate here to deal with this topic in detail.

There were from thirty to thirty-five such lineages among the Longhouse people at the time of fieldwork, varying in number of members from one to over one hundred. Figures 1 and 2 show the genealogical structure of two of these lineages. According to their own concept, from the standpoint of the

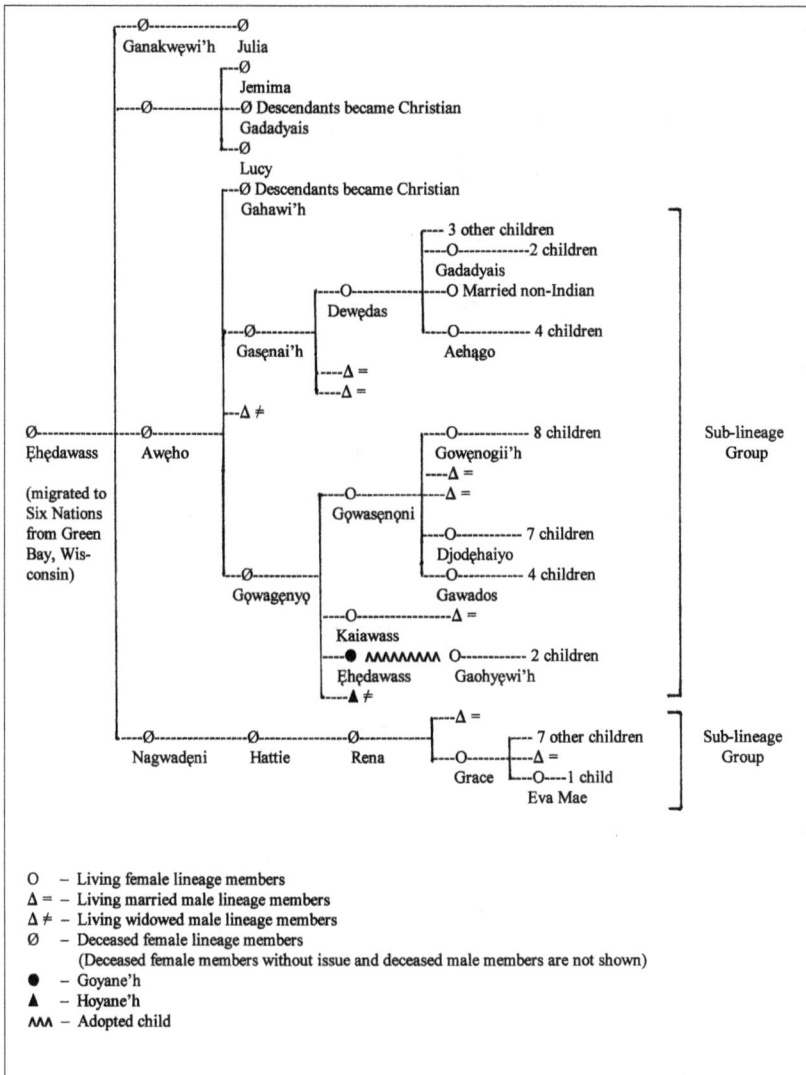

1. Lineage of *Howatsadeho* (*O'hhnyaji'h Gowa*, Oneida)

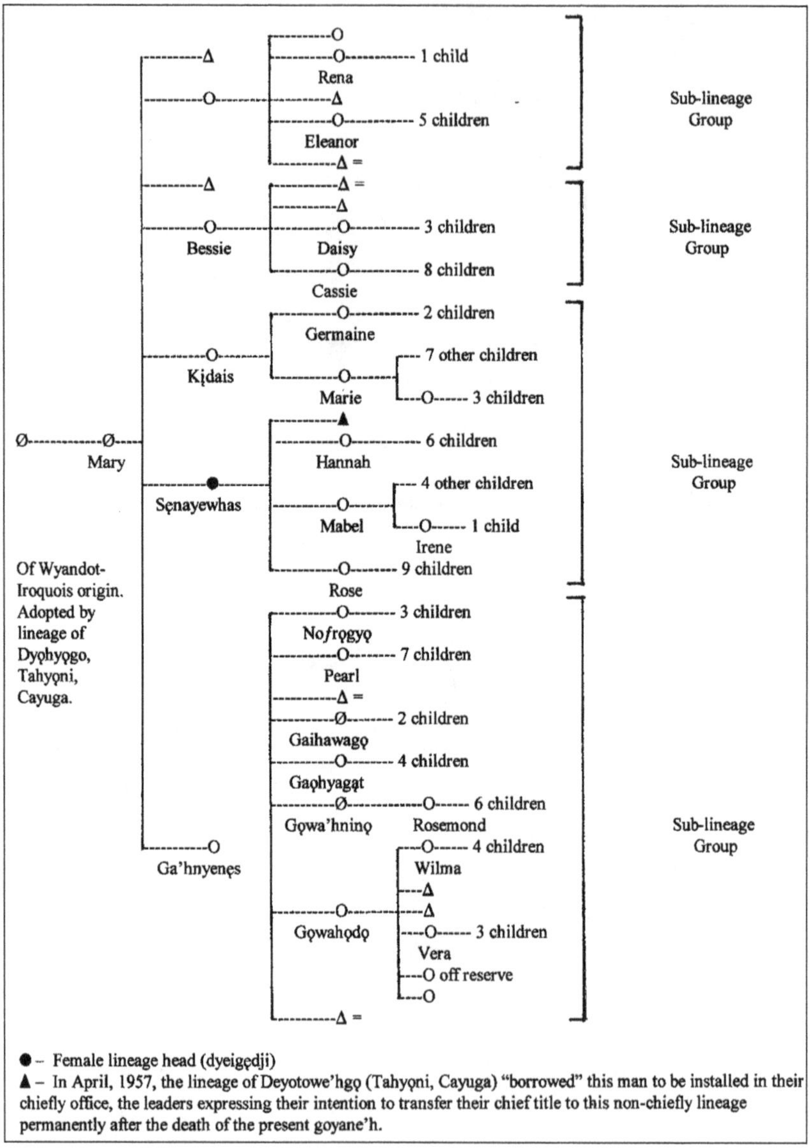

O
O ------- 1 child
Rena
△
O ------- 5 children
Eleanor
△ =

Sub-lineage
Group

△ =
△
O ------- 3 children
Daisy
O ------- 8 children
Cassie

Sub-lineage
Group

O ------- 2 children
Germaine
--- 7 other children
O
Marie └─ O ------ 3 children
▲
O ------- 6 children
Hannah
--- 4 other children
O
Mabel └─ O ------ 1 child
Irene
O ------- 9 children
Rose

Sub-lineage
Group

O ------- 3 children
No*frǫgyǫ*
O ------- 7 children
Pearl
△ =
Ø ------- 2 children
Gaihawagǫ
O ------- 4 children
Gaǫhyagat
Ø ------------ O ------ 6 children
Gǫwa'hninǫ Rosemond
─ O ------ 4 children
Wilma
─ △
△
─ O ------ 3 children
Vera
─ O off reserve
─ O
△ =

Sub-lineage
Group

Ø ------------ Ø ---
Mary

Bessie

Kįdais

● Sǫnayewhas

O
Ga'hnyenęs

Of Wyandot-
Iroquois origin.
Adopted by
lineage of
Dyǫhyǫgo,
Tahyǫni,
Cayuga.

● – Female lineage head (dyeigędji)
▲ – In April, 1957, the lineage of Deyotowe'hgǫ (Tahyǫni, Cayuga) "borrowed" this man to be installed in their chiefly office, the leaders expressing their intention to transfer their chief title to this non-chiefly lineage permanently after the death of the present goyane'h.

2. Non-Chiefly Lineage

politico-legal system, the existence of a lineage is recognized by the Longhouse people as long as it has a single member alive, for upon this person devolves the entire corporate weight of his lineage. This is illustrated in the case of one man who is the sole living member of his lineage. He himself bears the Onondaga chief title *Sagoggha* and discharges the responsibilities associated with the lineage ritual office of *hodrihǫt* (faithkeeper). Some years after the death of the lineage matron, who was also the last woman of his lineage, he became ill, and it was ascertained that his illness was a result of his neglecting the important feasts (*O'hgiwe*) for the dead of his lineage. Since the services of women acting in the office of *kogiwe* are essential for the proper performance of these feasts, he found it necessary to "hire" (*ęhǫwanha*) his own daughter to assist him in discharging this responsibility. The principle illustrated here tends to bear out the position taken by Professor Fortes (1959b, 207) that by the rule of descent, the children of the parent from whom descent is reckoned constitute the minimal element in the total system.

Lineage Name Sets

Each lineage has a set of names (*gawhadjiadogę godisǫna*) from which all the children born to its female members are named.[7] These names are kept by the female head of the group as an exclusive part of its corporate estate and may not be used without her permission. Names are borrowed (*gasęnaniheh*), however, and it is said of such a name that it is hung about the neck (*gahnya sodahǫ'h*) of the bearer and that the matron of the owning lineage still holds the name that is about the bearer's neck (*gadogę niyeha gasęna'h*). A name bestowed in this manner is only temporary and is returned to the owning lineage when a name becomes vacant in the borrowing lineage or upon the death of the bearer. Citizenship in the owning lineage is not conferred in this case as it is in naming lineage members or in outright adoption, the principle feature of which is the bestowal of one of its names by the adopting lineage upon the adoptee.

The internal structure of the lineage is objectified in its name set, which is differentiated based on gender (formerly generation also) and office. The names, whether individual male and female or official, have perpetuity in time, and to each is attached the full body of the rights and duties of citizenship or, in addition, the special rights and duties of office within the lineage; and they thus partake of the nature of *corporation sole* as defined by Maine (1920, chapter 4). A person is, as it were, born into the lineage name set at one end, experiences a series of formal successions through the network of name statuses, and dies out at the opposite end, while the names themselves persist. This process was, of course, most graphic when the three-generation categories of names were operative.[8] Yet political and jural activities continue to be governed by the principle of *corporation sole* and are concerned, to an important extent, with the filling of vacant names with individuals to carry on the obligations and privileges of citizenship and office within the lineage attached to each. Keeping the names filled is, in a measure, equated with maintaining the structure or system intact. It is this principle that lies behind the practice of adoption of captives in older times (see Morgan 1851, 341–44).

Name-giving (*gasẹnaọwe ohade*—path of lineage names) is always a public occasion occurring twice each year. Formerly, the name-giving speech was the duty of the child's mother's brother or of the male head of the lineage, who is also mother's brother or mother's mother's brother; and it is sometimes performed in this way at present. Usually, however, the lineage matron engages the male speaker of her side of the longhouse ritual group to give the speech. The ceremony itself is quite simple. For a girl child, the speaker directs his remarks to the women of the side of the dual division to which she was born. The child is held by the lineage matron for all to see, while the speaker announces the name and lineage of her father and also of the lineage into which she has been born. (This is a point of importance, because it symbolizes the fact that rights *in genetricem* never pass out of the control of the women of the lineage.) The speaker then announces the name that has been chosen by her lineage, pronouncing it several times, while exhorting the child to faithfulness to the Longhouse way. The speech for a male child is similar, except the speaker himself takes the child in his arms while addressing his remarks to the men. The name and lineage of the father are announced, and this is followed by the name of the child selected by his lineage. Thereafter, a male lineage relative of the child performs a rite called *ẹhọwadọtas* (see also Parker 1916, 43), in which one of the personal men's songs (*adọwa'h*) owned by the child's natal lineage is sung—the song to be taught the boy as he grows up.

Each person has actually two names at present (and likely a third, due to the great zest of the Longhouse people for nicknames): one is compounded of an English-language given name and patrifilial surname, with the other being the lineage name referred to above. The English-language name is used on the records of the Indian Department and in all ordinary intercourse; however on all formal Longhouse occasions of a political, jural, or ritual nature, the lineage name only is used.

The following case (using pseudonyms) illustrates how the names function to define citizenship within the lineage and how they are used by the lineage to assert control over the reproductive resources of its female members and over its human resources generally. Opal, a lineage matron (*goyane'h*), and her husband adopted a ten-month-old girl from Lucile, the child's own maternal grandmother. Opal gave the child an English-language name, Amanda, as well as a lineage name from her set, and raised her as her own child to fine young womanhood. Lucile, who had meanwhile become the effective female head of her lineage, due to the senility of the matron, saw that the girl was of fine character and desired to have her back again. On several occasions she sought to explain to Amanda why she had "adopted her out" and said that she had always hoped she would come back to them.

The lineage name given Amanda by the adopting lineage might, during her childhood, be regarded as "a name hung about the neck"; that is, temporary, not carrying with it full lineage membership. However, the test came after her marriage and the birth of her first child. The crucial question was, for whose lineage was she to bear children? In which of the two lineages involved were rights over her reproductive capacity vested?

This whole matter was brought to a head in the naming of Amanda's child. Both Lucile and Opal were clearly aware of the issues involved, and tension mounted as the time for the naming ceremony approached. Both women had selected names for the child, and when the day arrived, Lucile saw Amanda outside the longhouse with her baby and went directly to her. She reiterated the argument she had used before, saying that Amanda, and therefore her child also, were members of her lineage by birth and that "you can't change the blood," (*te'hdewadǫta dasaitgwesadeni*). She also reminded Amanda that she had (that is, was eligible for) lineage matronship (*goyanedah*) in her true blood lineage, and for these reasons, they should be the ones to name the child.

Before Lucile could conclude her conversation, Opal, seeing what was going on, quickly took a bottle of milk from her food basket, went straight to Amanda, gave her the milk and sent her into the longhouse under the pretext of feeding the baby. Lucile again presented her argument to Opal, who would hear no part of it. In desperation, Lucile repeated that the blood could not be changed and that the chiefs would never allow Opal to name the child, to which the woman replied that the chiefs had nothing to say in the matter and that Amanda would never consent to go back. Immediately she returned to the longhouse, went directly to her brother, who was chief of her lineage, and gave him the name she had chosen for the child together with instructions to give the naming speech as soon as it should become possible. Lucile, on the other hand, remained outside to plan her next move and was unaware of these arrangements. By the time she returned to the longhouse, the naming ceremony had got under way. When it came Opal's brother's turn to get up, he made the speech bestowing the name, while Opal held the child up for all to see, and Lucile was presented with a *fait accompli*.[9]

The incident raised some controversy, with some saying that the bloodline was unchangeable and others saying that it was the girl's right to choose. No one was heard to suggest that what had taken place should be revoked.[10] The adoptive mother commented that she had raised up a fine girl and now the grandmother by birth wanted to claim her back. Avoiding the points of contention, she ridiculed the name chosen by the grandmother's lineage. "What an ugly name, 'Guts-Lying-Out,'" she said in disgust.

As well as establishing the jural and social identity of the individual, the names also have ritual and cosmological significance. Each person is known to the spirits of medicinal plants, to the dead, the Creator, and all other supernatural entities by his lineage name. In its names, the lineage thus holds the key to the physical, social, and psychological well-being of its members. There is not space here to present the details of these aspects of the names.

Lineage Offices

It was indicated above that where a lineage possesses offices, these are associated with its set of names and are thus a part of its corporate estate. As a rule, each office is designated by a special name, which remains the same in perpetuity; however, while this is the rule without exception for all male offices, it is less often the case with female offices. The office of the lineage matron (*goyanedah*) was found to be unnamed in every case, and *godrihǫt* and *kogiwe* names have been "lost" in some instances, yet the offices themselves continue on as part of the corporate estate of the possessing lineages.

The three male and three female offices connected with each lineage possessing chiefship (*hoyaneda'h*) are the office of the male head or chief (*hoyane'h*); his "runner," messenger, or subchief (*haǫdanǫh*); the male faithkeeper (*hodrihǫt*); the lineage matron (*goyane'h*); the female faithkeeper (*godrihǫt*); and the female official (*kogiwe*) in charge of relationships with the dead. Where a lineage does not have chiefship, it has a recognized female head (*dyeigǫdji*— oldest woman) who is the cornerstone of its corporate activity in connection with funerals and rites for the dead. Such groups may also possess the male and female ritual offices of faithkeepers just mentioned.

The male and female officers of each lineage form the core of a kind of informal lineage council, in which older men and women also participate to deliberate lineage affairs. It is said of the officers that they "stand equally high" (netaditadide) or that "they listen to each other" (tonadatǫde). The advice or opinion of an older member may actually carry more weight than that of the officers.

Neither the hoyane'h nor the goyane'h wields any means of physical coercion. One goyane'h described the actual situation when she said, "Our chiefs are preachers and peacemakers. They inform the people how they should be" (ǫkiwhaganǫnyanih). They counsel, exhort, and remonstrate, with public opinion and supernatural forces as the sanction behind their actions. Except when acting in an official capacity, there is little to distinguish officers from other members of the lineage. Besides the duties within his or her own lineage, each officer assists the aggregate of all lineage officers in carrying out the activities of the more inclusive segments of society.

It is said of the hoyane'h that "he looks two ways," that "both earthly and heavenly duties lie before him" (ǫwhǫdjageha gaiwhio hodriwhagehǫ); yet politico-jural and ritual actions overlap and fuse into one. As one chief put it, "Our religion and our government, that's the same thing with us." The role of the hoyane'h in the naming ceremony was noted above. With the goyane'h, he is the guardian of lineage exogamy and assists in making funeral arrangements for lineage members. He has the duty to "preach good advice" (ǫsagotaha'hs) to those of his people who abuse one another; and with other lineage officers, he oversees lineage ritual. Beyond his own lineage, and with the chiefs of other lineages, he is the "custodian of all rites and ceremonies of the Creator" (Gaiwhio hodriwhagehǫ) and represents his lineage in the council of chiefs. The activities of this council as a focus of opposition to the Canadian government were noted in chapter 1. In addition to the activities mentioned there, the council installs chiefs after they have been chosen by their respective lineages, and it is custodian of the official titles of defunct lineages and has the right to reassign these titles. The council also performs a special condolence ceremony (hadinigǫdanyǫ) upon the death of all members of chiefly lineages. This action is, in effect, a recognition by other units in the system of the corporate identity of one of their number.

The haǫdanǫh ("he stands on the roots" of the tree of the hoyane'h) is to assist the hoyane'h in all his duties, and he may deputize for him. It is his duty, by a formal procedure, to communicate the death of the hoyane'h to the council of chiefs; and in the event the hoyane'h should be deposed, it is he, in company with the goyane'h, who carries out the final act of deposition.

The hodrihǫt (male faithkeeper) is said to "cover the tree of the hoyane'h." This refers to the fact that he is to assist the chief in all his ritual obligations. He obtains meat for ceremonies, cuts firewood, carries water, keeps buildings in repair, and distributes food in ceremonial feasts. In company with the goyane'h, it is his duty to "preach" to a wayward chief in an effort to get him to mend his ways.

During fieldwork it was confirmed over and over again that the best-informed person in matters of genealogy and in matters of jural, ritual, and moral importance was the lineage matron, or goyane'h. This arises out of the fact that she is the veritable pivot around which lineage organization, and therefore Longhouse society, turns. As guardian of lineage jural and moral norms, she is usually less hesitant to reprove wayward members than is her male counterpart, over whose moral conduct she is also to keep watch. Other lineage women often come to her with their own domestic problems. She is the repository of lineage names, and therefore title to all lineage offices is vested in her, and she is keeper of the shell beads (otgǫa'h) symbolic of these offices. Although she is assisted in making funeral arrangements by the hoyane'h, she carries the main burden of seeing that all parts of the funerary rites are properly performed. In this connection, she presides over the distribution of the personal belongings of deceased members of her lineage and performs the rite releasing their widows or widowers from the marriage. She also oversees the performance of the cyclical ceremonies, referred to as wiwhawędenyǫ.

In many instances, it is the goyane'h who discharges the duties of the office of godrihǫt (female faithkeeper), although this office is held separately in some instances. The principal duties of this office are the preparation of all vegetable food used in connection with the ceremonies of the annual cycle, the setting of times for the various ceremonies, and the raising of funds for maintaining longhouse buildings and for the holding of conventions (Gaiwhio odakhaohasǫ). The gonadrihǫt (pl.) also prepare and serve meals in connection with these conventions.

The kogiwe is in charge of all lineage feasts for the dead (adyęhakǫfrowanę ǫgwadriwhade sęnige'hwhadjiya). She meets with other lineage officers to set a suitable date, solicits assistance from lineage members in the form of food and cloth, or money with which these may be purchased (see list in chapter 3 for amounts of food and cloth used in one such feast), and "engages" (ęyǫdąnha'h—she hires) on behalf of her lineage the necessary singers and dancers for the performance of the ceremony. She also represents her lineage in the preparations for the O'hgiwe ceremony and also the less elaborate feast for the dead "of all the people" (gǫdyogwagwegǫ odyǫhakǫfra) held at the long-house ritual center. A more detailed appreciation of the duties attaching to these offices will be had from the description of the lineage activities given below.

Succession

Succession to the above offices is largely controlled by the women of the lineage under the leadership of the *goyane'h*, in whom the titles to all offices are vested. Successors are chosen by the women from among the members of the entire lineage group; and although male members of the lineage, especially respected elders, may be influential, the ultimate choice in the selection of a successor rests with the *goyane'h* herself. It is commonly said in explanation of this that "the woman is the main one to bring up the family and knows the hearts of them in choosing the chief." Related to her large role in selecting the *hoyane'h*, is her right to depose him (*desǫwanagahagwę*—the horns have been taken from him). This is a very grave matter and occurs only after due deliberation. A wayward and unrepentant *hoyane'h* is said to place his people at the edge of a deep chasm. Deposition, or the removal of the horns of office, is the last resort, the alternative to being carried into the pit of his wrongdoing from whence there may be no return. Although all members of the lineage are equally eligible for these offices, selection is ideally based on moral character and capacity for leadership and the ability to maintain the respect of other lineage members. It is not necessary that the order of succession to the office of *hoyane'h* follow the younger-brother-sister's-son pattern; yet in cases collected, there is a marked tendency for it to do so, and a *goyane'h* is apt to be sharply criticized by other members of her lineage if she installs her own son when older suitable men are available within the lineage. In keeping with the principle of *corporation sole* that permeates the system, the selection of candidates and their subsequent installation in named statuses is a principal task of government.[11]

Funerals

The corporate nature of the lineage group, as well as the distinction between its sphere of action and that of the domestic group, is clearly manifest in the funeral customs of Longhouse society, and this is seen most vividly in the death of married members of the group. When death occurs, word is first borne to the deceased's own parents (if they are alive) and, ultimately, to the female head of the lineage. When the members of the dead person's lineage appear on the scene, they are told by the surviving spouse, "I release the body, you make the arrangements," (sagatga'h hoyǫda is ǫsriwhaganǫni). This is a recognition of the claim of the lineage upon its dead; and from this point on, the lineage, in the person of its female head, assumes the responsibility for carrying out the necessary and proper funeral rites.[12] The initial arrangements include the notification of the opposite side of the dual division of the longhouse ritual group so they can proceed with their own duties, which include the notification of the longhouse group at large, making arrangements for the wake (tatiataita'h—they await the daylight), engaging grave diggers (hadiyadǫni), and notifying the speaker of their own side. Further, the lineage must engage the services of a mortician and "hire" two women to cook and to sew burial clothes and a man (ǫhadriwhastiis) to perform the general chores about the household.

If the lineage possesses chiefship, news of the death must be sent to the council of chiefs to enable them to arrange for the performance of their special condolence (hadinigǫdanyǫ). It is imperative that this notification be borne by a member of the deceased's lineage, and the chiefs adamantly refuse to receive messages otherwise brought to them. In July 1956, at a council of the chiefs, Chief Tadodaho was approached by a young man who had come to communicate the death of his father. The old chief told the young man that it was not his place to bear this message and refused to inform the council until he returned with his deceased father's lineage goyane'h, who then reported her uncle's death. Tadodaho then scolded her for not informing her lineage of the proper procedure in such matters.

Both the members of the lineage of the deceased and those of his or her own nuclear family are regarded as being in a state of mourning (gonatgaǫnio) for a period of ten days after the death, and it is the services rendered by the cooks, seamstresses, choreman, the undertaker, and the members of the opposite "side" of the longhouse group that allow them to keep their mourning restrictions. These restrictions are not very burdensome, requiring only avoidance of social gatherings and refraining from activities that would, if they became habitual, be detrimental. The members of the nuclear family of the deceased should remain at home for the ten-day period, and they should also retire while the death wake is being carried out, but should be awakened to witness the termination of the wake (ewasdǫtwata—the burning of the sticks [used in the ceremony]) at daybreak.

The lineage also arranges for a funeral feast, referred to as "eating the last meal with the deceased" (hesgagǫt dǫsgaǫdǫt), on the day of burial. On this occasion, the dead person is addressed on behalf of the lineage and asked to be content with what his people have done for him, since they have done the best they could. At the public funeral ceremony (aha'htiǫ'h—he spoke [referring to the speaker of the opposite side]), the members of the lineage of the deceased sit as a unit and are addressed as a group by the speaker as tsigawhadjiiǫ'h (the family that is left behind). They also view the body once more as a group at this time.

Mourning is terminated in a ceremony (hǫsakie whasę—lit. it has come ten) on the tenth day after death, although standards of decency require that the surviving spouse remain socially quiet for a longer period. This ceremony is also the occasion for the release of the surviving spouse (which will be described in the section on marriage in the following chapter), the distribution of the personal effects of the deceased, and a feast, all of which are principally the concern of the deceased's lineage.

The imposition of inheritance rules on Longhouse society by the Canadian government were noted in chapter 1. While these rules are followed for the descent of real property, farm implements, livestock, automobiles, money, and like items, the lineage maintains an element of control over the personal belongings (sęhodę hoyǫdʌk—lit. whatever he possessed; or gayędeʄra—belongings) of its deceased members. Articles of clothing; Indian costumes; ritual equipment, such as rattles, drums, and lacrosse racquets; blankets and other personal effects are the items usually distributed (dewadogwadǫ) in this manner. While the actual distribution is not confined to the lineage group, it is supervised by the lineage in the person of its female head; and it is significant, in this connection, that some of the personal belongings may be given to the help (cooks, seamstresses, and choreman) engaged by the lineage in return for their services. It is stressed that all of the personal belongings of the deceased should be turned over to the lineage for distribution in this way lest the spirit of the deceased be displeased and return to bring sickness and ill fortune to those responsible for withholding them, and there are cases where a second distribution has been held to relieve a person of maladies thought to have been caused by withholding items at the time of the original one.

The concluding part of the tenth-day rites is the feast spoken of as hęswasǫdahe (the chosen eve has come). The deceased's lineage must, at a minimum, provide such essentials as corn bread (onęhę onada'h) and corn soup (onęhogwa'h) for this feast, but as a rule, they provide much more in the way of pies, cakes, scones, doughnuts, and other foods the deceased was known to have been fond of during his lifetime. Affines and friends usually bring contributions of food as well, which are turned over to the lineage. The female lineage head presides over this feast, and after making up a plate of food and setting it aside for the deceased, she assigns the members of her own lineage only to distribute the remaining food to all present.

Although the lineage of the deceased makes the arrangements for his funeral, as indicated, it is generally felt that his or her own household should bear the bulk of the expense involved. This reflects the fact that the household group is the economic unit of the system. People explain that because the surviving spouse and children will inherit his land, house, livestock, farm implements, or like items, or "because his work was there" (his earnings), they should be the ones to pay the funeral expenses. Where the deceased has no significant estate, or where his or her own children are incapable of meeting expenses, it is a common thing for the members of the lineage (in most instances, own siblings) to bear them. If the deceased has land, but no money, the sibling or son or daughter putting up the money usually inherits the real property. Nearly all lineage members bring items of food for the necessary feasts.

Lineage ancestors

That the funerary rites of its members are the responsibility of the lineage is consistent with the belief that death does not extinguish lineage ties, and rites performed by the lineage on these occasions enable the proper passage of the deceased into "the world beyond the sky" (gaǫhyage), where he joins the ancestors (hǫdǫdjodǫǫ'h—they who have gone before). Symbolic of identity with the ancestors and of the continuity of descent, the lineage places in the coffin, in the hand of the dead person, a loaf of corn bread (ogęhęge watnadaǫt) made according to an ancient recipe and baked in ashes, which, it is thought, the deceased takes with him or her into the realm of the dead. Burial clothing must also be sewn by hand, symbolic of the ancient way.

It is the relationship between the living and the dead that gives ultimate continuity to the lineage. The nature of this relationship can be observed in a whole complex, which takes the form of beliefs, observances, avoidances, rites, and ceremonies. These are a part of a person's social and cultural heritage, and conditioning with regard to the dead begins almost simultaneously with birth. It is the belief of the Longhouse people that the ancestors have control over the social, physiological, and psychological well-being of the living. When neglected or offended in any of numerous ways, the dead may "get after" the living. They feed upon the substance of one's body, ultimately causing "strokes" or other internal hemorrhages. When proper relationships are maintained, they may "speak to a person in his mind," imparting valuable knowledge.

For these reasons, it is felt to be necessary for the living to maintain proper relationships with the dead. This is done by the lineage through the instrumentality of a rite called O'hgiwe.[13] Essentially, this rite is a gift exchange, in which the living members of the lineage offer food, drink, cloth, song, and dance to their ancestors in exchange for health, good fortune, and freedom from molestation. Less elaborate rites (adyę̨hakǫfrowanę̨ ǫgwadriwhade sę̨nige'hwhadjiya), consisting of a tobacco-burning rite (which is an address to the dead on behalf of the living by an appointed speaker) and the food offering only, are also held. The officiator in the tobacco-burning rite is always careful to include all the dead of the particular lineage concerned in such words as, "No one is being avoided [excepted] no matter how far back the family, for you all know that this ceremony has been held for many generations back. So now this far their word [carried on the tobacco smoke] goes, for they have meant it to be in honor of all of you." To neglect this would be a serious affront to the dead and would jeopardize the efficacy of the rite.

There is no set interval at which these rites are to be held. This is left to the discretion of the leading people of the lineage. The responsibilities and obligations connected with them rest solely upon the members of the lineage concerned. The role of the female official (kǫgiwe) in arranging these ceremonies was noted above. Lineage members must contribute the necessary food and cloth, and when the final distribution of these occurs in the course of the ceremony, this too may be done by lineage members only. Any departure from this deployment of responsibilities is thought to be offensive to the ancestors and would be certain to undermine the efficacy of the rite. Furthermore, where individuals are required to hold these placatory rites, the assistance of matrilineal kin in the preparation and distribution of food is felt to be essential.

Lineage Charms

At least some, if not all, lineages possess charms (otsinnagę̨da'h), which are said to have been handed down for many generations and which are kept in secret by one or more of its most trusted men or women. The placatory rites held in connection with its charms are some of the most sacred and exclusive held by the lineage, and it is extremely rare for anyone other than its own members to be permitted to attend these rites. These charms are said to "rest upon the blood of the lineage," or the "charm will follow the family" (ęgawhadjiaʃre atsįnagęda), and if they are not properly "tended" (ęyetinikowi'h— lit. to amuse), they will turn on the lineage, "sucking out the blood" of its members. It is frequently said of defunct or declining lineages that charms of this type associated with them were not properly transferred by their keeper before his death or were otherwise neglected and now feed (or fed) upon the blood of remaining members, causing them to die, one by one, of internal hemorrhage.

Lineages may also "own" (gonatgaawę) certain dances, which are carried out publicly on their behalf. The lineage of Chief Dyǫhyǫgo, for example, has three dances performed for them during the annual Great Green Corn and Midwinter festivals.

Kinship Terms within the Lineage

The unity of the lineage continues to be reflected in the kinship terminology used by its members. Basic to the system of terms used within the lineage is the set of relationships (grandmother, mother, child, siblings, and grandchild) contained in a given direct line of descent within the three generations normally present in the synchronic situation. The terms used in these primary relationships are extended, with appropriate distinctions being made for gender, to the siblings of the primary relative concerned and, by the principle of lineage unity, to all members of the lineage of the same generation as that of the primary relative. Thus, one's own mother is knoha ("ma," "mama," or "mother" are used in English language), while her own sisters are knohaʌ (little mother), along with all the women of the lineage of one's mother's generation. Her brother is knosę, and the same principle of extension applies in his case. The lineage hoyane'h may also be referred to as etįnosę (our mother's brother) as a mark of respect. The terms "aunt" and "uncle" are used in English speech for knohaʌ and knosę respectively, and are extended in the same way as the Native terms.

One's mother's mother is oksot, and so are her own sisters, as well as all lineage women of her generation. Her brother is hoksot, as are his generation equals within the lineage. These terms also apply to all lineage relatives above the grandparental generation. The term k'sot is usually applied regardless of gender to all these relatives. All lineage members of one's own generation are siblings (dęgaǫdęhnǫde). Distinctions are made, however, for younger brother (he'hgęę'h) and younger sister (kegęę'h), as well as for older brother (hagedjia) and older sister (ǫgedjia), although the term kdjiʌ is more often applied indiscriminately to both of these. These terms constitute the primary usages, but at present the term ǫgyase, primarily used for cross-cousins, is also used for these relatives outside one's own siblings.

A woman calls her own son hehawʌk and own daughter kehawʌk and applies the same terms with a diminutive suffix (hehawakʌ and kehawakʌ) to the sons and daughters of her own sisters and to those of all the women of the lineage of her own generation. For a man, his sister's son is heyǫwhadę and her daughter is keyǫwhadę, as are the sons and daughters of all the women of the lineage of his own generation. In English speech, "niece," "nephew," "sister's son," and "sister's daughter" are used by both men and women for their own and classificatory sister's children and are thence extended in the same way as are the Native terms. Both a woman and her brother say of her children's children, grandson (heyadre) and granddaughter (keyadre). These terms are likewise used for all children of the lineage of the second descending generation.

The present emphasis on the indices of differentiation in the terms for own mother and mother's sisters (own and classificatory) and in terms used by a woman for her own children and her sisters' (own and classificatory) children, and the use of dual terms for lineage relatives of one's own generation outside one's own siblings, reflects the fact that these relatives are usually members of separate households with a number of distinct economic and jural interests. Yet for the purposes and activities within the matrilineal sublineage and in some of the three-generation household groups, the attenuation of behavior between own and classificatory kin within the lineage may be slight. The behavior patterns associated with the various relationships will become clearer from the material given in the following chapter.

Lineage Exogamy

The lineage is an exogamous group, and its unity is clearly seen in this rule. Marriage within the lineage is likened to marriage with one's self, and this absurdity is brought to a focus in the question, "If you marry within your own lineage, 'where will your children's father's people be?'" (gainhǫ sehawaksǫ ǫgaǫdǫ sadǫnihǫnyǫge'h); the answer to which is, "In your own rectum," (saetkajn godǫnisę).

Lineage exogamy brings about jural relationships between lineages. One's father's matrilineage is a socially important group and is referred to collectively as one's agadǫnihonǫ (lit. the people of my father's sister). The father's sister (agadǫni) thus symbolizes the jural unity of the father's matrilineage.[14] Furthermore, a person may refer to, or address, any member of this group as his *agadǫnisę*. The relationship between a person and his father's matrilineage is discussed more fully in the following chapter.

A man or woman uses the term *knowhakiono* in reference to the entire matrilineage of his or her spouse, and this relationship comes into prominence in the funerary rites of every married person. It is to his *knowhakiono* that one must first communicate the death of his spouse and to them, in the person of the head woman, that he makes the statement, "Here is the body; you make the arrangements." Other jural matters associated with this term are discussed in the section on marriage in the following chapter.

The Sides of the Dual Organization and the Longhouse Ritual Group

Each of the four longhouse ritual groups (*ganǫses*) is characterized by a dual organization, and each o'hwhadjiʌ, or lineage, belongs to one or the other of the constituent sides (*honasesęǫ'h*) of a particular longhouse group. The model of these sides is that of a matrilineal descent group, but the rule of recruitment has been modified, in some instances, to meet changing circumstances. There are recent instances of whole lineages being transferred from one side to the other in order to balance out the number of members on each side; and although the members of a particular lineage tend to belong to a specific longhouse, it is possible for lineage members, and even officers, to participate in the activities of other longhouses with a minimum of adjustment.

The "sides" are fully corporate groups. Each has its own corps of officers (*hadiwhahędę*) made up of the hereditary officers of its constituent lineages. When additional officers are required, as they usually are, they are appointed by the incumbent officers of each side for life. Officers appointed in this manner are designated *onędodaǫ* (without roots), as opposed to hereditary officers who are *gwasǫwe* (real or genuine). The sides are designated by an eponym (Wolf and Turtle or Wolf and Deer) and are very much like a non-exogamous matrilineal clan, and tend to be regarded as such by the Longhouse people themselves. In fact, many people gave the eponym of their side of the dual organization in response to questions about clan membership.

The two sides of each longhouse group are associated with each other in a system of reciprocal services, which has been described by Morgan (1878, 88–98) and which has not changed greatly since his time. [15] Although Morgan described *Gayędowanę*, the fourth of the "four laws" (*Geiniyiwhagę*) operative between the "sides" of the dual organization, he appears to have regarded it as a "betting game" played for entertainment only (Morgan 1851, 307–12). Its proper context, however, is that of a ritual gift exchange by which the two

Table 23. Segments of longhouse society

Segment	Identification	Rights and duties
1. Sublineage (o'hwhadjiʌ)	Has female focus.	Exogamy. Jural and moral instruction. Frequent visiting. Reciprocal services. Borrowing of staples. Assistance in individual rites. Sharing of problems. Support in troubles with outsiders.
2. Lineage (o'hwhadjiʌ)	Eponym. Known ancestress. Lineage names.	Exogamy. Lineage names bestowing citizenship. Shell beads (otgɒa'h) symbolizing offices and corporate identity. Unit of succession. Arrange proper funeral rites for members. Release widows and widowers of members. Distribute personal property of deceased members. Rites for lineage ancestors. Possess lineage charms (otsinnagɛda'h) and placatory rites for same. Some have special dances and rites performed on public ceremonial occasions. adɒwa'h songs. Support in troubles with outsiders.
3. "Sides" (honasesɛɑ'h) of the dual division of the longhouse ritual group	Eponym.	Corps of officers. Rituals paraphernalia. Obligations to perform reciprocal services in ceremonial cycle, wakes, funerals, grave-digging and medicine rites. Ritual gift exchange with opposite side.
4. Longhouse ritual group (ganɒses)	Name of longhouse.	Corps of officers. Shell beads (gadjisdaįtgɒ), symbol of corporate identity. Land and buildings. Burial ground. Ritual paraphernalia.

"sides" renew their standing "contractual" relationship for reciprocal services. Further details of this matter do not fall within the scope of this study.

The officers of both sides (godrihǫdǫnyoh) of the longhouse form a council for the more inclusive group; and one of the council, traditionally a hoyane'h, is appointed to be the keeper of the strands of shell beads (gadjisdaįtgǫ) that symbolize the corporate identity of the longhouse ritual group. This unit has its own burial ground, buildings, and ritual paraphernalia. It is also, more or less, a localized group.

Professor Fortes (1953b, 35) has said that "a descent group is an arrangement of persons that serves the attainment of legitimate social and personal ends." In this chapter some of the most important politico-jural and ritual ends attained by the matrilineal descent groups of Longhouse society have been examined. It is important to note that the imposition of wills and a bilateral inheritance rule by the Canadian government and the individualization of economic activities have established an important field of action outside the direct control of the lineage.

In contrast to the external Longhouse system built up, as it is, on the rule of matrilineal descent, cognatic kinship is fundamental to the structure of the household group. Although matrilineal descent has considerable influence on jural and moral relations within the household, the jural and economic factors attached to marital status and parenthood impart to these relationships a large measure of autonomy in household structure. How the opposing factors of matrilineal descent, on the one hand, and conjugality and paternity, on the other, interact to make household structure what it is are examined in the consideration given to kinship and marriage in the following chapter.

Sisters Ruby (Johnson) Williams and Ariel (Johnson) Harris, on an outing in Niagara Falls. Though living in separate households, sisters maintain a close relationship throughout their lives. Photo courtesy of Ariel Harris.

Mabel (Turkey) Thomas and daughter, Eva. The crowning fulfillment of a woman's later years is to be surrounded by her daughters and their children. Photo by author.

Lineage matron, Margaret (Green) Johnson, and eldest daughter, Ariel (Johnson) Harris, in ceremonial dress for Green Corn ceremony. Mothers and daughters sit together on public ritual occasions, reflecting mutual confidence, affection, and the reciprocity of the domestic sphere. Photo by author.

First wedding to be held in a Six Nations longhouse: Lorna Jamieson and Edward Thomas following their marriage at Sour Springs Longhouse, 1 September 1956. Reproduced with permission of *The Hamilton Spectator*, Ltd.

Wedding feast for LeRoy Smoke and Doris Kick after marriage performed by Joseph Logan Sr., in June 1956. Pictured on either side of couple: (unknown), Harry Burning, Freeman Green, David Thomas (in shadow). Foreground: William Johnson, Jack Kick. Photo by author.

6. Kinship and Marriage

In part 2 of this study, considerable insight was gained into the nature of kinship within the household. Having now summarized the salient political, jural, and ritual aspects of Longhouse society, it is possible to assess more fully the relative weight of the various relationships in bringing about the overall configuration within the household. In this analysis, the main interest is with the jural content of these relationships, although moral elements and elements of personal sentiment are noted as well.

The Mother-Child Bond

All Longhouse people agree that one's mother is the most important relative one has. In discussing this fact, they invariably describe her role in bearing children and the nurture and care she gives in rearing them. "We have all got down from our mother's lap" (*agwegǫ etinwha ehoage ǫgwasnędǫ*), they say. This expression conveys somewhat the idea of the indispensability of the mother role and of the moral debt thus created, which can never be repaid. In the standard prayers uttered on all public occasions, the earth itself is referred to as "our mother, the earth" (*etinoha'h sę ǫwhądjade*); and it is said that people are similarly fundamentally dependent upon mother and earth for nurture and sustenance. A woman left on her own with her children will always find some means of providing for them, and a child whose mother dies is pitied.

Respect and affection, trust and confidence, are almost synonymous with the relationship itself, and no one in his right mind would ever abuse or disrespect his mother in any way. Mothers commonly give both sons and daughters moral instruction and are more concerned with their moral welfare generally than are fathers; and it sometimes happens that grown men, who have strayed somewhat away from the narrow path of the Longhouse way, are brought to contrition and repentance in the confessions (*ǫdatrewa'hdǫ*) that follow the preaching of the *Gaiwhio*, when the trials, sacrifices, and desires of their mothers in rearing them are recounted for them.

A woman is always addressed and referred to by her children as *knoha* or some English language equivalent, such as "ma," "mom," or "mama." She, in return, usually calls her son (*hehawʌk*) and daughter (*kehawʌk*), by their English-language given names, or by their lineage names.

Upon attaining manhood and the right to control his own earnings, a young man leaves his surplus money with his mother in complete confidence that it will be there when he requires it. He often gives her presents of food, clothing, money, or luxury items. Women are often jealous of their sons' wives because of the latter's claim on their sons and the division of loyalty this entails. Yet many men continue to seek counsel from their mothers even after marriage.

The crowning fulfillment of a woman's life, however, is to be surrounded by her adult daughters and their children, either in her own house or one near at hand. Although nowadays it is common for women to have their babies in a hospital, upon their return, they usually spend several weeks in their natal household in close companionship with their mothers. A woman's experiences in her adult life are apt to be quite like those of her mother, and a woman's mother is the first person she turns to for counsel in rearing her children or in marital problems. In speaking of their relationship with their husbands, women say, "You can always get another husband, but you only have one mother." It is a common sight to see a mother and her daughters sitting together on public ritual occasions, and this is a reflection of the confidence and affection they have and the reciprocal services they perform for each other in the domestic sphere.

As a person matures socially and participates as an adult in political, jural, and ritual matters, he continues to be closely identified with his mother and other matrilineal kin, and as noted, one's mother is the link through which citizenship and status in the external Longhouse system are determined. From the standpoint of the descent system, the mother and her children (in some instances a maternal grandmother, daughter, and daughter's children) of each household are identified with each other as a kind of minimal unit in the system.[1] In addition to the material given in the previous chapter, it should be noted that according to Canadian law, women may hold property on the reserve in their own right, which they may pass on to their children either by gift, will, or inheritance. Furthermore, some of her personal effects, which are distributed by the lineage, are invariably given to her daughters and appropriate items to her sons. Physical and psychological well-being, as these relate to lineage ancestors and charms, decree a close link with one's mother, and it is common for married sons and daughters to return to their mother's home to enlist her services in holding feasts for the dead (o'hdyehakọfṛa) and other medicine rites.

The generic term for mother (knoha) with a diminutive suffix (knohaʌ) is applied to one's mother's sisters and to all women of the lineage in one's mother's generation by their sister's son (hehawakʌ) or daughter (kehawakʌ). These women are usually members of separate households, yet they are shown deference, especially in lineage affairs. The relationship with one's own mother's sisters is most like that with the mother, and in some instances is very close. The term knohaʌ is also used at present for all other females (and for the wives of all male relatives) of the parental generation to whom one is related through either of his parents. These relatives are shown the same general deference and respect shown all people of the parental generation, but they lack the affection and confidence and the jural content of the relationship with the mother's sister.

Despite the generic similarity in the terms used for mother and mother's sister (and now as the term for mother's sister is used in the most extended sense), the bond with one's own mother is unique, both in its content of personal affection and in its political, jural, and ritual significance. The bond remains strong throughout one's lifetime, and mothers are seldom neglected in old age. A mother's ghost (oyadadrọk) is the one most often placated in personal feasts for the dead.

Paternity

Longhouse beliefs concerning the father's role in procreation were stated in the previous chapter. Paternity is also given social recognition in the naming ceremony, where the father's name and lineage are announced publicly. Informants said this may be done for the child of a single mother as well, unless the father were already a married man, although no case of this kind was actually witnessed in the field. The ideal is for the child's *genitor* and its *pater* to be the same person. Where the ideal does not obtain, as it often does not, children know their *genitor*, but have very little to do with him socially, and they suffer little stigma or jural disability under these circumstances.

A person has two kinds of kinship ties through his father—that with his father's matrilineage (his *agadọnihonọ*), personified in his father's sister, and those traced agnatically through the father. Theoretically, these agnatic ties are extended without limitation, but in practice, they are seldom remembered beyond a great-grandparent. One is linked with, but never becomes a member of, a corporate group within Longhouse society on the basis of paternal kinship, and this is the essential difference between kinship through the father and that traced through the mother.

Kinship relations traced through one's father are given institutional recognition. Some items of a deceased person's personal effects are always given to his or her age mates (ǫgyase) within his father's lineage group. In addition, failing a name (gasęna) in one's own lineage, it is said that the father's lineage is the proper group from which to borrow one, although there is no restriction to that effect at present. Such a borrowed name is referred to as gahnya sodahǫ'h, a name "hung about the neck," and does not confer citizenship, as in the case of the name from one's own lineage, and is returned to the agadǫnihonǫ when a lineage name becomes vacant or upon the death of the bearer.

Dream-discerning (ahǫwadiwęnahago'h), sometimes expressed as "taking the dream off his hands," is a kind of therapy among the Longhouse people and occurs on two days of the annual Midwinter Festival (gaiwhanęsgwagowa'h). Formerly, someone from one's agadǫnihonǫ was deemed the proper one to discern one's dreams, and in this way the members of the father's lineage featured in one's physical and psychological well-being (see also Hewitt 1910).[2] At the time of fieldwork, dreams might be discerned by anyone on the opposite side of the dual division.

A father's brother's son or daughter (dęgaǫdęhnǫde—siblings; now also ǫgyase—cousins) of a deceased person is given an item or two of his personal belongings in the distribution already noted; and there is a special dance (dʌksidosgeiha'h skadi gadjina) at the Midwinter ceremonies, in which the women seek out their father's brothers' sons or their father's father's brothers' sons' sons, and so on agnatically, as partners.[3]

These institutionalized practices maintain the connection with the father's lineage and serve to channel and maintain interpersonal relations with persons to whom one is related through his father, despite present reservation circumstances and the fact that modern environmental conditions allow a wide range of choice in nearly all social activities.[4] The following case illustrates the value placed on kinship through one's father as a personal bond of friendship. I had taken Lola, a lineage goyane'h, to visit her chief, who was living at the opposite end of the reserve. Lola explained on the return journey that it would be possible to drive by the home of a favorite mother's brother's daughter (ǫgyase, self reciprocal), Kathrine, and expressed the desire to do so. The ensuing visit was one of thorough delight on the part of both women, who obviously had great affection for each other. A meal was shared, and as the visit drew to a close, Kathrine took one of her dresses from a wall hanger, folded it neatly, and gave it to Lola, who accepted it with great pleasure. Kathrine later explained the giving of this gift as proper conduct towards one's agadǫnihonǫ, "especially a favorite agadǫnisę" like Lola.

The jural position of the father, which he imparts to his children, derives from both the Indigenous system and from the Canadian government. In opposition to the Indigenous matrilineal system, the Canadian government determines reserve membership, and therefore the legal status of Indian, by patrifiliation. Children are also given the surnames of their fathers on reserve membership lists, and these names therefore establish legal identity in all extra-Longhouse society affairs. Cayuga Iroquois children qualify for small annuities (amounting to between three and four dollars in 1957) on the basis of filiation with their fathers. Both sons and daughters may receive real property from their fathers either by gift or will. In the case of intestacy, after their mother's prior share of two thousand dollars value, siblings inherit equally with their mother in the remainder of their father's estate (Indian Act, sec. 48). Further, as noted in chapter 1, legal Indians are subject to the laws of the province in which they reside, and under this provision, a man may be held legally responsible for the care and support of his minor children. These are the principal legal aspects of paternity deriving from the Canadian system.

Within Longhouse society itself, a man does not define the status of his children in the external system. His authority and rights over his children are confined to the domestic sphere. Longhouse society recognizes the duty of a man to give care, protection, and economic support to his children. This was the most important aspect of fatherhood at the time of fieldwork, and the chiefs "preach" to men who neglect those duties. Fathers are shown deference and respect by their children. They may discipline them, but in practice seldom do so. In addition, a father plays no jural part in the marriage of his children. All this is in sharp contrast to the central importance of maternal kinship, both within the domestic order and in political, jural, and ritual matters.

The father-child bond lacks the general constancy that is both inherent in the mother-child relationship and imparted to it by the rule of matrilineal descent. There is much latitude for the play of individual personality factors in the relationship. While some men appear to have fairly close bonds of affection with their children, men generally rarely express affection or fondness toward them. The relationship with the father is closest during preadolescence. Children, especially sons, tend to disperse early, and there do not arise father and son combinations like those between a woman and her daughters. The fact that there are twice as many elderly men as elderly women living alone is significant in this connection.[5]

A man's funeral is arranged by his lineage. However, since his widow and his children are the heirs of his property, they are expected to bear the expenses if he didn't leave sufficient money to cover these himself.

One's father is both addressed and referred to as *ha'hni* in the Cayuga language, and as "dad," "daddy," "the old man" or similar terms in English speech. He, in turn, addresses or refers to his children by their English given names, their lineage names, or as "son" (*hehawʌk*) and "daughter" (*kehawʌk*). The generic term for father with a diminutive suffix (*ha'hniiha*) may be applied to one's father's brothers and his agnatic kinsmen of the same sex and generation. These kin are more often, at present, separated from the father terminologically by applying to them the term *knosę*, primarily applied to the mother's brother. In English, these latter relatives are called "uncle." They are nearly always members of separate households from ego and are shown the general respect and deference due all kinsmen of the first ascending generation. Kindness and consideration is fitting for both persons involved in this relationship. A Longhouse barber on the reserve required a very minimal charge for his services from fellow Longhouse people generally, but he cut his brother's children's hair free of charge.

Other Kinship Relations
Siblings

The relationship between siblings is primarily a moral bond deriving its strength from the fact of growing up in the same household as children of the same mother. The inference that it is the common maternal tie that is of first importance as a source of the strength of sibling ties is strengthened by the fact that paternal half-siblings, while they usually know of their relationship, seldom live in the same household and otherwise have very little to do with one another. Conversely, uterine siblings having different fathers are nearly always members of the same household and are scarcely distinguishable socially or jurally from full siblings.

The term *dęgaǫdęhnǫdę* (siblings) is used for both one's brothers and sisters, in either direct or indirect speech. Distinctions are made, however, between older brother (*hagedjia*) and younger brother (*he'hgęę'h*) and between older sister (*ǫgedjia*) and younger sister (*kegęę'h*). The age distinction in terminology is reflected in the fact that older siblings are often left in charge of younger ones while parents are away and that they are themselves often enlisted early in the economic support of the household group. The position of responsibility and respect for older siblings tends to carry over into adulthood, when they are a source of counsel and advice to their juniors. To call someone kdjiʌ (older sibling) is a mark of respect, and in the ceremonial thanksgiving prayer, the sun is referred to as "our elder brother, the great warrior" (sedwa'hdjia hoskęęn'hgeda gowa'h ądeka gagwa).[6]

As a general rule, siblings tend to live together in the same household from birth until young adulthood. There is early differentiation of tasks based on gender; and as they reach puberty, there is a reserve and sense of propriety between opposite-sex siblings, even though in many cases the entire family shares a common bedroom. Sexual topics are not discussed between opposite-sex siblings. It was difficult in fieldwork to get people even to talk about incest. Brother-sister incest is unthinkable, a sin (gaiwhiitgę) of the first magnitude. It was impossible to discover any cases where it had actually happened, although this may be attributable to the general reluctance to talk about it. It is thought that to be capable of committing such an act, a person would have to be mentally deranged; and offspring from such a union, it is thought, would be deformed or feeble-minded.

Even though siblings may quarrel and even fight among themselves, they have a strong sense of solidarity and loyalty to each other, as the following case illustrates. Two married brothers, Wilford and Frank, were at the home of their parents on one occasion. Wilford disciplined one of Frank's children, and this resulted in an angry exchange that deteriorated into a fight on the following day as they were assisting a third brother harvest grain. Some months later, Wilford separated from his wife and went away with a woman who was, at the time, living on a trial basis with Emmet, who was no relation to Wilford's family. Although this woman returned within a few days, Emmet's wounded pride caused him to seek revenge. An opportunity presented itself as he met Wilford in the doorway of the longhouse on a ceremonial occasion, whereupon he attacked and beat Wilford severely and would likely have killed him had he not been stopped by other men and women present. A short time later, Emmet was accosted seriatim by each of the younger brothers and a brother's son, over all of whom Emmet triumphed. The whole affair was put to rest when Wilford's eldest brother sought and effected a rapprochement.

In the course of their social maturation, the bond between brothers usually becomes attenuated. They do not, as a rule, cooperate to any great extent in work, and they maintain separate households. Even so, they come together on ritual occasions and may seek advice from each other, especially, as noted, from an older brother.

Sisters, too, come to live in separate households, yet generally speaking, they strive to maintain a close relationship throughout their lives. Their mutual identification with their mother provides frequent opportunity for visiting and for sharing their common experiences and problems. As noted earlier, it is a frequent occurrence in fieldwork to enter a household where a group of sisters have gathered to visit with their mother in their natal household, and the ties between female siblings feature strongly in the sublineage group referred to above. Even after the death of the mother, the pattern of cooperation and reciprocal services operative between sisters continues. They tend each other's children, give gifts to each other, give articles of clothing that their own children have outgrown to each other's children, and borrow staples and sometimes money. Most women agree that it is difficult to ask a sister to repay items lent her, although they would be accepted when returned voluntarily. A woman is closer to her sister's children than those of her brother, and for the Longhouse people, the mother's sister (or mother's mother) is the ideal person to take an orphaned child, since she is most like one's own mother.

Although all is not harmony between sisters, and estrangement and even cases of fighting are known to occur, for sisters to quarrel is felt to be disgraceful and does not appear to happen frequently. Few women have ties of companionship with other women who are not close kin, and in fact, real companionship is had only between sisters and, as noted, with a mother.[7]

As for the jural content of the sibling bond, a woman can, at present, assert no legal claim on her brother for support of herself or her children. Nor does a man hold any rights in his sisters or their daughters that would permit him to give them in marriage. The absence of these jural factors in the sibling relationship allows the conjugal bonds of siblings to take precedence over their ties with each other in arranging relationships within the household, and this fact is clearly reflected in tables 14 and 15 (see chapter 4).[8] As noted, it is a lineage responsibility to provide proper funeral rites for its members, and this often involves siblings, who make contributions of food and money for the necessary feasts. It was also noted that expenses for a casket and undertaker services are usually charged against the estate of the deceased or are the responsibility of the widow (or widower) and children, since they are the first heirs. Failing these, and if ready cash is lacking even when there is landed estate, siblings are first to respond.

In January 1957, when a lineage *goyane'h* and her brother learned that their sister was critically ill in a city about two hundred miles from the reserve, they spared no time and expense in bringing her back to the *goyane'h*'s household on the reservation, where they nursed her with various medicines (*onǫ'hgwatra'h*) and even consulted a white doctor off the reserve, only to have her die within a few weeks' time. The deceased sister had no real property, and the expenses for her funeral, amounting to over two hundred fifty dollars, were borne principally by her siblings, who were the *hoyane'h* and *goyane'h* for their lineage. They were assisted with gifts of food from other lineage siblings.

The kinship terms used for siblings apply to generation equals within one's own lineage and also to the children of one's father's brothers (all the men of the father's lineage of his generation), and to the children of all agnates of the father's generation. In fact, as an expression of closeness, they may be used for all cognates of one's own generation. The term *ǫgyase*, primarily applied to both matrilateral and patrilateral cross-cousins, is now also used for parallel cousins, both within and without the lineage. This usage tends to isolate one's own siblings as a distinct unit, but this isolation is not complete within one's own lineage.

Grandparents

The mothers and fathers of both parents are addressed and referred to by the terms *oksot* or *ǫgesot* (grandmother) and *hoksot* or *hagesot* (grandfather). English-language terms for grandparents are also used. These terms are extended to the siblings of one's own grandparents and to all members of their respective lineages of the grandparental generation and above. In fact, the grandparental terms may be applied to all people of the second ascending generation and above irrespective of known genealogical connection. The reciprocals of the terms for grandparents are *keyadre* (granddaughter) and *heyadre* (grandson), and these are applied to all relatives in the second descending generation and beyond.

As a rule, the relationship with maternal grandparents, especially with the maternal grandmother, is closer than that with paternal grandparents. The close bond between mother and daughter, described above, and association within the sublineage group, give rise to a close relationship between a woman and her daughter's children. A woman will discipline her daughter's children, but, as one woman put it, "I would never touch my son's children. They are another woman's children. I would leave that to their father."

The position of the maternal grandmother as an authority figure has a well-defined political, jural, and ritual basis within the lineage structure outlined in the previous chapter. It is also given an ideological foundation. The moon is referred to as "our grandmother" (*etisot sǫheka o'hnida'h*). It is said to control plant, animal, and human fertility: "our Grandmother Moon controls the birth of the generations" (*etisot sǫheka o'hnida dagǫnǫdǫge ǫgwe gonagradǫ hage*). This is symbolic of the fact that rights *in genetricem* over the women of the lineage are vested in their maternal grandmothers. It is true that today individual choice plays a large part in the selection of a mate, but maternal grandmothers still give moral and jural counsel at puberty and are the principal guardians of lineage exogamy, and they may also deputize for the mother in the marriage ceremony. They also arrange for the naming of their daughters' children; and it is, as a rule, a grandmother, own or classificatory, who releases one's widow or widower from the marital bond.

Grandfathers, especially the maternal, may also have a relationship of authority with his grandchildren, but this does not often occur except in the case of single daughters' children. His relationship with his grandchildren is generally one of easy-going equality expressed in teasing and joking.

Outside these contexts where grandparental authority operates, there is scope for the normal relationship between alternate generations to occur (Radcliffe-Brown 1950, 27–31). There is a saying that, "You are more stingy of your grandchild than your own child" (*heyohe sanǫste seyadre sęniyote is sehawak*). Fondness and kindness expressed in giving gifts and buying goodies is characteristic of this relationship. There is also a good deal of teasing and joking, but this appears to be elective rather than formal. It is usually grandparents who invent nicknames for their grandchildren.

Grandparents partake of the general respect accorded age in Longhouse society, which is demonstrated in the council of chiefs, where chiefs under fifty years of age scarcely open their mouths. All old people, and therefore grandparents, are regarded as repositories of wisdom and knowledge of the traditions, of medicines, and of the "right" way to perform a ritual or carry out a jural procedure. In this aspect they are symbols of security and of the continuity of social life and culture.

It was noted in chapter 4 that grandchildren are sometimes assimilated to a filial relationship with their maternal grandparents. This occurs only when a child is living in the household of its grandparent and appears to be related to the authority structure of the household concerned. Although grandparents, especially the maternal grandmother, have a well-defined position of authority in their own right, authority in domestic matters is ideally vested in one's own parents. The existence of a second parental relationship within a single household group has the potential of upsetting the established authority structure of the group, and it is the resolution of this potential that is effected by assimilating the grandchild to a quasi-filial status within the group.[9] In most instances, this practice relates to the relationship with the maternal grandmother, and this is primarily because of her central position within the household; but the usage also extends to the grandfather-grandchild relationship as well, especially in the case of single daughters' children. Otherwise, the grandchild may adopt one set of relationships toward its grandfather and another toward its grandmother.

The degree to which this assimilation occurs is related to the degree to which the "mother" and "father" statuses of the grandparents are still effective and how well the "mother" status of the child's own mother is defined. Assimilation of this type is most complete in the case of single daughters' children and less complete in the case of children of a married couple living with the parents of either and of the children of a separated daughter returning with her children to her natal household.

The expression "quasi-filial" status is used in this connection because it is doubtful that the assimilation is ever complete, at least as long as the child's own mother is alive. That this is so was illustrated in the case of a fifteen-year-old single mother whose child was, for all practical purposes in the day-to-day life of the household, indistinguishable from her younger siblings, yet at Christmas time in 1958, the single mother, no longer content to be included in the greeting received from her parents, sent her own individual greeting card to my wife and me, signed with her own and her child's name.

Usually, if new households are established when the children are yet young, a normal grandparent-grandchild relationship ensues along with the established terminological usage. There are, however, several instances of adults who were raised by maternal grandmothers who continue to address and refer to them as "ma" or *knoha*.

Mother's Brother

The most important thing to note about the relationship with the mother's brother is the absence of his influence in the composition and structure of the household group, as reflected in tables 14 and 15. These circumstances are related to the absence of jural content in the relationship. A person does not inherit land or income property from his mother's brother, although he may inherit some of his personal belongings. Nor can a woman assert jural claim of her brother's economic services in support of her children. A man does not have jural authority to dispose of his sister's daughters in marriage, although he may watch over the selection of a mate to see that it does not violate lineage exogamy. A mother's brother, in the person of the lineage chief (hoyane'h), may also "preach" to a sister's son and daughter who are negligent of their domestic duties.[10] These factors ensure that a man's primary orientation in domestic matters is toward his own children.

From the standpoint of the domestic group per se, the position of the mother's brother resembles that of the father's brother; but from the standpoint of lineage activity, it differs markedly from that with both the father and his brothers. Men are always identified with their sister's children rather than their own in the lineage activities outlined in the previous chapter. Mother's brothers may be lineage officers, and as such, warrant the respect and deference of their sisters' children. It is common on public occasions to see mother's brothers take their sisters' children to dance and sit with them during the ceremonies. A mother's brother is still deemed to be the proper one to perform the adǫwa'h rite upon the naming of his sister's son and to teach him his own adǫwa'h song. A proper mother's brother will also contribute to the wedding feast of his sister's daughter, and upon his death, some article of his personal effects may be given to his sister's sons. The nature of the jural content of his relationship with his sister's children makes of him a trusted friend and a refuge outside their natal household.

The term knosę is used in both direct and indirect speech for one's own mother's brother and for all men of the lineage of his generation. Reciprocally, all these men use the terms keyǫwhadę for sister's daughters and heyǫwhadę for sister's sons. The English-language words equated with these terms are "nephew" and "niece."

The term knosę is also primary usage at present for father's brothers and for the husbands of both father's and mother's sisters. Again, while these relatives merit a show of respect and deference, they do not feature in lineage activities as does a mother's brother. The term "uncle" is used in English speech for these relatives.

Father's Sister

The father's sister is deemed to be a close relative, but her influence in her brother's household is limited by the primary orientation of a child towards its mother and its maternal grandmother. A brother's child, in this respect, is like a son's child—"the child of another woman." For this reason, a father's sister would seldom discipline her brother's child. Since a woman has no claim on her brother for support of her own children, she is not brought into regular conflict with his children on this score. Affective ties with the father's sister tend to reflect those with the father. She is to be treated with respect and kindness and is to be shown deference. She may also give presents to her brother's children. This practice was institutionalized in former times but is elective at present. The high incidence of conjugal separation tends to attenuate the relationship with the father's sister.

The father's sister stands for the corporate identity of the father's lineage; and although the term most often used for her today is knohaʌ—the same term used primarily for mother's sister—the term agadǫni may also be applied to her by her brother's children, for whom she uses the terms keyadawę (brother's daughter) and he'hyadawę (brother's son). Consistent with the use of knohaʌ for the father's sister, she also uses the terms kehawakʌ and hehawakʌ for her brother's children. Some items of a woman's personal belongings are always given to her brother's children (goyadawęsǫ) upon her death. Some of the younger members of Longhouse society do not know the term agadǫni for father's sister, but all know agadǫnihonǫ, the term derived from it used for the "father's people" or father's lineage group.

The terminological usages connected with the father's sister also apply to the father's father's brother's daughter (likewise to all the father's female parallel cousins), the father's father's father's brother's son's daughter, and so on, tracing genealogical connections agnatically. Such relatives are recognized to warrant respect and kindness of the same general type shown a father's sister, but in practice, there is little contact with them. In English speech, the term "aunt" is used for all these relatives.

Kinship Terms

Professor Fred Eggan (1960, 196) has said that Morgan's

> view of kinship was forever complicated by the fact that the Iroquois system of terminology, with its balanced bilateral character, did not rest conformably on a matrilineal clan system, as he supposed. Hence he was not able to isolate types within or outside the classificatory system, nor to see the correlation of unilineal clans with "Omaha" and "Crow" systems. The task of understanding the Iroquois social system and its development still faces anthropologists and Morgan's critics have added little to our basic knowledge.

The range within which present-day Longhouse Iroquois recognize kinship has been briefly outlined in this and the previous chapter. It is not the purpose here to enter into a discussion of Morgan's treatment of Iroquois kinship, rather only to suggest that the apparent anomaly in the Iroquois system of terminology is cleared up when it is seen that the system is built up not only on the basis of matrilineal descent, but in addition, on the complementary recognition of filiation with the father. Not only does a person have institutionalized relationships with members of his father's matrilineage, but institutionalized interpersonal ties also occur on the basis of agnatic relationships (in which a kind of shadow lineage is thus outlined). It is these features that are given terminological recognition to give the overall system its "balanced bilateral character." In the traditional system, and to a considerable extent at present, nuclear family relationships are identified terminologically with relationships within one's own matrilineage, with relationships within the field of agnatic descent, and, to a lesser extent, within the father's matrilineage. The terms used for these relationships are given in figures 3 and 4 below. It is beyond the scope of the present problem to deal further with these matters.

The principal jural and affective features of the relationships within the household and the terms associated with each have been noted. It should be pointed out, however, that in daily intercourse it is general usage to refer to and address kin of one's own and descending generations by personal names rather than by kinship terms. On the other hand, kinship terms are always used in addressing and referring to kinsfolk of ascending generations. They are used more frequently in reference than in address and their use is always a mark of respect.

One of the most important aspects to note about the present terminological system is the tendency to isolate the relationships within the nuclear family. This has always been possible by the use of a diminutive suffix with primary terms when used in the generalized sense; and as noted in the previous chapter, this device is still used within the lineage to differentiate wider lineage relatives from own nuclear family kin, the one exception being the use of the cousin term (ǫgyase) as an alternate term for generation equals within the lineage outside one's own siblings. Terminological isolation has become more complete in the case of the father. While his own brothers, the male members of his matrilineage of his own generation, and his male agnates of his own generation may all be called ha'hniiha (lesser father), the term knosę is deemed more appropriate for these relatives at present, thus affecting terminological isolation for one's own father (ha'hni). Traditionally, the children of all the men included here are siblings (dɛgaọdɛhnọde), but they tend to be designated by the cousin term (ọgyasɛ) at present, even to a greater extent than do generation equals within the lineage. Both terms are used, however. The degree to which the children of those latter relatives are separated or identified with own children in the terms applied to them can be seen from figures 3 and 4.

In summary, it can be seen that while nuclear family relationships are more sharply distinguished terminologically at present, there continues to be basic terminological continuity between the matricentral cell of each household and the matrilineage, although the use of some dual terms and the increased emphasis on the diminutive suffix as distinguishing factors denote a loss of lineage solidarity. The fact that terms such as knosɛ and knohaʌ, primarily lineage terms, are now applied respectively to father's brothers and sisters, denotes a decline in the terminological exclusiveness of the lineage; but the fact that they replace terms outside the lineage, rather than the reverse, indicates their continued viability in their primary context. Terminological continuity in relationships traced through the father have been more extensively undermined.

These usages clearly reflect the jural and economic factors attached to the various relationships examined in the forepart of this chapter and the large measure of autonomy imparted to the nuclear unit by the jural and economic matters attaching to the conjugal bond and to parenthood. They also reflect the continued importance of factors attached to matrilineal descent.

Marriage

In part 2 of this study it was shown that some form of conjugal union is of fundamental importance in the household life and structure of nearly every household and that marriage (gana'hgwa'h) is the normal state of adult men and women in Longhouse society. The age at which men and women marry was noted, and data were given on residence arrangements after marriage. The domestic roles of husbands and wives were also described, and some numerical data were given on the durability of conjugal ties. While marriage is thus an event and a developing process within the domestic order of relationships, the particular form that it takes, as pointed out by Fortes (1958; see also Radcliffe-Brown 1952, 42), is determined by forces emanating from the politico-jural domain. For a fuller understanding of marriage, and therefore of the structure of the household, it will be necessary to consider it from the standpoint of its jural and ritual content.

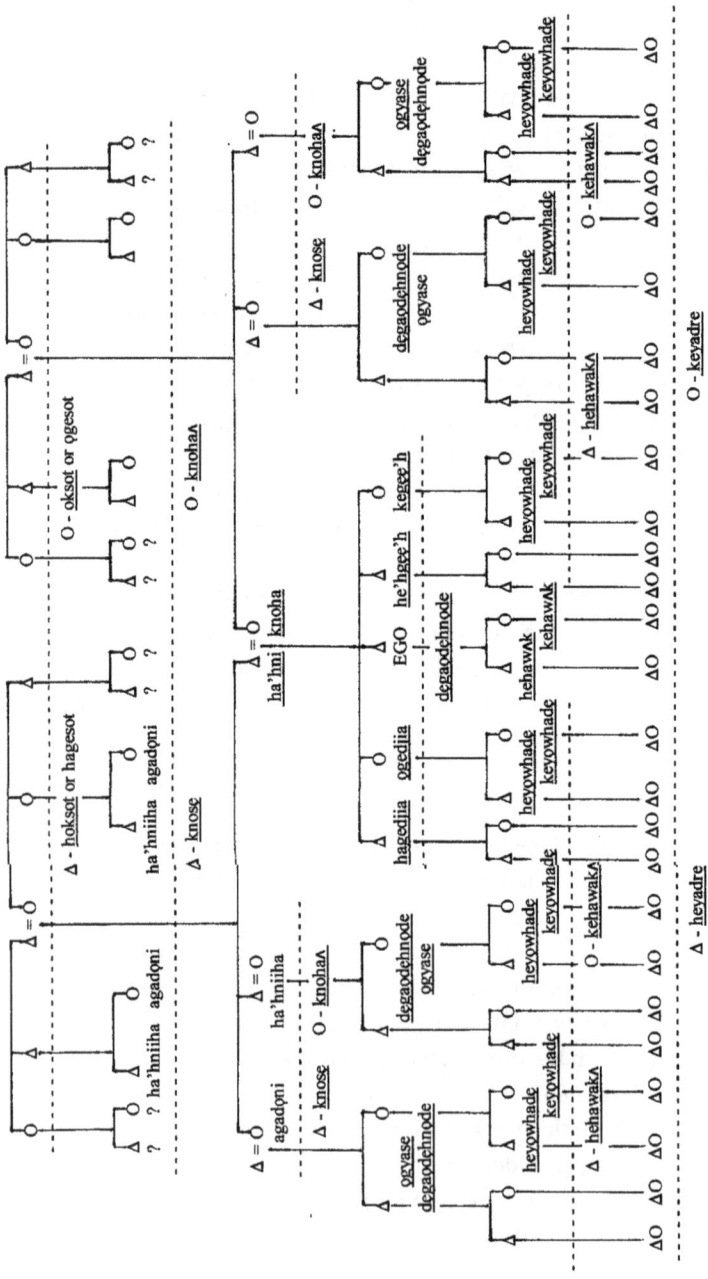

3. Paternal and Maternal Kin, Ego: Male. Note: Terms used most frequently at present [1958] are underlined. Where traditional terms differ from these, the traditional terms are shown nearest the relative concerned. In-law terms not included.

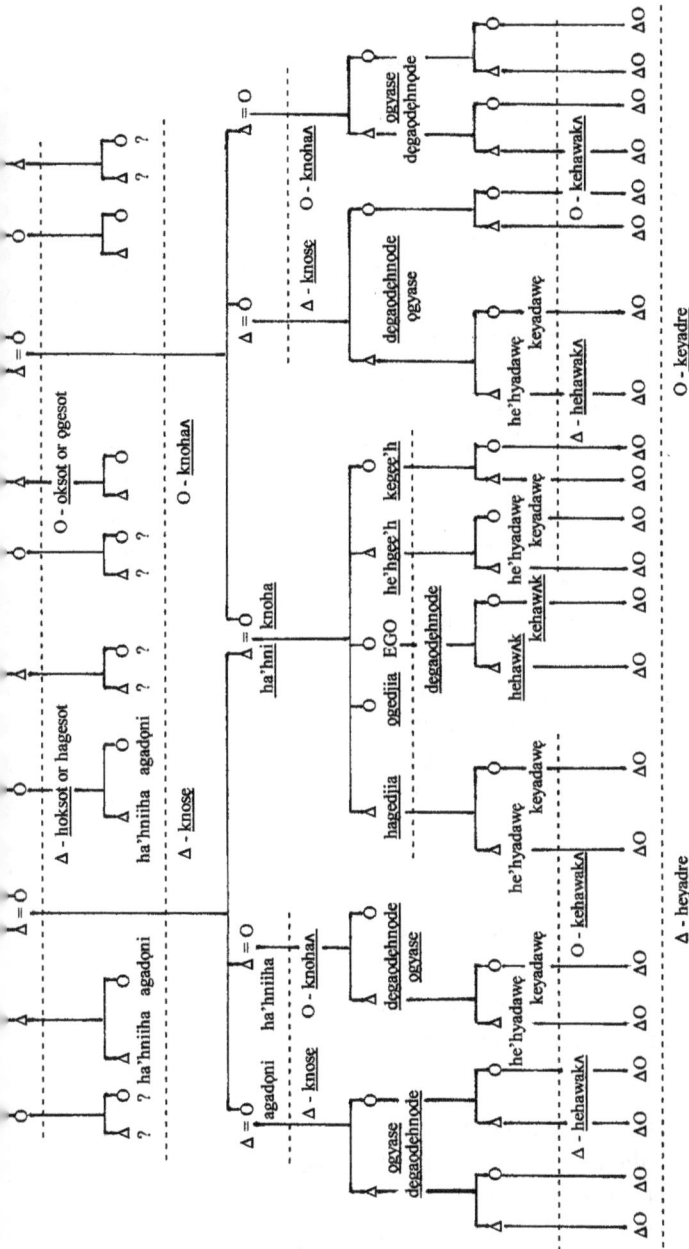

4. Paternal and Maternal Kin, Ego: △ Male, ○ Female. *Note:* Terms used most frequently at present [1958] are underlined. Where traditional terms differ from these, the traditional terms are shown nearest the relative concerned. In-law terms not included.

Characteristic of the duality of the social space of Longhouse society, the jural forces under which marriages are initiated and develop in time emanate from both the Indigenous system and from the Canadian political and legal systems. It is necessary, therefore, to give an account of the political and legal institutions of Canadian society that affected Longhouse marriages at the time of fieldwork.

Under Canadian law, a woman who marries an Indian man becomes a legal Indian herself, and an Onondaga Iroquois woman marrying a Cayuga Iroquois man becomes a Cayuga, along with all her children by this man, and all qualify for small Cayuga annuities on this basis. If a Longhouse woman marries a nonmember of the reserve, she forfeits her reserve membership, whereas a man doing the same, imparts his status to his wife. A person's legal spouse is his or her first heir in cases of intestacy, although both men and women may dispose of real property held in their own name independently without reference to his or her spouse. Also according to provincial law, which applies in this respect to Indians, a woman may, at least theoretically, sue her legal husband for nonsupport in a provincial court. Actually, among the Longhouse people such action is seldom, if ever, taken, and claiming this right under the provincial system is strongly disapproved as action inimical to their own system.

These rules make of marriage an important concern in the administration of Indian affairs. From the early reservation period until the first decades of the present century, Longhouse people were required only to communicate the facts of their marriage to the Indian Office. Since then, however, in an effort to enhance the adequacy of their vital statistics, the Indian Office has sought to have marriages performed by a person especially designated in each longhouse ritual group and to have the requisite information be submitted on prescribed forms. This has tended to establish the longhouse ritual group as the unit from which marriages derive their legality, rather than the respective lineages of the bride and groom, yet the lineage group retains an important jural interest in the marriages of its members.[11]

Courtship

Formerly, marriages were arranged by the mothers and maternal grandmothers of the couple, and there were some arranged marriages in existence among the Longhouse people at the time of fieldwork. Present economic and jural circumstances, however, permit a rather wide scope for individual election in matters of courtship and the selection of a marriage partner, and most people agree that it is better to let the young people choose for themselves. Yet the field data show that individual choice operates within moral and jural limitations laid down by Longhouse society at large.

Upon reaching puberty, young people are given moral and jural instruction, usually by their mothers and maternal grandmothers. Young girls are told that it is now possible for them to "get in a family way," and they are cautioned about the difficulties pregnancy at this stage in their lives might entail, that having a child might make it difficult to find a man later on. That sexual relations will occur during this period is accepted, and the counsel given is, therefore, more directed to whom they must not have sexual relations with rather than that they must not occur at all. Young men are also cautioned against having sexual relations with girls during their menstruation lest they get a wasting sickness called todraǫ.

There follows a period of intrigue, and that it involves sexual experience is seen in the large number of single mothers in this age group. Young men, in the incessant and spirited joking and rivalry that goes on whenever they get together in aggregate, call each other by numbers representing the number of their sexual conquests—a kind of coup-counting. In some instances, when pregnancy occurs from these casual affairs, marriage follows; but as a rule, there is no intention to marry.

These activities tend to shade into more stable patterns. A young man may begin to stay at the household of a young woman if her parents permit, or work on fruit farms and in canning factories may afford opportunities for young people to get together in a kind of quasi-cohabitation or a period of trial marriage; and if the couple prove compatible and they meet no opposition from the old folks, a ceremony is arranged for or, as sometimes occurs, they continue to live together without ceremony.

When one man, who had been married for four years at the time of field-work, began in earnest to look for a wife, he made himself useful at his present wife's mother's home by drawing in wood from the bush and cutting it into stove lengths and by doing other chores about the house. The duration of his visits were extended until, on one occasion, his wife's mother called the couple together and asked them if they would look after her house while she went to the fruit country to work—that he might as well stay, since he was always there anyway. About a year later, his wife's mother's brother, who was a chief, arranged for a group of other chiefs, one of whom was designated to perform marriages, to come to his sister's house to marry the couple.

In speaking of the younger generation, elders frequently say, "They choose whomever they want to [for a mate] nowadays." The young people, however, supply a counter statement and say, "Just let us make the wrong choice, and they soon put us straight."

Marriage Regulations and Preferences

In accordance with the incest taboo, marriage (*gonyas*) within the nuclear family is forbidden. Incest is described as "biting into your own family" (*ahadatwhadjiagiih*) or "to meddle in your own family." It is a "thing contrary to the family system," a sin (*gaiwhiitgę*) that no one in possession of his faculties could commit. It is believed that offspring from a union of this kind would likely be deformed, mentally unsound, or "odd" (*gaya'hdogę*). These sentiments are extended to members of one's own matrilineage in a somewhat attenuated form, although the rule of lineage exogamy is given a separate formulation, as noted in the previous chapter, in which marriage within the lineage is likened to marriage with one's self, a total absurdity. One informant stated that he had seen a child born of such a union that had no bones.[12] There is general agreement concerning these rules, and genealogies show that lineage exogamy is virtually complete.

The regulation of marriages outside the lineage is less clear. Many Longhouse people say that lineage exogamy is all that is necessary, while others say that marriage between nonlineage kin should be restricted to third or fourth cousins. Genealogies show, however, that marriages between second cousins who are descendants of a brother and a sister are common, whereas marriages between agnatic kin of any degree of nearness or remoteness appear to be rare. This correlates with the fact that agnates of one's own generation are termed siblings.

Preference is expressed for marriages within Longhouse society on the reservation. Young people are instructed at puberty to confine their association to the Longhouse sector of the population of the reserve, and marriage outside Longhouse society with either Christian Iroquois or with white people is also denounced during the preaching of the *Gaiwhio*. One Longhouse woman described a dream in which her mother, who had been dead for some seven years, appeared and expressed joy at her daughter's having married a Longhouse man. Mothers express the preference for local marriages when they tell their sons that they "will use up all their money on the road and never be able to get a house," if they marry Longhouse girls from the States or even other reservations in Canada. As noted, women who marry out in this way lose their reserve membership.

One man was heard to instruct his son, "If you should marry a white girl, she would always be telling you that you are a no-good Indian, and you would be calling her a dirty white man." The chiefs passed a resolution in their council in the summer of 1956 to the effect that either a man or a woman who marries a white person should automatically lose his status in Longhouse society. These regulations and preferences tend to keep the bonds of kinship and affinity generated by marriage within Longhouse society. The strength of the stated preferences for Longhouse and local endogamy can be seen from table 24. The figures in the table are taken from the census of 150 households and represent the most recent unions of the household heads, their married children, and other married members of their households, amounting to 244 unions in all. Since the interest here is to show the preference for a conjugal partner, the figures represent the actual number of choices made by Longhouse people rather than the number of unions only.

The Marriage Ceremony

The marriage ceremony is quite simple, and arrangements for it, as in the case noted above, are made by the bride's near kin—her parents and members of her sublineage group. It is, as a rule, held at the bride's parents' home although two weddings took place at the longhouse during fieldwork. Bride and groom are seated side by side with their respective mothers seated beside them. After the standard prayer (ganǫhǫnyǫk) used on all ceremonial occasions, the officiating chief, or other officer designated to perform marriages, delivers a speech of exhortation to the couple referred to as "placing their minds at one" (gadogę ǫwadǫ godinigǫha'h). Points made in this speech having value for the present analysis will be given in the section on the jural content of the marital status below. After this speech, the other chiefs present, and perhaps respected elders, address the couple, developing favorite marriage themes or dwelling further on the points of the main address. At the conclusion of these speeches, the couple stand and, in turn, are given a strand of shell beads (otgǫa'h). With this in hand, they declare their intention (ne gai whaniyata ęsninyak—they endorse it) to abide the charge given them. Thereafter, the couple remain standing while all present file past, shake hands and offer their own personal words of encouragement (gastiyaǫnyǫk) to the couple. Meanwhile, a table has been prepared, and the couple, with their mothers and the chiefs, eat together,

Table 24. Choice of conjugal partners

	Longhouse	Church	White	Total
On reserve	280	39	0	319
Off reserve	7	4	4	15
Total	287	43	4	334
Percent	86.0	12.8	1.2	100.0

whereupon near and then more remote kin and, eventually, all present are fed. This ends the ceremony, which was, in the five cases witnessed in the field, followed by the opening of presents by the bride and groom given them by kin and friends. In three of the cases observed, wedding cakes were cut and served to all present. Old people usually deplored these appendages as being "the white man's way."

Jural Aspects of Marital Status

There is great emphasis on the equality of husband and wife in marriage. It is said in the speech of exhortation, just referred to, that their minds are as one (*skanikwat*) and that there is to be "no master in the house" (*tęhdeskot hądǫ tawaddǫ*). The high degree of equality between spouses is related to the very important role accorded women in political, jural, ritual, and economic affairs and is a function of the system of matrilineal descent of Longhouse society. It also explains the absence of any dramatic transfer of rights in the marriage ceremony. There are, however, well-defined expectations and privileges involved, and these are set forth in the hortatory speech of "placing the minds together." Well-defined procedures exist for dealing with actions that upset these expectations. The rights, duties, and privileges acknowledged in the marriage are the right of the couple to establish co-residence, the right of the husband to the domestic services of his wife, and mutual sexual privileges. Rights *in genetricem* remain vested in the women of the lineage.

The right of the couple to establish co-residence is acknowledged in the exhortation that they are to "make their own way" (*ęgaǫdadyadagęnha'h*) as a distinct unit and be equally responsible for maintaining their own household in the days ahead. It is also identified by the fact that it is often denied couples who have not been married, of which there occurred several cases during fieldwork. The mother of one young man set up an independent household in a house inherited from her mother when her children began to reach maturity. The young man continued to spend time at the houses of each of his parents; and when he sired a child by a Longhouse young woman, urged on by his father, he managed to bring her to his father's house, only to have her mother come and take her home again. Had the couple been married, there would have been no question of their right to set up their own household or to live together, whether they had their own house or not. The conferral of this right amounts to a recognition of the transition to the status of wife (kegędji) for the bride and the status of husband (he'hgędji) for the groom. This is often of more consequence in the case of the girl, since she is usually residing in her natal household at the time of marriage. It is also of significance in this connection that when young men move out of their natal households to establish their economic and jural independence, this nearly always culminates in marriage and the recognition of adult status. If a man sires several children by a woman, co-residence is usually acquiesced in by both parents and lineage.

A man is entitled to the domestic services of his wife. This is clear from the statement that she should "look for ways in which to make him comfortable" (i'hdesgwayǫ'h ǫgisak sǫnhǫ skǫnǫ ahanǫdǫnyǫ'hhak). (This does not, however, include the right to the fruits of her economic activities outside the household.) Some informants said that this right is given emphasis in the meal provided by the bride and her kin. In former times, it was also emphasized by the practice by the woman of serving her husband's meals separately. It oftentimes happens at present, if her husband has special guests, that a woman will serve them first, she and her children eating later. It is also for this reason that a woman usually consults her husband before taking work outside the household that would upset the routine of her domestic services.

Reciprocally, a woman has a claim on her husband for economic support in the household.[13] Informants agreed that this claim is included in the charge that the couple are to be equally responsible for maintaining their own household. This claim is the basis of much of the tension between a woman and her husband's mother (and sometimes sisters), especially during the early part of marriage. When one newly married man continued to give money to his sister, who was a single mother, this was quickly quashed by his wife's mother, who reminded him forcefully that his duty was to provide for his own wife and child. Another Longhouse mother raised her children in her own household and was only visited periodically by her husband. When her eldest son began working out, it was a great boon to her. She managed to keep him at home until he was well into his thirties, at which time he married. The reallocation of economic responsibilities thus entailed dealt the security of this woman's household a severe blow, and it continues to be a source of tension between her and her son's wife, of whom she is very critical. "I always think of how much better I cared for him than she does," the woman said. "I suppose it's something like we are in love with the same man." She attempts to resolve the problem by avoiding her son's wife.

Young married couples often complain that someone is using witchcraft to break up their marriage. Often, the one felt to be behind the witchcraft is the husband's mother or the woman who has raised him, although this is not usually spoken of openly. These problems are symptomatic of the fact that after marriage, a man's first economic duty is to his wife and children, thus alienating his support from his mother.

There is also the expectation of mutual sexual privileges, and this is in-dicated in the statement of the main speech, when it is said that the couple should not "pass from one [mate] to the other" (gǫdefra'h). In the marriage speech these privileges are linked with the central purpose of marriage, "the generation of children" (eksasǫa'h dǫyagodaǫhǫgai'). When a couple are living together before marriage, as often happens, they have no such claim to ex-clusive sexual privileges. The withholding or diversion of sexual favors by either is a way of showing that the relationship has no capacity to endure. Prior to his present marriage, one man had attempted to establish a union with another young woman. He stayed with her in her mother's household for longer periods, performed odd chores about the house, and had begun to extend economic support to the group. Upon returning from work on one occasion, he discovered that the young woman had gone away with another man. He later warned her that she could expect no support from him if this continued, but when she ignored him, he had no recourse but to find another partner. Sexual fidelity is probably higher among women than among men, but a man who is notoriously free in sexual affairs outside his marriage would not keep his wife long and would have no sympathy from her kin in his effort to get her back again if she left him.

The procedure in case of default is the same in all of these matters. For example, if a man's wife leaves him, thus denying him her domestic and sexual services, she forfeits any claim to his economic support. If he desires to get her back, he may appeal to her parents or the female head of her lineage, who will, if they deem her to be in the wrong, "preach" to her and try to effect a reconciliation. A group of chiefs may be called in to preach to her as well. In doing this, the chiefs usually display the otgǫa'h and remind her of the "day of her marriage." The same procedure is followed in the case of the husband's being the offender.

There is a wide scope for individual election in present circumstances, which limits the effectiveness of the above procedures, and if a person is deemed to be at fault by his or her spouse's kin, he can expect little sympathy, although the chiefs may act independently in an effort to effect a reconciliation. In cases of people having no organized lineage, an appeal can be made directly to the chiefs.

That it is the marriage ceremony that confers these rights and expectations can be seen in the fact that they are not involved in the casual affairs of youth, and men or women living together in trial unions have no recourse if one or the other of them chooses no longer to continue their relationship. In addition, the chiefs refuse to act in cases of common-law or "living together" unions. However, as noted above, if a couple have been together for a long time and have reared children together, it is said that the "children make the marriage," and the same conditions apply as in case of marriage.

Rights In Genetricem

As noted, the couple is told that the central purpose of their union is pro-creation, and the *Gaiwhio* states that a woman who bears twelve children and raises them is assured of felicity in "the world beyond the sky" (*gaǫhyage*). These offspring are claimed by the lineage of the bride, however, which means that rights over the reproductive capacity of its female members are vested in the women of the lineage. This fact is symbolized by the presence of the mothers (to the exclusion of the fathers and mothers' brothers) beside their children during the marriage ceremony and is underlined by the fact that failing a mother, the maternal grandmother (as occurred in one instance during fieldwork) or a mother's sister may take her place.

Rights over the offspring of its women are asserted initially by the lineage in the naming ceremony, as described in the previous chapter. This factor reinforces the mother-child bond within the household and orients the whole Longhouse system around its women members. It is probably this circumstance that lies behind the feeling that women should control the earnings of their children and manage Family Allowance payments, that a woman would discipline a daughter's children (but not her son's), and the fact that children nearly always go with their mothers upon separation.

Termination of Marital Status

The status conferred at marriage is to last as long as both the partners are alive. In the marriage speech it is said that since the couple have decided to place their minds together, they should remain thus "according to the number of their days" or according to the prescribed way (ẹtgayane'hhẹ'h). Death is ultimately the only recognized termination of the marital status. In keeping with this rule, upon the death of one of the spouses, there is a ritual termination of the marriage and of the affinal relationship between the two groups united by it, but this does not, of course, extinguish the kinship ties generated by the marriage.

This termination begins when the surviving spouse turns over the body of the deceased to his or her own lineage, who make all the arrangements for a proper funeral. At the "ten-day feast" (họsakie whasẹ) the principal people of the two lineages joined by the marriage in question meet. The surviving spouse sits initially with the deceased's lineage (his or her knowhakiono) whose head woman (goyane'h), or oldest woman (dyeigẹdji) in the case of a non-chiefly lineage, places him (or her) on a chair in front of the group, combs his hair, and ties a silk kerchief around his neck. This is referred to as "relieving his (or her) grievance" (agaọdadyadadrọgo) preparatory to being returned to his own lineage. When this grooming is completed, the head woman presents the survivor with four or five yards of cotton print cloth (nigahnesa) as an earnest (gowẹna—lit. her word) confirming the release (saọdadatga'h) of the surviving spouse from his (or her) marriage ties and obligations. Subsequently, the goyane'h or the oldest woman from the survivor's lineage comes forth and leads him back to his own people. At the following Green Corn Festival (djiskne ọdekwaohes gakowane'h) or at the Midwinter Festival (gaiwhanẹsgwagowa'h), the surviving spouse "speaks up" (dọdaiwẹnitgẹ), publicly terminating mourning, and "releases the body" (saọtiyọdaisʌt) of the deceased. Again, this release is confirmed by the return of four or five yards of cloth to the lineage matron of the deceased spouse's lineage (knowhakiono). This cloth is also referred to as the "word" (owẹna'h) of the survivor confirming the release. With this the marriage and affinal obligations are terminated.[14] These customs show that ultimately it is the lineage from which the marital status derives, and it alone can terminate the relationship once it has been established.

Separation

Longhouse people are resolute in the stand that they have no divorce, and the chiefs adamantly refuse to perform a second marriage as long as both the original partners to a marriage are still alive. Separation and subsequent unions frequently occur, however, and it is these circumstances that lie behind the "getting together" (adyọdranegẹ) or common-law unions noted in chapter

4. Twenty-five of the thirty-two (78 percent) existing common-law unions recorded in tables 19 and 21 are of this type. Yet regardless of how many separations and unions occur subsequent to the jurally recognized marriage, this tie must be ritually terminated upon the death of one of the partners in the manner described above, and there are cases of men and women who had been separated for twenty-five or thirty years being released from their original marriages.

The only explanation of these apparently anomalous circumstances elicited from the Longhouse people was that "it is the Creator's law." Two other factors are apparent, however. One is the continuity of a definite set of affinal ties, with their jural and ritual content. In addition, the custom maintains a distinction between jurally authorized marriages and unions in which the partners merely "live together" (see Fortes 1962, 9). Both of these factors would appear to be of special importance in a society where separation is easy and frequent, as it is among the Longhouse people. The jural statuses of neither spouse nor of their children changes greatly from one union to the next after the original marriage (although there may be some economic disadvantage for the woman), and it is likely for this reason that no real stigma or social disability attaches to this action.

As noted earlier, about 50 percent of all adults in the census had had previous unions at the time of fieldwork. The jural position of the spouses in the marital relationship sheds some light on this feature. The emphasis on the equality of the spouses in marriage was noted, and it was also seen that a woman has full rights over the fruits of her wage-earning activities outside the household. There is no mention of the right of the husband to remove his bride from her natal home to his own house, rather only the right of the couple to establish their own household as husband and wife. Nor does the husband (or his kinsmen) have any rights in the generative powers of his wife, these being vested rather in the wife's lineage. While the husband's legal status as Indian and member of the reserve is imparted to his wife and children, these are not crucial, since the wife likely was already Indian and a member of the reserve prior to her marriage; and a woman's children by more than one union can claim reserve membership through her. This brings the conjugal relationship to rest primarily upon the reciprocal domestic, economic, and sexual rights and privileges, as well as the ties of personal sentiment, of which there is very little outward show between husband and wife. If this reciprocity breaks down for any reason, there is little beyond mutual interest in the children that can keep the conjugal relationship intact. It is significant that the causes most often given for conjugal separation are drinking and "running around" with other men or women. In the latter case, however, it would appear to require almost a withdrawal of sexual favors altogether in order itself to cause separation. The fact that both men and women carry various roots as love medicine (onǫhwhet) to "keep their wives (or husbands) around" is related to the tenuous nature of the conjugal bond.

With the cessation of childbearing and the subsequent decline in sexual interest on the part of women, and with the maturation of the children, the effectiveness of the economic and sexual reciprocity is very seriously undermined, and the conjugal bond is divested of its main basis. It is often said that a woman leaves her husband because "she grew up on him" (ǫhǫwhadoga'hs). It is like coming of age. She frees herself from the authority of her husband in the domestic group—authority made effective by her dependence upon him for economic support during the period of childrearing—and establishes herself independently as a unit in the matrilineal system. It is the mother-child bond that is most often exploited in separations. A woman may set up her own household with her own children, some of whom are able to assist her economically, or she may return to her own mother. The latter is the course most often taken by younger premenopausal women, whose parental households are usually always open to them upon separation. A woman never forfeits her status as daughter in her mother's household.

Affinal Relationships

In the speech of the "placing together of the minds," the new couple are told to "love and respect each other's families" (ayetsiwhanǫkwak sniwhadjiyasǫ), and this is often a favorite theme of the chiefs and elders who address the couple after the main speech has been completed.

Parents-in-law

As noted earlier, the ideal of establishing co-residence in their own house is seldom obtainable at first for a newly married couple, and this means a period of living with parents-in-law, either for the husband or the wife. A preference for uxorilocal residence during this period was also noted on the grounds that it requires less of an adjustment to take in a son-in-law, since his work keeps him out of the house. Of living in the husband's parents' household, it is said that the new wife is "living in another woman's house," or "it is like there are two wives in the same household." This latter arrangement also brings together in the same household two women with conflicting interests in the same man. A son of marriage age is often a very important economic support to his mother, and by virtue of the status conferred at marriage, a man's wife has first claim on his economic services. The conjugal tie is here brought into conflict with that between mother and son.

In a rather typical case, Ned brought his bride, Della, home to his parents' household. He was a principal factor in the support of the household economy, and his mother and sister resented Della greatly. Trouble was not long in coming, and Della fought with Ned's sisters and told him that she was going home, but he persuaded her to stay. When winter arrived, Della had no coat, and her husband gave her money with which to buy a new one. Upon discovering the purchase, Ned's sisters informed their mother, who took the coat upstairs and shook it in Della's face, saying, "Maybe you'd better put this on the table for breakfast." After this experience, Della left the household and returned to her mother's sister and her husband who had raised her, refusing to go back to Ned until they were able to get a house of their own.

Cases of this general type are common among the Longhouse people, and few women consent to reside for long in their husband's mother's household. Women agree that it is difficult to avoid troubles with a son's wife when you live in the same household "even when you try." As noted earlier, one woman said, "It is something like being in love with the same man."

Because his position is less central within the household, the relationship of a woman with her husband's father is not fraught with these same tensions. However, the relationship is one of very considerable reserve and respect for both of the persons involved.

When living with the wife's parents, circumstances are less tense. The adage that "when your son marries, you lose him, but when your daughter marries, you gain a son," is cited to sum up this situation. Again, because of her central position in the household and because of the strength of the mother-daughter ties, it is the relationship with the wife's mother that is of most consequence. Young men are subordinate to their wives' parents. When in the house, daughter's husbands are shy and retiring. They seldom speak directly to their parents-in-law, rather addressing them through their wives when this is necessary, and tend to spend much time away from the household. Men seldom have close dealings with their wives' fathers under any circumstances.

When a couple moves into their own household, there is less opportunity for trouble to arise, but the general pattern of shyness (odihgrofrah) toward and avoidance of parents-in-law continues. As a marriage matures, there is some relaxation in the relationship, although parents-in-law are always treated with a good deal of respect.

A man uses the term haknenhǫs for his wife's father and ǫknenhǫs for her mother. They, in turn, address and refer to him as henainhǫs. For a woman, her husband's father is hagesęǫ and his mother is her ǫgeseyǫ. She is their keseiǫ. The respective terms for parents and those for son and daughter may also be used. The behavior patterns described here are most applicable to the relationship with one's spouse's own parents and with one's own children's spouses; however, the same general pattern applies to the siblings of parents-in-law and son- and daughter-in-law, but it is attenuated rapidly thereafter.

Siblings-in-law

Like relationships with parents-in-law, that with siblings-in-law is also marked with considerable reserve despite the mitigating principle of generation equality. There is little of privileged familiarity and joking between siblings-in-law. They are seldom members of the same household for extended periods; but when they are together, they are, as a rule, on their best behavior. A woman is cordial toward her husband's sister, but the two women are seldom companions and are likely to be sharply critical of each other when apart. In one such relationship, the woman complained that her brother's wife was very cross and made trouble if he attempted to help his mother by giving her money or buying presents for her. She suggested further that her sister-in-law really had little to complain of, since the child, for whom her brother was providing, was likely not his child at all.

There is little contact between a woman and her husband's brother; but when they are together, there is a marked reserve between them. This applies also to the relationship between a man and his wife's sister.

On one occasion, a young man was heard to joke with his wife's sister soon after she had given birth to a baby boy. The baby, he said, had plainly not been sired by the woman's common-law husband, but was rather his own child, which anyone could plainly see by the curls in its hair. This is definitely not general behavior between opposite-sex siblings-in-law, but is rather the result of an individual personality characteristic. Sexual topics with such affines are, as a rule, avoided.

A man is also circumspect toward his wife's brother, especially so if he is an elder brother. They are cordial toward each other but again, are seldom companions.

A man's wife's sister is his ǫgyanyę, and he is her ǫgyagyo'h. He and his wife's brother are ǫgyagyo'h to each other. A woman and her husband's sister are ǫgyanyę to each other, and her husband's brother is her ǫgyagyo'h. Sibling terms may also be used for these affines.

The Two Sets of Parents-in-law

The respective mothers of the bride and groom, who sit beside them during the marriage ceremony, are *agyadęnǫk* to each other. The root of this term is the same as that used for siblings, and informants translated it to mean "someone of whom you are very fond," or "very dear friends." The word in its plural form, *agwadęnǫk*, may be used to include both sets of parents linked by the marriage, as well as their own and lineage siblings.

The most obvious aspect of the behavior connected with this relationship is the avoidance (*tiyǫgweyę*), which centers around the two mothers-in-law, but which also includes the two sets of parents. It may also, in considerably more attenuated form, extend to the siblings of the parents. In discussing this feature of affinal relationships, one young woman informant said, "It's a funny thing with us here. It seems that two women can be good friends; their children marry, and it's *tiyǫgweyę* from then on." Again, this principle appears to be related to the fact that the marital status establishes first claim on the economic support of the husband with his wife and on the domestic services of a woman with her husband. It was shown earlier that even when a young man leaves his home to establish his jural and economic independence, the tie with his mother is seldom broken and that he continues to be an important element in her security. This applies also to a woman and her daughter, and it was shown how mothers sometimes prevent young, unmarried daughters from going to live with a man in his house.

The alienation of the son by marriage is often a severe blow to a woman's position. It was stated above that a woman is very often critical of her daughters-in-law, and these same circumstances extend to the two mothers-in-law, who are generally very critical of each other. In a case that occurred during field-work, a woman accused her daughter's husband's stepmother and sister of "coaxing his money away from him," when he should be using it for his own family; and they, in turn, spoke of how he (since he was living in his wife's mother's household) was supporting her, as well as his wife and children.

Eleanor was a member of Gloria's father's lineage, and the two women were fast friends. When Eleanor's daughter, Mae, became pregnant by Gloria's son, Gerald, Eleanor and her husband did not approve of the union. The couple eloped, however, and upon returning to the reserve, went to live with his parents. By the time Mae had her first child, her parents had forgiven her;

and by the time the second was born, rapport had been established with her husband. Yet the mothers of the couple continued to avoid each other despite their long-standing friendship. During the autumn of 1957, my wife and I were visiting Gloria and her daughter-in-law, Mae, who made it known that since her husband was away working in New York State, she was going home to stay with her own parents for a period. She was anxiously awaiting the arrival of her parents to drive her back to their home and sighted their car as soon as it appeared in the lane. The car parked a good distance from the house, and though both parents were in the car, they sat and waited for their daughter to come. Mae had a large bag of clothes besides her two children to manage, and she called to her father, who came to the porch, took up the bag and went back to the car, whereupon she joined them and they drove off. Gloria sat disinterestedly through this whole operation, as though her daughter-in-law had suddenly moved into a separated realm. Her only comment after they had gone was, "They didn't like it when they got married, but they have forgiven them now that the children have come." Eleanor commented later that she would be happy when her daughter got her own house so she could visit her more often.

The connotation of the term *agwadęnǫk* is clearly an expression of the ideal relationship between the parents of bride and groom, and it is only maintained through the principle of *tiyǫgweyę*. It can be seen that one of the principal forces behind the ideal of having a separate residence after marriage lies in the need to resolve the conflict inherent in the opposing ties of kinship—the ties between mother and children, on the one hand, and those of marriage and affinity, on the other.

False Faces (*hẹnadoíi*) emerge from Sour Springs cookhouse where they have donned ceremonial attire before performing a medicine rite. Photo by author.

House rendered uninhabitable by neglected ancestral spirits is allowed to fall into ruin. Such houses, in certain instances, are initially in better condition than some houses still in use. Photo by author.

7. Summary and Conclusion

Household structure of the Longhouse Iroquois and its development in time were described in part 2 of this study. In part 3 an explanation of this structure has been sought in an analysis of the jural content of the various relationships of which the group is composed. Because the jural attributes that make up the various statuses (in the sense of Radcliffe-Brown 1952, 37) within the group derive from the external system, it was necessary also to give a brief account of the system of matrilineal descent. Certain elements of the various statuses making up the group derive from the Canadian system, and these were also taken into account. In chapter 3 the notion of the division of economic responsibilities between the sexes in Longhouse society, together with an assessment of the relative contributions of men and women to the domestic economy, were given.

It should be fairly clear at this point that the weight of the jural and economic factors attaching to parenthood and the conjugal bond supports the ideal of a household based on the nuclear unit of husband-father, wife-mother, and their own children and has endowed this unit with a very considerable measure of autonomy. The strength of these factors is reflected in the composition of the group, especially at its inception and throughout the expansion phase of its development. It comes into being as an already-expanding, two-generational unit primarily dependent upon the husband-father for its economic support. It appears that it is largely this fact that justifies his authority within the group, although his position is sanctioned by both Longhouse society and rulings of the Canadian government. The weight of these matters is further reflected in the absence of the avuncular factor in the composition of the group, in the limited number of collateral kin of either spouse present at any time throughout its development, and in present usages in the system of kinship terminology.

Yet in matters pertaining to citizenship, the regulation of marriage, succession, the inheritance of personal belongings, the provision of proper funerary rites, and the maintenance of physical and psychological well-being, as these relate to lineage ancestors and lineage charms, the members of the household conform to rules arising in the lineage system, which rules are often overseen by lineage officers. For every male officer, except one, in the Native political and ritual systems there is a female counterpart, and there is the important female office *kogiwe* in charge of relationships with the dead for which there is no male counterpart. Whenever a man participates in ritual or jural activities in the external system of Longhouse society, he is of necessity separated from his wife and children, whereas a woman always has her children with her. In these matters the membership of every household is split by the rule of matrilineal descent, and the mother-child bond is reinforced by the descent rules.

It is in the context of these diverging forces that the matrilineal sublineage group emerges in its proper structural perspective as an intercalary unit between the household group and the lineage. It is a kind of domestic subdivision of the lineage. A person is identified with this group early in life, and, as seen above, the sublineage may have a good deal of influence in the households of its members (table 23).[1] The kinship ties upon which this group is based (figures 1 and 2) are, as a rule, the mother-child bond (own and mother's) and sibling ties (own and mother's), and this relational network arises as a kind of compensatory factor to mitigate the strength of the conjugal ties of its members. This is consistent with the facts of the dependence of a woman and her children on the economic support of the husband-father, while at the same time being integrated into the external system by the rule of matrilineal descent. It is also consistent with what has been said above that the household group and the sublineage should become synonymous at certain points in the developmental cycle, and this actually occurs in many of the three-generation households, especially those with female heads, but also in some with male heads.

As the household group matures, social, economic, and jural factors working through the mother-child bond gather force, and this brings about a reorientation of relationships within the group. As the disabilities incumbent upon her by virtue of her role in the birth and care of children diminish and finally end, the wife-mother and her children are less dependent on the husband-father for their support. A woman is now free to work out of the home for wages and will often be assisted economically by grown-up sons and daughters. As the children mature socially and jurally, they too become more involved in their own right in activities connected with matrilineal descent. It is significant in this connection that when young men assert their jural and economic independence from the domestic group, they do so by moving out of their natal households and in many instances go to live for a period with matrilineal kinsmen.

It is at this point that the conjugal bond begins to give way, and the analysis of the jural content of the marital status has made it clear why this is so. The incidence of female headship and the number of three-generation households also increases. When the husband-father remains a member of the three-generation group, he is often socially, economically, and jurally defunct for the other members of the group, and ties with him are brought to rest on their affective content only, which is in many cases not great.

If Longhouse households are viewed in terms of the analytical model set forth by Professor Fortes (1958, 8–9)—that is, as comprising three orders of relationships, consisting of the cell of mother and children; the nuclear unit of husband-father, wife-mother, and their own children; and a domestic order, which among the Longhouse people includes relationships beyond the nuclear unit in about 40 percent of the households—the overall structural form of the group and the polar forces, in terms of which it develops in time, are drawn into clearer perspective. From what has been said, it is clear that the cell of mother and children is linked with the external politico-jural and ritual domain through the mother, or in some instances the maternal grandmother, thus separating this unit from the husband-father cum male head, whose jural authority is largely confined to the domestic order of relationships. The principal jural identification the father has with his children outside the domestic unit is in the Canadian system. At the same time, Longhouse society must oppose the validation of this link in order to maintain its own identity. These structural circumstances combine to lend point to the playful taunt sometimes held up to a man by his wife and children, "one lonely Turtle among all us Wolves." There are circumstances under which, and times when, the husband-father becomes almost dispensable.

The polarization of forces basic to the structure of the household is symbolized in the persons of the husband and wife of every marriage, as the counsel given in the marriage rite shows when it is stated that the pair "are to sit side by side" (gadogǫ ǫgaogę'h)—to sit level with each other in their new venture—and that "there shall be no master in the house" (tęhdeskot hǫdǫ tawaddǫ). These phrases connote a certain sensitivity to the forces underlying household life.

The structural position of women remains well-defined throughout their lives. They have the well-defined status as mothers, are practical coordinators of household affairs in the internal domain, and are the connecting link for their children in the external Longhouse system. A corollary of this position is their general alertness, forcefulness, and independence and the fact that they generally overshadow men in their understanding of jural, ritual, and genealogical matters. The fact that they are less vulnerable to drinking than men may also reflect their structural position. The problem men have with alcohol and the fact that they are inclined to spend a good deal of their earnings outside household interests reflect their peripheral and somewhat ambiguous social and jural position. This inference is lent plausibility by the fact that upon succeeding to official position within their own lineages or within the longhouse ritual group, men often stop drinking and perform their duties in an exemplary manner.

The intensity and frequency of conflicts occasioned by the diverging ties of matrilineal descent, and those arising out of the conjugal bond and paternity, have been lessened by the removal of the principal matters of inheritance from the lineage and by the individualization of economic activities, thus separating rather clearly the fields of action within which these forces are operative. Nevertheless, a great many of the day-to-day interpersonal problems arising in Longhouse society are attributable to the orientation and the stresses brought about by these opposing factors, as the following cases illustrate.

In the autumn of 1957, Delbert was killed in a road construction accident about a year after his marriage. He and his wife had been living with his mother who now sought to have her son's automobile, which was of considerable economic value, distributed with his personal belongings at the ten-day feast. She was opposed in this by her son's widow, who easily won out with the help of the Indian Office, which enforced the Canadian government ruling that the widow has first claim on the property of her deceased husband.

Mildred, who succeeded to the position of goyane'h for her lineage after the death of her mother, desired to raise up her eldest son as hoyane'h for the group. She was supported in this by the other members of her lineage, but was opposed by her husband, whose own lineage had become defunct and who had an abiding grievance against the chiefs. He swore that he would "never let a son of his" become one of their number and threatened to "make trouble" for her if she went ahead with her plans. Mildred's lineage group was few in number, and her son was the most suitable candidate available. Although her husband had succeeded in stalemating her plans, she set up her own separate household during the time of fieldwork and will likely go ahead with the installation.

Another woman, whose lineage kin lived on a reserve in New York State, had a terminal illness. She refused to go to white doctors for treatment, and the fortuneteller (dehayadoweta) whom she consulted on the reserve told her that because of neglect, her matrilineal ancestors were "getting after" her (hemorrhages are invariably regarded as symptomatic of the displeasure of the dead or of lineage charms) and that she must hold an O'hgiwe feast for them. To carry out the feast, her common-law husband enlisted the aid of his mother, although she was somewhat reluctant, saying that the feast would be without efficacy if his wife's "family" (o'hwadjiʌ) did not make the preparations. When the woman continued to wane after the feast, her mother-in-law's point was taken as proved and a second feast was held with the help of lineage kin from the States, but it was then too late.

Belva, whose husband, Ray, had a serious drinking problem, provided the main support for their eight children, with the aid of the sizable Family Allowance she controlled. After a prolonged absence, Ray returned home, demanding that she give him the monthly Family Allowance and saying that since the children were his, the money rightfully belonged to him. She refused and, instead, left the house with the money, hoping to take refuge with her mother's sister, who lived about five hundred yards away and who was the focus for her sublineage group. Ray then threatened her and became enraged when she continued on despite his threats. Thereupon, he returned to their house, loaded his rifle, called a final time for her to come back, and then shot and killed his wife. This case is highly atypical and not representative of the norm, but it is included to demonstrate the tensions inherent in the conjugal bond carried to the extreme.

It was shown in chapter 3 that the earnings of some Longhouse men compare favorably with those of many middle-class Canadians, yet there is very little social differentiation based on economic wealth among them. Occupational specialization is also minimal in Longhouse society. The husband-father is not able, therefore, to define the social status of his wife and children in the wider society on these bases. The answer to why the full range of possibilities inherent in his present position remain unexploited lies in the mechanisms through which the continuity of society at large is achieved. This will become clear from the brief consideration of some of these mechanisms that follows.

Kinship, in the broad sense, still provides the organizational framework through which many important social interests of both individuals and groups within Longhouse society are fulfilled. However, rulings of the Canadian government (such as those deposing the lineage chiefs and the authorization of wills and a bilateral rule for the descent of property) and individualized wage-earning activities within the Canadian economy have given rise to fields of action outside the lineage system, over which it has only indirect control. These factors clearly pose a threat to the descent system and the social and economic homogeneity that allows kinship categories to be an effective basis for ordering relationships. Many of the institutions, beliefs, and practices in Longhouse social life at the time of fieldwork can only be understood when seen in the context of the struggle of Longhouse society to maintain itself. Some of the ways in which opposition to the Canadian government is manifest were discussed in chapter 1. A few of the most important additional factors follow.

The Concept of Sin and the Gaiwhio

Much of what is regarded to be sin (*gaiwhiitgę*) in Longhouse society has to do with the adoption of white customs and differentiating one's self socially from one's fellows. At the time of fieldwork, many Longhouse people felt that it was wrong for them to have their teeth preserved by the white man's dentists, and they related cases where the gold and silver fillings in the teeth of men and women who had done so turned molten hot in the last hours before death, causing excruciating pain to them. Likewise, the hair of Longhouse women who had permanent waves at the white man's beauty salon was said to turn into stiff wire and pierce their heads in the last hours before death, causing terrible pain. Some women told me that they had actually seen this happen and had heard the women concerned confess this sin in great anguish. It was also a sin to make light of another's dress, not to offer food to visitors, or to refuse to eat food when offered.

One of the principal functions of the conventions for the preaching of the *Gaiwhio*, noted in chapter 1, is the constant identification and underscoring of actions regarded as sin. One principal burden of the *Gaiwhio* is to draw, in terms of fire, a line of demarcation between the white and Iroquois societies. As one young woman put it, "All things that come from the white man are sin for the Indian—cards, liquor, fiddle dances, money. This is what the old people tell us." In addition, the white man's attachment to "worldly things" (*owhędjageka*)—manifest in his greed for land, his ostentation, and his business activities—all involve reprehensible actions preached against in the *Gaiwhio*. Consistently, the white man, worlds without end, can never enter heaven.

Conventions for the recitation of the *Gaiwhio*, lasting four or five days, are held on alternate years at each of the longhouses, or more often, if the people feel the necessity. A portion of the *Gaiwhio* is set forth in the forenoon of each day, and the afternoon is given over to "repentance" (*odatrewa'hdo*). The people are called upon to confess their sins, while holding the longhouse *gadjisdajtgo*, a strand of shell beads that is the sacred symbol of longhouse group identity. Those appointed to conduct this session do not hesitate to single out individuals, and known offenders are exhorted strongly to repent. Many a Longhouse person has felt his society, as it were, reach out through the instrumentality of these conventions and pull him firmly back to his own.

Witchcraft

Despite the fact that witchcraft (*gotgotra*) is denounced in the *Gaiwhio*, it was rife among the Longhouse people at the time of fieldwork.[2] Witches (male or female) are thought to be the embodiment of asociality. They are said to suffer banishment in the hereafter, and to call someone a witch (*gotgoh*) is the only form of invective in their language. In keeping with this appraisal, a person who attempts to introduce innovations deemed to be antithetical to the social system is either branded a witch or, sooner or later, has witchcraft directed against him. Witchcraft is, in this way, an important force for maintaining the system.

The most severe case of witchcraft observed in the field involved the deaths of at least three people, blindness for one, sickness and accidents for several, and the moving of residence of another. In the welter and acrimony of the accusations that surrounded these events, the man and his wife accused seemed to be living quite normal lives. They participated in ceremonial life faithfully, and on the long summer evenings, numbers of men would gather on the grass in front of their house to play croquet.

It was not until the accusations could be seen in the context of their economic activities that any regularity was detected. In every case where the couple had been accused, they had sold, or had attempted to sell, either goods of their own production or those they had obtained outside the reserve to their fellows for a profit. In one instance, they sold a woman a pair of shoes, which caused lameness, eventual disability, and death; in another, they sold a man's suit and hat, which produced blindness in the purchaser. A woman bought a pig's head from them with which to hold a medicine feast and after using it began to vomit blood. One man refused to buy some corn from the couple, accusing them right to their faces of being witches and telling them to "peddle your wares somewhere else." This man died soon afterward of coronary thrombosis, and this intensified the accusations. In yet another instance, the couple traded a man out of his house and land in an exceptionally one-sided deal. In effect, they were attempting to carry on a petty distributive operation for profit. As often as they entered into these transactions, they were accused of being witches.

In the course of time, the man involved suffered an illness causing partial paralysis. This was interpreted by the Longhouse people generally as an indication that the power (otgǫ'h) of his own charms had been "turned back on him" by someone having greater power. In an effort to elude these circumstances, he sold his house and erected a shanty on a plot about half a mile away. The distortion of a system of homogeneous relationships caused by the introduction of vendor-vendee relationships and the profit motive is obvious and is clearly resisted by Longhouse society in this way. All such attempts call into operation machinery for the consolidation of the system.

Jealousy (go'hnosę) is said by the Longhouse people to be the most frequent motive behind witchcraft. Possession of a considerable sum of money, having too good a job, too nice a car, house, clothing, garden, cow, or poultry, all seem to create the expectation of witchcraft in both the possessor and society at large. There is an endless number of cases that illustrate these circumstances. A case in point is that of a man who had received specialized training for his job. During his lifetime he had become almost the epitome of what his social system forbids. He had "soft," steady work with a relatively high level of income, possessed a smart, nearly new automobile, and had built quite an imposing house, which he was furnishing in a manner quite different from his fellows. He also dressed and groomed himself quite distinctively. In addition to this, he set up a provisional shop in his home, where he sold his services to men on the reserve in evenings and on weekends. He manifested a sensitivity to his position. He charged less than half the price for his services on the reserve than he got off the reserve and said of this that he was "not going to take advantage of my brothers just because I have had a chance to learn a skill." He was cautioned by his elder brother to be more careful regarding money and was taunted by his neighbors, especially by one, who told him constantly about witch lights seen on and about his house at night. Along with his wife, he defensively denied this, saying, "It's this witchcraft that I can't believe in. People have told me that they have seen witches [at his place, which he omitted], but I have never seen one, and I have really looked." While denying the efficacy of witchcraft verbally, he consulted a fortuneteller in connection with some "dizzy spells" he was having, and he held certain rites that were to placate charms said by the fortuneteller to have been held by his late father.

This man was killed in an accident shortly after the period of fieldwork. In a letter received from his wife, informing us of his death, she stated, "I never believed in witchcraft. I think I told you that. Well, so many people said this must be . . . that I should get my fortune told. I went to three different people that use different methods. They told the same. Said that this had been done through jealousy. Even went so far as to kill my husband."

Events like this one are both far-reaching and profound in their influence. They usually juxtapose a multitude of events in a causal relationship leading to the final result. They can also bring about a thoroughgoing reorientation in the economic activities of kin, neighbors, and friends of the victim. It was noted in a brief visit to the reservation later, that this man's son, who was following fast on his father's example, had given up a well-paying job and a new automobile, television, electric refrigerator, and other items of furniture, which he was buying on time payment. However, despite his precautions, he too encountered a similar fate to that of his father.

Consistent with the present emphasis on social and economic homogeneity were the means used by longhouse ritual groups to raise the necessary money for their operation. These are bingo games, raffles, field days, and collecting donations (gawhisdaohǫ), which some jokingly refer to as "begging," all of which assure the anonymity of the giver and keep these contributions from being used as a means for establishing status by conspicuous giving.

The Sale of Ritual Objects

Selling one's services to the white man is the principal means of economic sustenance for the Longhouse people and is regarded as a practical necessity. This applies also to the sale of goods that are the product of a handicraft and that have utilitarian value, such as baskets, beaded belts, walking canes, and handles for hammers, axes, and other hand tools.

In a different category is the production and sale of objects related to the ritual system. To traffic in these objects for profit is fraught with dangers. The objects themselves may "turn on" their maker, bringing illness and possible death to him or his family. Neighbors may also observe his operation and become jealous.

Elaborate steps are taken to separate an enterprise of this kind from its context in the traditional system. This is seen in the work of one man who sells carved false-face masks (*hadoii gagǫsa*) to purchasers from Quebec to San Francisco. He explained that, first of all, he does not make the "faces for the white man" from the legendary basswood, but rather of pine. Then, when the mask is completed, he omits the burning of tobacco and a speech telling it who its owner is to be and what it should do for him; neither does he allow it to enter a ceremony. Furthermore, such masks must not be anointed with oil (*o'hna'h*), ashes, or fed their favorite food, a sweetened mush (*wadǫsǫ o'hdjigwah*) made from roasted, ground corn. Another man who sells lacrosse racquets similarly disengages his operation from the "genuine" one.

The objects thus made are clearly intended to be only surrogates. Yet one can never be certain that he has not offended the real object, which offence is readily detected in misfortune or the illness of one's self and family. These rudimentary productive operations again highlight the means by which the Longhouse system keeps in check the activities of its members and maintains its own integrity. Some appreciation of the effectiveness of these sanctions in controlling the economic activities of Longhouse men and women can be gained from the fact that of the twenty-one businesses on the reserve—ranging from a mortuary service, bus line, café, and general store, to a billiards room—all were confined to the Christian sector of the population at the time of fieldwork.

Charms

Charms (*otsinnagǫda'h*), formerly used in hunting and in warfare, also exert a great influence on the homogeneity and continuity of Longhouse Iroquois social order. These charms are possessed by both individuals and lineage groups. That they have always stood for a good deal more in the social life of the Iroquois than their ostensible practical use is suggested by their continuation even after the demise of warfare and the hunting economy. Longhouse informants said that the Seneca prophet *Skanyadaiyo* tried unsuccessfully to abolish them sometime between 1790 and 1815 (see also Parker 1912, 29–30, 114).[3]

Their indestructibility was pointed out by one informant who said, "This is something our forefathers did a long time ago. They got this medicine to use in hunting so they could survive. It was their way of making a living. Now that the game is gone, there is nothing for it to do. The people now can do nothing about it, only try to keep it satisfied. If they don't take care of it, it turns on them; and many times they turn it to evil purposes." There is also a current legend that establishes a precedent for their "getting after" people as well as game. Longhouse people maintain that through their mystical power these charms "turn on" their owners who neglect to amuse them with special songs, dances, and feasts, and also "turn on" those to whom they are directed by their owners, almost, as it were, in self-defense. Invariably, the victims are individuals who have violated accepted social usages and norms. Charms, which at present may actually be lost, still underlie many of the personal medicine and luck rites (ǫdwęnǫgotanǫ) of Longhouse people today. In these ways they bind Longhouse people to their traditional social order.

It should be noted here that the components, such as songs, dances, or other ritual actions, of the various public ceremonies may also be connected with the health, safety, and general well-being of individual members of society, who must, on occasion, have the particular song, dance, or other ritual act carried out on his behalf to insure his physical well-being.

The Ancestors

Perhaps the factor of greatest importance in the continuity of Longhouse society is the relationship between the living and the dead. The dead are felt to stand back of the entire social order. It is often expressed, as it was by one informant, that "it is the dead people who are responsible for what goes on now among the living. Our ancestors from way back cause us to do what we do today." The dead always stand for the correct way of performing rites or executing a jural or moral rule. Their pardon is always begged in speeches connected with ceremonies held for them for any discrepancies or omissions that might have occurred. "Old food" (in the sense of being traditional) such as corn soup and corn bread must be used in these ceremonies, symbolizing the continuity between the past and present social order.

On one occasion, a certain chiefly lineage held an O'hgiwe feast for the dead of their lineage; but rather than carry the rite on through the prescribed way, they abbreviated it. A short time thereafter, the brother of the lineage kogiwe had a stroke, which brought partial paralysis and temporary loss of speech. He attempted to communicate with his sister, but found this impossible until, on one occasion, he discovered he could whistle, whereupon he whistled some of the songs that had been omitted in the recent ceremony for the dead. The group got together and held a second feast, even though it cost between thirty and forty dollars. This time they were careful to adhere to the old rules.

The ancestors are linked in this way with a kind of ideal form of the social order and are the most incontrovertible index of the social identity of the Longhouse people. In 1956 Longhouse marriages came under fire from the provincial government, and at the same time, the chiefs were carrying on court proceedings, seeking to be recognized by the Canadian government as the legal government of the reserve. During this time of crisis, the chiefs met often to carry out very secret and exclusive rites in connection with the dead chiefs, in which (I was told by one of their number) they burned tobacco for their predecessors, asked their support, and feasted them with "old food." Thus, in times of stress, when their social identity was threatened, they sought to insure its continuity by intensifying the bond with their forebears.

Ancestors are felt to have power of life and death over the living. Laxity in moral, ritual, and jural obligations are thought to be punished by them. When the lineage of Deyotowe'hgǫ began to make preparations to raise up a new chief in early 1957, one of the leading men of the group told me that they had been without a chief for three years and felt they would incur the displeasure of their dead if they were to delay further in installing a successor. He and his sister estimated that it had cost them between $150 and $200 to hold the installation ceremony.

There was a woman who had been negligent of her mother prior to, and during, the illness that led to her death in 1956, leaving the burden of her care to her mother's sisters. She also contributed little to her mother's funeral. Before a year had passed, she became ill, and this was interpreted to have been caused by her mother's ghost for the gross breach of proper moral conduct in her relationship with her mother. In a state of deep anxiety, she enlisted the assistance of her mother's sister in order to hold a special feast (o'hdyęhakǫfra) for her mother, the expenses for which, amounting to over forty dollars, she bore herself in an effort to restore her relationship.

When one Cayuga chief was installed, he succeeded also to custody of a set of shell beads (otgǫa'h) used by the Cayuga chiefs in their condolence rites (hadinigǫdanyǫ). In the same year, he sold these to a Toronto museum collector. Some time thereafter, he began to feel that he was being bothered by witches and the dead. He began to wander from place to place, carried bones with bits of meat on them, and sprinkled salt around his bed before retiring at night. He also became "strange in his mind." Several Longhouse people explained that the dead chiefs had "turned on him" in consequence of his disloyalty.

It should be noted that a witch may also "hire the dead" (honawędaǫ ahǫwadinha) to molest people. This is done by burning tobacco and giving them food.

The Fortuneteller

It is important in the present context to say a word about the role of the dehayadoweta ("investigator") or fortuneteller, as he is called in daily parlance. Individuals acting in this role are, generally speaking, of very conservative temperament and are usually ripe in years. It is the dehayadoweta (who may be either a man or woman) who selects the categories in terms of which individual crises are dealt with. What this amounts to is the relating of personal illness, the sickness or death of family, marital troubles, accidents, failure of gardens, death of animals or poultry, and many other misfortunes to the activity of witches, or to the neglect of charms, personal medicine or luck rites, ceremonial obligations, or the ancestors. The causal nexus is invariably felt to be the violation of moral and jural norms of society or the neglect of objects, ceremonies, and beliefs that stand for them.

When a certain man's mother died, he kept her fur coat, thinking to sell it rather than turn it over for the distribution of her personal effects at the ten-day feast. When he began to wane shortly thereafter, he went to a white doctor who found nothing wrong with him. A dehayadoweta told him that his illness was due to the displeasure of his late mother, which was connected with his violation of the rule for the distribution of her personal effects. He was advised to hold a second feast, which he did, whereupon he regained his strength.

I have seen people shot through with fear and anxiety after a consultation with a dehayadoweta; and conversely, I have seen existing anxieties vanish almost immediately. There can be little doubt as to their ability to direct the course of the social life of the Longhouse people. The important point here is that they drive home the fact that the troubled person can only get relief in his crisis by conforming to the accepted moral and jural norms and ritual usages of Longhouse society. In carrying out their prescriptions, a person intensifies his bonds with the Indigenous system. The chiefs, and old people generally, have a kindred influence in directing the activities of the people, however their counsel lacks the specific sanctions of that of the dehayadoweta.

According to the hypothesis advanced by Professors Fortes and Evans-Pritchard (Fortes and Evans-Pritchard 1940, 16–22; Fortes 1949a, 344–47), ritual objects and actions, myths, ceremonies, beliefs, and ancestors stand ultimately for the moral and jural norms upon which the social order of a given society rests. That this is so for Longhouse society can be inferred from the empirical data given above, which show that the violation of the moral and jural norms that underlie the social life of the Longhouse people arouse the displeasure of charms, ancestors, and other supernaturals. Through their mystical power over the physical well-being of individuals and groups, they bind them to the social order for which they stand.

In discussing the importance of medicine rites and feasts for the dead for the Longhouse people, one woman said, "When they get after a person, if he doesn't put up the proper ceremony right away, he will just die, that is all. We have seen it happen! It is the same with the dead people. That's why we can't let our religion go; we've got to keep these things up. Perhaps if the people in Ottawa could have explained to them what our beliefs are, they wouldn't try to force us to give them up. That's what [white] people just don't seem to understand." Little wonder that they equate the demise of their system with the end of the world.

The importance of such mechanisms as these in maintaining intact the social order of societies without centralized governmental institutions is apparent. However, for Longhouse society, their importance is further enhanced by its present de facto political position and the constant threat to its integrity posed by white society and culture generally. This great structural importance of ritual institutions is also one of the most significant factors in the continued viability of offices within the lineage, some of the most important duties of which are connected with ceremonial affairs.

The aggregate of rights, duties, and sentiments thus maintained by the mechanisms described above are those arising out of kinship and working through the matrilineal descent system of Longhouse society. What this comes down to is that under present circumstances, kinship continues as the basic structural factor in Longhouse society and appears ultimately to take precedence over principles of achievement, such as economic wealth and occupational specialization. Inadequate as this statement is, it gives some idea of the intricate way in which Longhouse society is organized to meet present-day exigencies and how, in perpetuating itself, it perpetuates the marginality of the husband-father in the household—first by maintaining the matrilineal descent system and then, in the process, by preventing him from exploiting the full range of possibilities inherent in his present position. Longhouse society seems to sense that as long as the hearts of the mothers are turned to their children and those of the children are turned to their mothers, their system can endure.

The use of numerical data to elucidate such aspects of household structure as the gender and age of household heads and the generation depth and genealogical composition of the group, as well as such matters as the age and conjugal status of men and women in Longhouse society, was helpful in identifying the polar forces that underlie household structure and its development in time. The consideration given to the economic roles of men and women and the analysis of the jural content of the relationships that make up the group, and the above brief discussion of other limiting factors arising in the external system, have provided an explanation of the relative strength of matrilineal descent and the maternal bond, on the one hand, and paternal and conjugal ties, on the other, in determining household structure and the course of its development in time.

Professor Fortes's statement (1949b, 84) that "structure appears as an arrangement of parts brought about by the operation through a period of time of principles of social organization which have general validity in a particular society" is amply validated for the structure of Longhouse Iroquois households on the Six Nations Reserve.

Afterword

M. Sam Cronk

Nearly fifty years have passed since Merlin Myers began fieldwork at the Six Nations Grand River Territory. His ethnographic research on Hodinǫhsǫ:nı́ social organization, demographics, household structures, and naming practices is little known within the academy, and perhaps even less so at Six Nations. Myers's research is part of a unique body of anthropological and historical literature that has documented the lives, languages, and histories of this singular community for more than 170 years. Hundreds of academic publications and more than a dozen dissertations have analyzed various aspects of life on the reserve, drawing on the expertise and generosity of a relatively small group of Longhouse people for information, analyses, and friendship.

Although patterns and structures of social relationships have been constant tropes in the canon of Iroquoianist literature, few published works in the twentieth century assess clan and lineage in detail at Six Nations. Substantive genealogies developed by Annemarie Shimony have been used extensively by the hereditary Grand Council of the Confederacy to select clan mothers and chiefs; much of her research was intended for community use. More recently, Mohawk historian and philosopher Deborah Jean Doxtator completed a groundbreaking work as her dissertation at the University of Western Ontario, "What happened to the Iroquois Clans? A Study of Clans in Three Nineteenth-Century Rotinonhsyonni Communities" (1997). Unfortunately, she passed away before revising her research for publication. It is significant, then, that Myers's text (among others) comes to light.

One of the strengths of Myers's work is its wealth of detail. The myriad of household facts and figures that form the basis of his analyses are otherwise missing from the Iroquoianist literature; this information cannot be culled easily (if at all) from extant census records or similar documents. Cayuga concepts about family relationships and cultural practice integrated throughout his text are also valuable, as is the understated narrative of reciprocity and exchange among the Myers' and their Hodinǫhsǫ:ní hosts. The history of this complex, century-old network of relationships among anthropologists and ǫgwehǫweh at Six Nations has yet to be adequately addressed in any publication.[1]

Mohawk anthropologist Audra Simpson has observed that "anthropology tells us as much about academics and their times as it does about the subject under study" (Simpson 2000, 1). Not surprisingly, the discipline of anthropology has changed profoundly since Myers's research in 1958. Although many fundamental principles endure, the impact of Cultural Studies, Gender Studies, Marxism, Postcolonialism and Postmodernism, reflexive practice, and hegemonic praxis, has indelibly shaped anthropological discourse, as well as our critical assessment of earlier research.

Response to anthropologists' work by the Hodinǫhsǫ:ní has also changed. There is far greater control now exerted by both the hereditary council and the elected band council as to the nature of research conducted at Six Nations. Most Longhouse ceremonies are now closed to non-Native people in at least seven Iroquoian communities. In direct response to often unwelcome scholarly inquiry, the study of ceremonial masks, songs, and speeches associated with traditional curing societies has been proscribed by the hereditary council in both Canada and the United States. A statement issued by Tadodá:ho' in 1995 explains this decision.

> The non-Indian public does not have the right to examine, interpret, or present the beliefs, functions, and duties of the secret medicine societies of the Hodinǫhsǫ:ní. The sovereign responsibility of the Hodinǫhsǫ:ní over their spiritual duties must be respected by the removal of all medicine masks from exhibition and from access to non-Indians. [Grand Council 1995]

At the same time, several generations of First Nations scholarship have emerged. Hodinǫhsǫ:ní anthropologists, historians, and linguists such as Simpson, Doxtator, Reginald Henry, Amos Keye, Frances Froman, Lottie Keye, Alfred Keye, John Mohawk, Christopher Jocks, Sue Hill, David Maracle, and Gerald Alfred, among others, have reshaped the landscape of Canadian ethnohistory and anthropology.

Of course, the community at Six Nations has also changed. Language fluency has decreased dramatically, although significant measures are now in place to reverse this loss. Subsequent occupational and educational opportunities have affected household structures. Federal regulations, such as Bill c-31, which in 1985 removed key discriminatory practices in Canada's Indian Act, altered the legal definition of who is—or is not—an "Indian."[2]

One of the most profound events for Canadian Iroquoian communities took place at Oka, Quebec, during the summer of 1990. Confrontation erupted when Mohawks at Kanesatake (Oka) tried to block the expansion of a non-Native golf course on their traditional burial grounds. When Quebec police attempted to remove the blockade, a member of the Sureté was killed. This began a seventy-seven-day armed siege known as the Oka Crisis (Pertusati 1997). The Canadian army surrounded Kanesatake. The nearby Mohawk community of Kahnawake blockaded highways and bridges into Montreal as Canadians watched the spectacle of Québécois burning effigies of Mohawk warriors on the nightly news. In support, members of the Longhouse community at Six Nations blockaded roads along the Grand River; similar blockades took place across the country. The Canadian flag was removed from many of the public buildings at Six Nations and other settlements—a significant gesture. Since that date, the sense of autonomy and self-determination of Six Nations as an independent nation-state has been clearly and vigorously expressed in diverse political and cultural forums. Relationships with the Canadian government, with academic institutions, and with non-Native academics have been redefined by the Hodinǫhsǫ:ní according to the concept of the Two Row Wampum: as partnerships, ensuring access to and control of Iroquoian resources by their communities.

Community Profile: Six Nations Grand River Territory in 2002

Six Nations is an integral part of the contemporary Hodinǫhsǫ:ní Confederacy, one of eighteen Iroquoian settlements located in Wisconsin, Oklahoma, New York, Ontario, and Quebec. It is now the largest reservation in Canada with approximately 20,000 band members. At least 9,500 live on the 45,000-acre settlement, with an additional 10,500 band members "on the list." Approximately 30 percent of the community is under the age of twenty-eight, according to the Six Nations Tourism office. First Nations business, cultural, and political organizations connect this dynamic community to other Indigenous groups throughout Canada and the United States.

Many belong to one of the Baptist, Anglican, or Protestant churches at Grand River, but perhaps five thousand people identify themselves as "Longhouse." They follow the Great Law of Peace and the Gaihwi:yo:, the Good Message of Seneca prophet Handsome Lake, and taking part in calendric ceremonies held at the four Longhouses at Six Nations and at other Hodinǫhsǫ:ní settlements.

The traditional hereditary council of chiefs and clanmothers exists along-side an elected band council, a structure recognized by the Canadian federal government. The administration consists of twelve councilors and a chief councilor, elected biannually. Although the organization and modes of oper-ation of these two governing bodies differ considerably, they have common goals: the recognition of First Nations autonomy and the cultural and eco-nomic viability of the Grand River Territory.

The village of Ohsweken is the administrative hub of Grand River Territory, featuring a library, an arena and other sports facilities, men's and women's shelters, medical and birthing facilities, a seniors' residence, band council offices, a land claims office, a bank, and a business plaza. More than three hundred local businesses are owned and operated by community residents, including a tourism facility, gas stations and repair shops, restaurants, internet providers and multimedia design firms, art galleries, plant nurseries, and clothing stores.

Just north of Ohsweken on Chiefswood Road is the Ohsweken Motor Speed-way. Nearby is Chiefswood, a historic site and the homestead of Mohawk poet E. Pauline Johnson. Across the roadway is Chiefswood Park, site of the annual Champion of Champions Powwow, which brings together Indigenous dancers and drummers from across North America the third weekend each July.

A locally owned news weekly, *Tekawennake News*, has been published at Six Nations for more than twenty-five years. In 1987 the Aboriginal Communi-cation Society—with members from both Six Nations and the adjacent New Credit Missisauga Reservation—launched a local radio station, CKRZ 100.3 FM, "The Voice of the Grand," which broadcasts eighteen hours each day. With its mix of local news, popular music, and Indigenous programming (includ-ing the ever-popular "Mohawk Bingo" and traditional music show "Gayowah 101"), CKRZ is designed to foster greater self-awareness among ǫgwehǫweh and to encourage Iroquoian and Algonquian language and cultural retention.

Language preservation is an urgent concern for Longhouse people. Less than 4 percent of ǫgwehǫweh at Grand River are now fluent in an Iroquoian language, and Delaware and Tutelo are no longer spoken there; most fluent speakers are over sixty years old. The loss of an original language profoundly affects every aspect of Indigenous traditional identity and culture. It represents a loss of connectedness not only within the nuclear family but also with the physical and spiritual environments to which they belong. According to the prophecies of Handsome Lake, it also foreshadows the destruction of the earth.

At Six Nations, there are now seven schools, including two new immersion programs providing instruction in either Cayuga or Mohawk language from kindergarten through grade 12. Additionally, the Six Nations Polytechnic Institute, a community-based development center, offers university-accredited courses in both Cayuga and Mohawk as well as bachelor's degrees in education and certification in health sciences, computer systems, and early childhood education. As with the immersion programs, the goal is to address local issues and needs from Indigenous perspectives.

Among several technological organizations promoting cultural retention is Ohwejagehka: Ha'degænage, a nonprofit organization established to help preserve and nurture Iroquoian languages and songs. State-of-the-art digital recording technologies are used to document traditional events, while online resources offer immediate access within the community to significant cultural materials.

Located in the nearby city of Brantford, Ontario, the Woodland Cultural Centre is another dynamic facility, highlighting exhibits of First Nations art and culture. The Centre's language program has developed standardized Mohawk, Onondaga, and Cayuga orthographies, created multimedia dictionaries, promoted numerous conferences and workshops on language and culture, and has documented every Longhouse speech and ceremony for community use and study. Merlin Myers's work—texts and photographs—could prove a welcome addition to their resources.

Notes

1. Qgwehạweh is a Cayuga word that translates as "real, or first, people"; it is one of many ways of referring to the Indigenous people of North America.

2. Bill C-31 sought to abolish a discriminatory practice of enfranchisement that had been in effect since the original Indian Act of 1867. Thousands of descendants of enfranchised men and women regained their status, joining the band roles at Six Nations and other reservations across Canada.

References

Alfred, Gerald R. 1995. Heeding the Voices of Our Ancestors: Kahnawake Mohawk Politics and the Rise of Native Nationalism. Toronto: Oxford University Press.

Bilharz, Joy. 1998. The Allegany Senecas and the Kinzua Dam. Lincoln: University of Nebraska Press.

Doxtator, Deborah Jean. 1997. "What Happened to the Iroquois Clans? A Study of Clans in Three Nineteenth Century Rotinonhsyonni Communities." PhD diss., University of Western Ontario.

————. 2001. "Inclusive and Exclusive Perceptions of Difference: Native and Euro-Based Concepts of Time, History, and Change." In *Decentering the Renaissance*, ed. Germain Warkentin and Carolyn Podruchny, 33–47. Toronto: University of Toronto Press.

Foster, Michael K. 1974. *From the Earth to Beyond the Sky: An Ethnographic Approach to Four Longhouse Speech Events*. Canadian Ethnology Service Paper no. 20. Ottawa: National Museums of Canada.

Grand Council of the Six Nations. 1995. *Policy Statement on the Use of Medicine Society Masks*.

Jocks, Christopher. 1994. "Relationship Structures in Longhouse Tradition at Kahnawa:ke." PhD diss., University of California, Santa Barbara.

Johnston, Charles M. 1964. *The Valley of the Six Nations: A Collection of Documents on the Indian Lands of the Grand River*. Toronto: University of Toronto Press.

Landsman, Gail H., and Sara Cibroski. 1993. "Representation and Politics: Contesting Histories of the Iroquois." *Cultural Anthropology* 7(4):425–47.

McNab, David T., ed. 1998. *Earth, Water, Air, and Fire: Studies in Canadian Ethnohistory*. Waterloo, Ontario: Wilfrid Laurier University Press.

Pertusati, Linda. 1997. *In Defense of Mohawk Land: Ethnopolitical Conflict in Native North America*. SUNY Series in Ethnicity and Race in American Life. Albany: State University of New York Press.

Rogers, Edward S., and Donald B. Smith, eds. 1994. *Aboriginal Ontario: Historical Perspectives on the First Nations*. Toronto: Dunburn Press.

Simpson, Audra. 2000. *Making a Tradition of the Past: Ely S. Parker, Lewis Henry Morgan, and the Writing of Iroquois Confederacy*. Unpublished ms.

Weaver, Sally. 1978. "Six Nations at Grand River." In *Handbook of North American Indians*, William C. Sturtevant, gen. ed., vol. 15, Northeast, ed. Bruce Trigger, 525–36. Washington: Smithsonian Institution.

Notes

1. The Tuscarora tribe joined the original five tribes, or "nations," in about 1714 (Beauchamp 1905, 148), after which they were known as the "Six Nations." The reserve takes its name from the fact that groups from all six tribes settled there. It is also designated "Grand River Reserve" in the literature.

2. More complete accounts may be found in the following works: Colden 1747; Stone 1838, 2 vols.; Morgan 1851, book 1, chap. 1; Beauchamp 1905; Wraxall 1915.

3. The issues involved leading to the establishment of a specialized agency for dealing with Indian affairs are discussed in Wraxall (1915), and an opposing view is set forth by Colden (1747).

4. The difficulties encountered by the Six Nations people in their effort to gain recognition of their claim to perfect title to the land of the Haldimand Grant are discussed by the following writers: Stone 1838, vol. 1, 397–427, appendix xxxix–xliii; Dunham 1945, 170–71; Noon 1949, 85–88. Since the rights of the members of the Six Nations people in the land of their reserve continue to be defined by the Simcoe deed, it will be helpful to give relevant excerpts here. The deed states that " . . . for the purpose of assuring the said lands [as defined in the Haldimand Grant] to the said Chiefs, warriors, women and people of the Six Nations, and their heirs and securing to them the free and undisturbed possession and enjoyment of the same, it is our royal will and pleasure that no transfer, alienation, conveyance, sale, gift, exchange, lease, property or possession shall at any time be had, made or given of the same district or territory, or any part or parcel thereof, by any of the said Chiefs, warriors, women or people, person or persons whatsoever, other than amongst themselves . . . but that any such transfer, alienation . . . [etc.] be null and void and of no effect whatever, and that no person or persons shall possess or occupy the said district or territory or any parcel thereof, by or under any pretense or any such alienation, title or conveyance, as aforesaid, or by or under any pretense whatever . . . that if at any time the said Chiefs, warriors, women . . . [etc.] of the Six Nations should be inclined to dispose of and surrender their use and interest in the said district or territory or any part thereof, the same shall be purchased by us, our heirs, and successors, at some public meeting or assembly, of the Chiefs, warriors, women . . . [etc.] of the Six Nations . . ."

5. Tribal distinctions are not of great consequence in the social life of the people at present. The Indian Office arranges reserve members on its band or membership lists according to tribes, and members of the Cayuga tribe receive annuity payments; however, tribal identity for these purposes has been determined patrifilially according to Canadian law since 1868 (Indian Act, sec. 11). The hereditary chiefs still sit by tribe in their councils, and certain lineage chief titles

are recognized as belonging to matrilineages of a certain tribe. There are, on the other hand, no occasions when a tribe meets as a separate and exclusive body.

6. Nearby Brantford was a terminus for the Underground Railroad during the slavery period in the United States. After reaching Brantford, runaway slaves often drifted out among Indians in the area. The census of 1880 (Warner, Beers and Co. 1883, 490) lists nineteen Africans in Tuscarora Township, the principal area covered by the reserve, as well as numerous Europeans.

7. The lack of institutional ties between the two groups would appear to have been further demonstrated in March 1959, when a group of Longhouse "warriors" sought forcibly to oust the elective council from the council house at Ohsweken and restore the hereditary chiefs to power. They were later driven from the council house by a contingent of Royal Canadian Mounted Police armed with truncheons and loud speakers.

8. Dominion Bureau of Statistics, "Agricultural Census" (Ottawa 1921, 1931, 1941, 1951).

9. Longhouse people do not admit to being without recourse before the Canadian government. In discussing prevailing circumstances with a Longhouse friend who is a chief and leader among his people, he suddenly and very candidly asked, "Do you know where our power is? It is in the tobacco. We can burn tobacco, and in the prayer that we say while it is burning, we can cause almost anything to happen, even destroy whole cities." After citing instances of its use against the Americans in the War of 1812, he went on to say, "We still have this today and can use it if we choose to. It is out of mercy that we don't use it." Young men sometimes ask the old chiefs to use this power and settle their problems once and for all, to which the chiefs counsel patience and add the censure that only white men would thus be so ruthless and uncivilized! Their tobacco (oyę'hgwaowe) is, for the Longhouse people, a vehicle of communication between themselves and all forces and agencies in the supernatural world. It is thought to have a compelling power (ǫgwayada gęnhafra) over all supernatural entities, by which they may be brought into the service of the Longhouse people. Consistent with this is the reference to Church people as those who have "thrown their tobacco over the fence" that separates Indians from white people.

10. When viewed objectively, the reserve has economic advantages in the sense that its lands are tax free, that the purchase price of possessory rights to land is very low, and that rental charges are almost nonexistent among the Longhouse people; but they seldom think of their relationship to the land of the reserve in these terms. Several Longhouse people suggested to me that I might live on their land as long as I should like, and even offered to help me build a house.

11. According to Hewitt (1902), the Iroquois understand orenda to be a supernatural force present in all persons or objects and represents the spiritual force accounting for all human accomplishments.

2. The Household

1. Longhouse people include both witchcraft and sorcery in the term gotgǫtra. The word has its root in the word for caul (gotgǫhsǫ), and persons born with a caul are thought to be true witches. By far the greater part of the activity designated by the word gotgǫtra is sorcery, in the technical sense of a person directing the power (otgǫ'h) of charms against other persons with the intent to do injury.

3. Some Economic Features of the Household Group

1. See also Speck, 26–27.

2. Nevertheless, women who are unable to conceive may go to great lengths to bear children. One young woman stoically submitted to drinking the warm blood of a freshly killed deer, after all other fertility methods known to her had failed.

3. It is relevant also to note here that some women possess a knowledge of "bad medicine" (onǫ'hgwatra'hetgę'h) with which to cause abortions. Statistics are difficult to come by in such cases, though one hears of women making a meal to feed the spirits of fetal children buried in the "back yard." It was also said that women sometimes confess at the Handsome Lake Code Convention (Gaiwhio odakhaohasǫ) that they have used such medicine, but I did not personally hear such a confession.

4. During the summer 1957, one of the hereditary chiefs received an offer from a civic official in the state of Virginia, U.S.A., in which a local government proposed to pay the chief a generous sum of money if he would bring a group of his people to the town and there perform a reburial of some bones that had been discovered when an ancient grave site had been accidentally excavated. In a letter refusing the offer, the chief stated that the presence of the spirits of the dead would surely bring a frost that would destroy the crops in the surrounding area. He made a counter offer suggesting that the occasion be postponed until November, at which time he would be happy to come.

5. It is estimated from the census data that drinking limits the value of male earnings for over 50 percent of the households. In about half of these the limitation is quite severe, and in the other half it is considerable.

6. The "law of hospitality" described for the Iroquois by L. H. Morgan (1881, 45–47) is still operative. The aspect of the law most stressed at present is that of giving offence by not accepting hospitality when it is proffered. In this sense, it becomes a test of the nature and degree of homogeneity actually obtaining within the society.

7. An estimate of the level of income of Longhouse men can be had by comparing the figures in table 7 with salaries of schoolteachers in the Province of Ontario, which ranged from $2,400 to 3,000 for beginners to $4,800 with seniority during the period of fieldwork.

8. This is the only instance known to me of a Longhouse person's holding a life insurance policy, and it was probably purchased at the behest of his creditors as surety against possible default in payment by death.

4. Composition of the Household Group

No notes.

5. Some Politico-Jural and Ritual Aspects of Matrilineal Descent

1. It was noted in the field that younger informants were usually not familiar with this explanation. Correlated with it, however, is the belief that somatic defects follow the agnatic line and that children born of unions contracted within the lineage may be born without bones. This topic requires further exploration.

2. The term o'hwhadjiʌ is also used at present to designate the unit of a conjugal pair and their children. All informants agreed, however, that technically the father does not belong to one's o'hwadjiʌ (tęhdehayada'h sęgawhadjiade—he is not part of the family), since family line (o'hwhadjiadade) is equated with bloodline (otgwęsadagyeh). O'hwhadjiagwęnio (main family) and gaiwhadjiya gwagǫ (entire lineage) are also used to designate one's lineage when greater precision is required. ǫgwanǫskǫ ǫgwadęnǫksǫ (the relatives in one house) may also be used to distinguish the members of the nuclear family.

3. Since the deposition of the hereditary chiefs in 1924, and the subsequent general loss of interest in chiefship by Christian Iroquois, the endeavor to maintain the overall traditional structure has been largely confined to Longhouse society. This is clearly indicated in cases of succession to various chief titles, and two cases of reassignment of the type described above occurred during the period of fieldwork.

4. The census data collected in the field show that about one-fourth of all the members of Longhouse society fall into this category, although matrilineal descent clearly dominates the overall structural form of society. There are cases where wives from outside the reserve have been given place on their husbands' "side" of the dual division; yet the children of these women conform to the matrilineal rule, and lineage groups have formed around these women in some instances.

5. Although these bear tribal names, tribal diffusion has become common throughout the reserve, and this is reflected in the fact that Longhouse persons of mixed tribal identity attend and officiate in all longhouses.

6. This is the unit Morgan designates by the term *gens* (compare Morgan 1878, part 2, chapter 2).

7. Although several writers have studied Iroquois names, their full jural significance has not been described (Morgan 1878, 78–80; Goldenweiser 1912, 469–70; Cooke 1952). The system of names was originally, and is primarily still, a lineage phenomenon. However, in the case of members of Longhouse society who have no organized lineage and in the case of some fragmented lineage groups, names are bestowed by the next most inclusive segment, the "sides" of the dual organization of the longhouse ritual group, which have "keepers of names" for this purpose.

8. Goldenweiser (1913, 367) collected some names when the generation distinction was still recognized. A few older people at the time of fieldwork remembered the custom of changing the names of the individual at successive stages in his or her life; for example, the bestowal of a child's name in infancy, an adult name at puberty, and yet another upon reaching old age. The demise of this custom appears to be related to the expansion of the sphere of activity of the domestic domain, where generation differences are more patent, against that of the lineage domain. This, in turn, is related to changes in the economic and social environment and to the demise of warfare.

9. The nature of lineage loyalty can be appreciated when it is realized that the chief involved in bestowing the name had lived off and on in a common-law relationship with Lucile, who remarked about their relationship, "I suppose you could call him my boyfriend."

10. Some years later this case was resolved. Prior to her death, Opal advised Amanda to return to her biological lineage in order to assure harmonious relationships with members of her adoptive lineage. Although she understood Opal's desire to spare her from possible future discord, Amanda was bound by love and loyalty to her adoptive mother and lineage. It was with considerable reluctance and regret that she complied with Opal's counsel, thereafter receiving names for her grandchildren from the set belonging to her biological lineage and ultimately becoming head female faithkeeper for its appropriate longhouse moiety.

11. For a description of the installation ceremony, see Morgan (1851, 114–25), Beauchamp (1907), and Fenton (1946).

12. I was brought rather abruptly to a realization of these rights of the lineage in funeral matters. Shortly after arriving in the field, I sought to attend the "ten-day feast" (hęswasǫdahe) held for a man of the lineage of Dyǫhyǫgo. I had met the deceased's wife, who was friendly, and on the day of the ceremony, I joined a party of chiefs (several of whom also were sympathetic to my attendance), who were on their way to perform the condolence rite. However, I had not reckoned with the lineage. Upon arriving at the house, all seemed to be clear for my attendance, when the lineage goyane'h appeared and informed me that this was "a sacred affair of her family" and that I would not be permitted to enter. The deceased's wife and the chiefs were powerless to intercede.

13. See Fenton and Kurath (1951) for a description of this rite.

14. The term most often used at present for father's sister is knohaʌ. The term agadǫni may also be applied to her, and it is this latter term that is the basis for the usage described here.

15. See also Speck (20–29).

6. Kinship and Marriage

1. These circumstances tend to confirm the point made by Fortes (1959b, 207).
2. For details of the rite, see Speck (122–23).
3. It is possible that marriage with agnatic kinsmen was restricted in the past, as was told Goldenweiser by one of his informants (unpublished mss. in the possession of W. N. Fenton). Genealogies I collected suggest that marriages between the descendants of two brothers of any degree of nearness or remoteness seldom occur, but I did not discover a rule to this effect.
4. Morgan (1851, 91) noted the value of paternal kinship in establishing a field of relationship outside the lineage (tribe) and as an important factor of integration and solidarity at the more inclusive tribal (national) level. Another factor that serves these same ends at present is the custom of "ceremonial friendship" (honatsi). Ostensibly for therapeutic purposes, two people of either gender (not members of the same lineage) are ritually linked in a bond of "friendship." They exchange gifts; hold a special medicine rite together each year; have special moral duties and obligations to each other; assume each other's own kinship ties, adopting the appropriate terminology; and upon the death of either, the bond is ritually terminated. At the time of fieldwork, such bonds united Longhouse people from a number of separate reservations. There were Longhouse people on Six Nations Reserve who made use of these ties to compensate their having no fixed abode, moving for a period from one set of these ties to another.
5. Much of Morgan's characterization of the father-child relationship remains valid (see Morgan 1851, 325–27).
6. See glossary for translation variations.
7. While mother-daughter and sister bonds are preeminent, it has become clear over the course of time since fieldwork that some women form other close female friendship ties as well. These may be with an associate worker in the longhouse, or a fellow employee, or, when living away from the reserve, an unrelated Six Nations woman having similar life experiences, and so on.
8. There are cases among the older members of Longhouse society where men have raised their sister's children and where a man's loyalty to his sister and her children has been the cause for conjugal separation.
9. This interpretation follows that given by Smith (1956, 143) of a similar set of circumstances in his British Guiana material.
10. In pre-reservation times, land was female property and passed from a woman to her daughters. In addition, title to all lineage offices was and is vested in the women of the group, as are rights over lineage women. These factors, even in traditional times, would have made of the mother's brother–sister's children relationship something less onerous than that which has been reported of matrilineal people like the Ashanti (Fortes 1950, 272). After the reservation period, when land became associated with male activities, the Canadian government established the rules for the descent of property. This weighted the paternal bond against that with the mother's brother, and the individualization of economic activities has nearly excluded the mother's brother's influence in his sister's household altogether.
11. The extension by both federal and provincial governments of social security legislation benefits, such as Mothers' Allowances, Unemployment Insurance, Workman's Compensation, and Veterans' Pensions to Indians, the amount of and the eligibility for which varies with marital status, has increased the need for more precise vital statistics. In 1956 the Ontario provincial government passed legislation bringing Longhouse marriages directly under their licensing system and also requiring the registration of the Longhouse officials designated to perform marriages, declaring at the same time all Longhouse marriages performed after July 1, 1956, to be illegal and the children born thereto as illegitimate unless the above requirements

were complied with. Longhouse chiefs agreed to submit statistical information to the federal government, but adamantly refused to register their officers with the provincial government or to use the latter's marriage licenses (even though the province offered to supply them free of charge), arguing that the conduct of their marriages was their own affair and that compliance would jeopardize their own sovereignty. Some Longhouse people, however, took the precaution of being married a second time by provincial justices of the peace.

In December of 1956, a young man who had recently been married in a Longhouse ceremony was accidentally killed at his work in a nearby stone quarry. When his wife sought to claim his job insurance, her claim was rejected on the grounds that her marriage was not legal. The chiefs, with the help of a Toronto lawyer, made this a test case, in which it was upheld that the province had no right to pass special legislation respecting Indians. The Ontario law was repealed and Longhouse marriages were thus permitted to continue.

12. This is connected with the contribution thought to be made by the father in the procreative process.

13. In former times, upon marriage, the acquisition of these rights by a woman was symbolized by the presentation to the bride's lineage by the groom of presents of skins and meat. According to Stites (1905, 87–95), during the first year of marriage, the wife had the right to all the produce of her husband's hunting, thereafter, however, he was obliged only to share it with her. In return, a woman was required to carry fixed quantities of firewood to her mother-in-law and assist her in her fields at fixed intervals throughout the year. Although her husband could take a *femme de campagne* on a hunting expedition while his wife remained at home, this woman had no claim on either the skins or meat taken and could be dispossessed by the legal wife upon the return to the village.

14. In former times, if it were desirable to continue the affinal tie, another spouse was put in the deceased's place after a period of mourning of one year. If at the ten-day feast the survivor heard the words *ghǫwadyęnawat* ("they are going to keep him") spoken, he or she would know that the relationship was to be continued. This rite is called *sahǫwędrǫhʌs* ("to put another in his place"). During the interim, the surviving spouse had a claim on the deceased spouse's lineage for economic support or domestic services. If the affinal ties were terminated at the end of the year's time, this claim ceased. There were offspring of such marriages on the reserve at the time of fieldwork, but the practice has been discontinued.

7. Summary and Conclusion

1. The interest of the women of this group in the children of its female members was demonstrated on one occasion when my wife and I were present in a household where a young woman had returned only a few days before from the hospital with her newly born baby. Several members of a matri-sublineage were also present, some of whom were classificatory grandmothers to the child. The women sat reminiscing experiences with their own and each other's children and admiring the new babe, when a health nurse from the hospital came to examine the child and to begin its immunization. (Some Longhouse households did not permit this.) The nurse, in a very authoritarian and forceful manner, began to perform her duties, when, with the exception of the child's own mother, the women of the sublineage arose and left the room in a group, using the principle of avoidance in this ad hoc manner when their own relationship to the child was thus challenged.

2. See the footnote in chapter 2 for the connotation of the term *gotgǫtra* in Longhouse society.

3. It is of interest to note here that silver coins and whisky are reckoned to be the most effective counteractors of all types of Native medicine, including those of witch or sorcerer. Only one

means was heard of by which an *otsinnagęda'h* could be rendered innocuous, and that was by taking it to a lonely spot in the swampy part of the bush and there carrying out the rite over it, which ends with the burial of the charm together with a silver coin. For the *Qgwehǫwe* silver coins and whisky have deep relational significance, and their use as counteracting agents probably reflects a very profound and general feeling of the incompatibility of the two systems of their present world—the substance of the one nullifying the substance of the other.

Glossary and Pronunciation Key

This glossary utilizes orthographies from three sources and is intended to represent variety existing in pronunciation and interpretation among Cayuga-speaking peoples at Six Nations Reserve. It features the work of Lorna Hill, a team of Six Nations linguists and teachers, and the *English-Cayuga/Cayuga-English Dictionary* (2002).

Lorna Hill is a Cayuga language teacher, a language consultant for linguistic anthropologist Michael Foster, the head female faithkeeper of the Wolf moiety at Sour Springs Longhouse, and serves, along with her son, Samuel Thomas, as a representative of Iroquois people at the Indigenous People's World Forum. She provided invaluable service editing Merlin's translations, as well as editing and converting his phonetic script, sometimes altering tense or gender to fit the flow of the text, and locating typographical and other errors. I have elected to use her orthography in the body of the text, both to pay tribute to her for the great service she rendered Merlin as his language teacher during fieldwork and to provide a voice for Cayuga speakers in the upper, Sour Springs area. (It should be noted, however, that spellings in the text that do not conform to Hill's orthography are those utilized by other authors.) Her spelling is based on the modified phonetic system she developed during her fifteen-year assignment by the Board of Education in the Niagara Falls, Ontario, school system to teach Cayuga language under the auspices of a federally funded program, during which time she received her Native Language Teacher's degree. In this glossary her spellings appear first in each entry, followed by the Six Nations version in parentheses (see example below).

The linguistic team at Six Nations transcribed (often closely, sometimes loosely) Merlin's phonetic script into the spelling system devised initially in the early 1980s by the late Reginald Henry, linguist and head male faithkeeper of the Deer moiety at Seneca Longhouse, which is now used by teachers in the Six Nations Cayuga immersion school. It is a somewhat more analytical phonetic system, representing Lower Cayuga pronunciation. I have elected to use it in this glossary, as a counterpart to the Hill orthography. These spellings appear in parentheses immediately following the Hill version. Example: *gowęna* (*gawę́:na'*) her word. A few entries were not included in the team's working copy of the text and consequently have no analytical counterpart.

The *English-Cayuga/Cayuga-English Dictionary* is also based on the Henry phonetic orthography, and all Cayuga-speaking consultants are from the Lower Cayuga area (xii). Therefore, where there is a one-to-one, or quite similar, correspondence to the Hill entry in either spelling or meaning, I have used the dictionary spelling and meaning for the analytical counterpart rather than the Six Nations team spelling only. Example: *haknęnhǫs* (hakné:nhǫ:s—my father-in-law) (m.s.) my father-in-law.

Where both Merlin's and Lorna's meanings coincide, only one meaning is given; where they vary slightly in expression or differ markedly, both meanings are given, Merlin's appearing as number one and Lorna's number two. Example: *godiyanesǫ* (*godiyanǫ̜sho'*) 1. lineage matrons 2. the matriarchs; clan mothers holding chief titles.

Lorna identifies nasalization of four vowels, <ą>, <ę>, <į>, and <ǫ>; prefers the use of <wh> as in English, <u>wh</u>at, rather than the phonetic <hw>; expresses elongated vowels by doubling them, such as *kegęę'h* (my younger sister); similarly doubles consonants to express elongation where this is detectible, as in the personal name *Kaiawass*; uses the Upper Cayuga sound combination <ʄr>, as in *odihgrǫfra* (shyness), rather than the Lower Cayuga <sr>, *adî'grǫhsra'*; uses the symbol <ʃ> for the sound of <sh> as in <u>sh</u>ow; makes use of the phonetic <ʌ> for the sound of <u>, as in <u>up</u>; and uses the phonetic combination <dj> rather than <j>. As in English texts, Lorna does not indicate accented vowels or syllabification. The Six Nations team does not typically identify stress marks in their transcriptions either, whereas the dictionary orthography indicates accented vowels in almost all cases (except for a few in which elongated vowels or vowels ending in a glottal stop obviate stress marks). For the purposes of this book, then, syllabification is not indicated in either the team or the dictionary entries included in the glossary. The pronunciation key below compares most aspects of the two orthographies discussed here, and the reader is referred to the dictionary for more extensive orthographic information.

Pronunciation Key

Lorna Hill	Six Nations Team/Dictionary	Pronunciation
		Vowels
a	a	sounds like <a> in f<u>a</u>ther
ą	n/u	sounds somewhat like <a> in <u>a</u>nchor
e	e	sounds like <a> in d<u>a</u>y or <e> in gr<u>e</u>y
ę	ę	sounds somewhat like <e> in <u>e</u>nd or p<u>e</u>n
i	i	sounds like <i> in cap<u>ri</u>ce or <e> in sc<u>e</u>ne
į	n/u	sounds somewhat like the diphthong <ai> in k<u>i</u>nd
o	o	sounds like <o> in <u>o</u>pen or r<u>o</u>ve
ǫ	ǫ	sounds somewhat like <o> in <u>o</u>nly or <u>o</u>wn
ʌ	n/u	sounds like <u> in t<u>u</u>b or <u>u</u>p
	u	sounds like <u> in tr<u>u</u>e or fr<u>ui</u>t
ii,	:	indicates lengthened vowels
		Consonants
d	d*	sounds like <d> in <u>d</u>id before voiced vowels and like <t> before whispered vowels
ʄr	n/u	sounds like <fr> in <u>fr</u>om or <u>fr</u>eight
g	g*	sounds like <g> in <u>g</u>et before voiced vowels and like <k> before whispered vowels
h	h*	sounds like <h> in <u>h</u>and; is pronounced separately
dj	j*	sounds like <j> in <u>j</u>oke or <u>j</u>am
k	k	sounds like <k> in <u>k</u>eep
n	n*	sounds like <n> in <u>n</u>oon
r	r*	sounds like <r> in <u>r</u>ain or t<u>r</u>ip
s	s*	sounds like <s> in <u>s</u>ide
ʃr	sr	sounds like <shr> in <u>shr</u>imp or <u>shr</u>ed
ss	n/u	indicates lengthened consonant

t	t	sounds like <t> in top or tin
ts	ts	no English equivalent; pronounce one after the other without vowel sound in between
w	w*	sounds like <w> in window
wh	hw	sounds like <wh> in when or where
y	y	sounds like <y> in yawn or the <y> sound in fury
'	'	glottal stop
_		underlined letters are whispered, as in "ensakotahas," to preach good advice

* indicates there is further information in the dictionary about these letters
n/u indicates this symbol is not used in the dictionary

The glossary has been alphabetized according to the English alphabet, irrespective of nasalization, glottal stops, or other diacritics. Abbreviations occurring in parentheses include o.l., indicating "old language"; com., referring to "common usage"; f.s. to "female speaking"; m.s. to "male speaking"; and spec. to "specifically."

adǫwa'h (adǫ:wa'—men's chant)1. (o.l.) personal warrior song; now, personal male thanksgiving song. 2. specific male songs dedicated to the Creator; also used in male name-giving.

adyęhakǫfrowanę ǫgwadriwhade sęnige'hwhadjiya (adyagǫsrawaneh ǫgwatsriwadeh sanikwajia) 1. lineage feast for the dead. 2. big feast for the dead for all my family.

adyǫdranegę (ajondranége') 1. common-law union 2. to sit side by side, as in marriage; (com.) she sat beside it/someone.

Aehągo Female lineage name belonging to Hǫwatsadęhǫ, Big Bear lineage, Oneida.

agadǫni (agadónih) 1. (o.l.) father's sister or classificatory sister; also applied metaphorically to Three Brothers moiety of Confederacy chiefs. 2. my father's family, not including my father.

agadǫnihonǫ (agadǫnihǫno:) 1. father's sister's people; father's matrilineage; sometimes also applied to father's kindred. 2. all my father's family.

agadǫnisę (agadǫnishę:) 1. members of father's matrilineage; sometimes also applied to father's kindred. 2. I have relatives on my father's side.

agaǫdadyadadrǫgo (agaǫndajado'kdrǫgoh) 1. relieving her grief. 2. they massaged her body.

agaǫdǫgwedaǫgoh (agaǫdǫgwe'dáǫgo') 1. adoption. 2. they adopted a person.

agęwhadjiya; (com.) **akwadjiya** (agahwají:ya') 1. my family; may refer to nuclear family (minus the father), sublineage, or matrilineage. 2. my own personal family, as either child or parent.

agwadęnǫk 1. reciprocal term for both sets of parents linked by marriage. 2. I/we are linked/related.

agwegǫ etinwha ehoage ǫgwasnędǫ (agwé:gǫh etinhwa ehoa:ge ongwasnędo:) we have all climbed down from our mothers' laps.

agyadęnǫk (agya:dę́:nǫhk—my relative) 1. reciprocal term for mothers of bride and groom; my relative or very dear friend. 2. we (two of us) are related.

ahadatwhadjiagiih (ahadathwajiagái:) 1. incest within the matrilineage; biting into your own family. 2. he bit/attacked his family.

aha'htią'h he spoke/he talked.

ahǫwadiwęnahago'h (ahǫadiwę'ahayǫ') 1. dream-discerning. 2. they interpreted his dream.

atadwęnadeni (dẹhadwęnádẹnyǫhs—lit. his voice is changing; he is reaching puberty) 1. puberty. 2. he changed his voice.

Awęho female lineage name belonging to Hǫwatsadẹhǫ, Big Bear lineage, Oneida.

ạyetsiwhanǫkwak sniwhadjiyasǫ (swajiyakiǫnk etsiwanǫnkwa'ak) love and respect each other's families.

dʌksidosgeiha'h skadi gadjina (sgadigají:nah—a social dance done with a paternal cousin) 1. agnatic kin dance, lit. 2. chicken dance fashion, male on one side (also personal feast).

Deganawida (Deganawídah) 1. legendary founder of League of the Iroquois. 2. the Peace-maker.

dęgaǫdẹhnǫde (degadẹhnǫ́:de:—my sibling) they are siblings.

dehayadoweta (taya'dowęhta') he tells fortunes; he thinks it over; (com.) he thinks about it.

Deskahe'h (Dehsgáhe:'—Not Sitting On It Any Longer) Cayuga chief title meaning More Than Eleven.

desǫwanagahagwę (dẹsǫwana'gaha:gwa:') they removed his antlers(his title was removed).

dewadogwadǫ (dewadogwáhdǫh—distribute) distributed.

Dewędas female lineage name belonging to Hǫwatsadẹhǫ, Big Bear lineage, Oneida.

Deyotowe'hgǫ (Deyotowéh:gǫh—Double Cold) Cayuga chief title meaning Cold On Both Sides.

Deyotsǫdaigǫ (Deyodạhsǫdáegǫh—Dark Dance [for the Little People; restricted]) 1. Blow-out-the-lights medicine rite. 2. personal feast; Dark Dance, meaning "bound by dark-ness."

djigo'hses (jigǫhses) pike(food fish).

djiskne ǫdekwaohes gakowane'h Harvest Ceremonies, "Big Green Corn" in August.

Djodẹhaiyo female lineage name belonging to Hǫwatsadẹhǫ, Big Bear lineage, Oneida.

dǫdaiwęnitgę she spoke again, meaning the widow releases her deceased spouse and can appear in public again; (com.) she replied; she spoke again/once more.

dyeigẹdji (egẹ́hjih—she is old; an old woman) the eldest female.

Dyǫhyǫgo (Deyǫhyǫ:go:—It Touches the Sky) Cayuga chief title meaning Reaches the Sky.

Dyǫnhegǫ (gyǫnhéhgǫh—what we all [incl.] live on; Our Sustenance) 1. Spirit of Vegetation. 2. Our Sustenance; Three Sisters: beans, corn and squash; (com.) that which we live on, which keeps us alive.

ęgaǫdadyadagęnha'h (diyadagęnha') they will make their own way; they will help them-selves.

ęgawhadjiaʃre atsịnagęda (ę'gahwajisre' otsinhagę'nda') 1. the charm rests upon the blood of the lineage. 2. "charm" will follow family.

ęhadriwhastiis (ahatrwa:ste:s) 1. chore man. 2. he will perform the necessary tasks; (com.) he will tend to matters at hand.

Ęhẹdawass female lineage name belonging to Hǫwatsadẹhǫ, Big Bear lineage, Oneida.

e'hnyǫǫ (ehnio) white woman.

ęhǫwadǫtas (ayǫhwadǫta'as) 1. bestowing an adǫwa'h song in the naming ritual. 2. he will be honored with a male song by a member.

ęhǫwadyenawat (ęsagiahnawat) 1. they are going to keep him. 2. (com.) they will hold him back; they will hold him from freedom.

ęhǫwanha (eho:węnha') he will be hired/appointed.

ęhǫwhadoga'hs (ęhǫwadǫ́:gahs) to grow up on him.

eksasǫa'h dạyagodaǫhạgai' the generation or begetting of children.

enǫsagwęniyo (ęnǫhsagwani:yo:) she is the head of the house.

ęsagotaha'hs (ęnsakọtahas) he will preach good advice to her/them.

ęsgaiwhįdʌkwęk (ęsgaihwáędak) responsibility will be (refers to transfer of responsibility to females for ceremonies other than Harvest and Midwinter).

ętgayane'hhę'h (etgaiyanehe) it will follow the rules; (com.) it will follow the way/path.

etinoha'h sę ǫwhądjade (etínoha' ohwéjade'—our mother, earth) Our Mother the Earth.

etįnosę (etíno'sęh) 1. Our Uncles (mother's brothers), honorific kinship term for lineage Confederacy chiefs; also applies to 2. Our Uncles, pertaining to two males (Wolf and Turtle) chosen to open and close the stirring ashes ceremony at Midwinter; (com.) our uncles on our mother's side.

etisot sǫheka o'hnida'h (etíhso:t sǫhekhá:' ęhní'da:—our grandmother, moon) Our Grandmother Moon.

etisot sǫheka ohnida dagǫnǫdǫge ǫgwe gonagradǫ hage Our Grandmother Moon controls the birth of the generations.

ewasdǫtwata (owádǫdáhkwa') burning the sticks; morning ritual of a wake.

ęyetinikowi'h (ayetinigo'owi:) we will amuse them.

ęyǫdąnha'h (ęyǫndęnha') she will hire.

ęyǫ'hdok (ǫhdó:gahs—she is reaching puberty; she is maturing) she will mature/grow up.

Gadadyais female lineage name belonging to Hǫwatsadęhǫ, Big Bear lineage, Oneida.

gądefra'h (gę'ęndsra) 1. pass from one [mate] to another. 2. promiscuity.

Gadjinǫdaohe'h (Gaji'nǫdáweheh—Coming On Its Knees) Cayuga chief title meaning Gathering Worms.

gadjisa (Gajíhsa'—Husk Face; False Face) cornhusk medicine mask; (com.) cornhusk mat; anything made of cornhusks.

gadjisdajtgǫ (gadjistę'ntgǫ') 1. a wampum strand symbolizing (and part of) the corporate estate of each longhouse. 2. wampum strings known as the "fire" of the longhouse.

gadogą ągaogę'h (gadǫ:ga agaǫ:ka) 1. to sit level with each other. 2. they will sit side by side; they will live together.

gadogę ąwadǫ godinigǫha'h (gado:gę: ęwá:dǫ' ogwani'gǫ́ha') their minds will be as one.

gadogę niyeha gasęna'h the name still belongs to the matron of the lineage; she still holds the name.

gądyogwagwegǫ odyąhakǫfra (gędiogwagwe:goh dehagǫ:sra') Longhouse community feast for the dead.

Gahawi'h female lineage name belonging to Hǫwatsadęhǫ, Big Bear lineage, Oneida.

gahnya sodahǫ'h (ęyisǫhnya'soda') name hung about the neck; being bound to a situation.

Ga'hnyenęs female lineage name belonging to a non-chiefly lineage (see fig. 2).

gaihǫdadǫ (gaihǫdadon) 1. "shaking the word" rite. 2.(personal feast) "shaking the matter."

gainhǫ sehawaksǫ ągaǫdǫ sadǫnihǫnyǫge'h (ganho sehawaksǫ agadǫnihǫno') 1. Where will your children's father's people be? 2. What position will your children be in their father's family?

gaiwhadjia gwagǫ the entire lineage.

gaiwhanęsgwagowa'h (Gaihwanǫhsgwa'gó:wah—Midwinter Ceremony) Midwinter ceremony; matter of greatest importance.

Gaiwhawagǫ female lineage name belonging to a non-chiefly lineage (see fig. 2).

gaiwhiitgę (gaihwané' aksra'—sin) a bad thing; a sin.

Gaiwhio (Gaihwi:yo:) 1. Code of Handsome Lake. 2. the good word/message.

Gaiwhio hodriwhagehǫ (Gaihwi:yo: hodriwagi:yo:) 1. custodian of the Creator's rites. 2. his responsibility is to carry out the rules of the Great Law.

Gaiwhio odakhaohasǫ (Gaihwi:yo: odakhao:hasǫh) 1. Code of Handsome Lake convention. 2. preaching of the Great Law of Peace; convention.

Gaiwhio wiwhagowa'h (Gaihwi:yo: esgwago:wah) the Great Law of Peace; (com.) a good matter/message.

Gakowanę (Gagówanęh) 1. Big Green Corn Ceremony. 2. Harvest Festival; (com.) it eats a lot.

ganahaowi (Ganaháowi:'—Midwinter Ceremony) "stirring the ashes" day during Midwinter Ceremony.

gana'hgwa'h (ga'náhkwa'—marriage) the marriage situation.

Ganakwęwi'h female lineage name belonging to Hǫwatsadęhǫ, Big Bear lineage, Oneida.

ganifrage gwii gayadagwęnio (kanira gagwai kayadagwęni:yo:) 1. the father furnishes the body. 2. person's body is provided by the father's side.

ganikdah (gąhihta') 1. mortar. 2. hollowed-out log used for making corn flour; a pounding block.

ganohage gwii gatgwęsagwęniyo (knǫ:ha'gagwai gotgwasagwęni:yo:) 1. the mother supplies the blood. 2. person's blood line is provided by the mother's side.

ganohage gwii gayadagwęnio lineage follows the mother's side.

ganǫhǫnyǫk (ganǫhǫnyǫhk—the Thanksgiving Address) the Thanksgiving Address.

ganosanǫn (gano:hsanǫ) water lily plant.

ganosęfra (ganóhshęhsra'—envy) envy; jealousy.

ganǫses (ganǫhse:s—Longhouse) Longhouse.

ganǫsot (ganǫhsa'—a house) house.

Ganregwae (Ganre'gwá:'e:'—Eagle Dance, Strike the Stick) Eagle Dance.

Gaǫhyagąt female lineage name belonging to a non-chiefly lineage (see fig. 2).

gaǫhyage (gaǫhyage') heaven/in the sky.

Gaohyęwi'h female lineage name belonging to Hǫwatsadęhǫ, Big Bear lineage, Oneida.

gaoǫtǫwisas (ǫtǫ:wí:sas—seed songs [for women]) 1. planting ritual; lit. a group of women. 2. females.

gasęna (gahsę́:na'—a name) the name.

Gasęnai'h female lineage name belonging to Hǫwatsadęhǫ, Big Bear lineage, Oneida.

gasęnaniheh (ęhsęniha') a borrowed name.

gasęnaǫwe ohade (gasę'nǫha:de') path of lineage names.

gastiyaǫnyǫk (gahsgyáǫ:nyǫ:—words of encouragement) encouragement.

Gawados female lineage name belonging to Hǫwatsadęhǫ, Big Bear lineage, Oneida.

gawhadjiadogę godisąna that name belongs to a particular family.

gawhadjiia (gahwajiyá:de'—a matrilineal family) 1. the family (may apply to nuclear family minus father, sublineage, or entire matrilineage). 2. the family.

gawhisdaohǫ (agaihwisto:hek) 1. gathering donations. 2. act of collecting money.

gaya'hdogę odd; singled out; (com.) a certain body/item set apart from others.

gayędefra (gę'ęndsra) the act of owning; belongings.

Gayędowanę (Gayędowá:nęh—Peach Pit Game) 1. the Bowl Game, fourth of the four laws of the Creator. 2. the Great Bowl Game.

Geiniyiwhage (Geí: Niyoihwá:ge:—Four Ceremonies) 1. Four laws of the Creator. 2. the Creator's four chosen ceremonies; (com.) four matters; four items.

Geiniyǫwedage (ge:iniyǫgwe'dá'gé:h) 1. four messengers. 2. the Four Guardians; (com.) four people.

godiyanesǫ (godiyanęsho') 1. lineage matrons. 2. the matriarchs; clan mothers holding chief titles.

godrihǫdǫnyoh all the faithkeepers as a group.

godrihǫt (godrihǫ:t—female faithkeeper) female faithkeeper; (com.) that is what she does/occupation.

go'hnosę (gǫnóhshęsra'—jealousy) she envies; jealousy.

gonadrihǫt (gonádrihǫt) female faithkeepers; (com.) that is what they do/occupation.

gonatgaawę (gonatga'awę') they (females) own.

gonatgaǫnio (gǫnatgaǫ) 1. mourning. 2. they are bereaved.

gonyas (gonya:s—she's getting married) the act of marriage.

gotgǫh (goná:tgǫh—witch doctor; bad medicine people; a force to be reckoned with; ominous) 1. witch or sorcerer. 2. person with unnatural powers.

gotgǫhsǫ (gotgǫhsǫh) a caul.

gotgǫtra (gotaǫhtra') 1. witchcraft or esp. sorcery. 2. her charm piece.

Gǫwagęnyǫ female lineage name belonging to Hǫwatsadęhǫ, Big Bear lineage, Oneida.

Gǫwa'hninǫ female lineage name belonging to a non-chiefly lineage (see fig. 2).

Gǫwahǫdǫ female lineage name belonging to a non-chiefly lineage (see fig. 2).

Gǫwasęnǫni female lineage name belonging to Hǫwatsadęhǫ, Big Bear lineage, Oneida.

gowęna (gawę́:na') her word.

Gowęnogii'h female lineage name belonging to Hǫwatsadęhǫ, Big Bear lineage, Oneida.

goyadawęsǫ 1. (f.s.) brother's children; also classificatory brother's children (e.g., the children of father's parallel cousins: father's brothers' sons' children and mother's sisters' sons' children). 2. her mother's family.

goyanedah (goyá:nę'da:) 1. matronship; office of lineage head matron. 2. the title the matriarch holds for her family's chief.

goyane'h (goyá:nęh—clan mother) 1. lineage head matron. 2. matriarch; clan mother holding her family's chief's title.

gwasǫwe (gwahs ǫ:weh—really) the real thing; genuine.

hadihnyǫǫ (hadihnyǫ'ǫh) white men.

hadinigǫdanyǫ (hadinígohdạnyǫ') they are doing Condolence.

Hadiwęnodages (Hadiwęnódagye's—Thunderers) the Thunder Bearers; (com.) they are chanting/speaking as they go along.

hadiwhahęde (hadihwahę'nde') 1. longhouse corps of officers. 2. they are in charge of matters.

hadiyadǫni (hadiyadǫni') 1. grave diggers. 2. they are digging a grave.

hạdǫdjodǫǫ'h (hę:dǫdsǫdo'ǫ:) they who have gone before; deceased.

hadoii gagǫsa false-face mask.

Hadoii Gowa'h (hado'i:s ǫwehgó:wah) the Great False Face.

Hadyatrǫne'h (Hagyá'drǫhne'—He Will Put Bodies One on Top of the Other) Cayuga chief title meaning He Piles It Up.

hagedjia (hehjí'ah—my older brother) my older brother.

hagesęǫ (hagehsé:yoh) 1.(f.s.) my father-in-law.

hagesot (hagéhso:t—my grandfather) my grandfather.

Hahihǫ (Hahí:hǫh—Onondaga chief—He Is a Spiller, He Is Spilling It) Onondaga chief title meaning He Is Spilling It.

ha'hni (ha'nih—my father) my father.

ha'hniiha (ha'níha'—my godfather) my "little" father/uncle; my father's brother.

hahnyǫǫ (hahnyǫ'oh) white man.

Ha'hstawędrota (Hahsdawędrǫ́:ta'—Attaching Rattles) Mohawk chief title meaning He Attaches Rattles.

haiwhasaoha (haihwahswá:wa' [M. Foster]) he preaches the Gaiwhio.

haknęnhǫs (hakné:nhǫ:s—my father-in-law)(m.s.) my father-in-law.

Hạnahidos (Hęnáhi'dohs—Gourd Society Dance [part of Shake Pumpkin]) they shake pumpkin.

Ha'nikwahetgę (wahé:tgęh—evil [in mind]) Satan; Devil; one with an evil mind; (com.) he has a bad mind; his mind is not at its best.

hanǫsagwęnio (honǫhsagwani:yo:) he is head of the house.

haǫdanǫh (háǫdanǫh—He Is the Watcher of the Log; a sub-chief) he guards the tree; title [office] of a Confederacy chief's runner.

hehaw^k (hehá:wahk—my son) my son.

hehawak^ (hehawá:k'ah) 1. (m.s.) nephew; spec. brother's son or the son of any male cousin; (f.s.) nephew; spec. sister's son; also (o.l.) son of parallel female cousin, or son of any cross cousin; now often applied to a son of any cousin. 2. (f.s.) my sister's son; my nephew.

he'hgęę'h (he'gę:'ęh—my younger brother) my younger brother.

he'hgędji (hegęhjih—my husband) my old man/husband.

he'hyadawę (heyá'd'awę'—nephew) 1. (o.l., f.s.) brother's son or classificatory brother's son (e.g., the sons of ego's parallel male cousins: father's brother's son's son and mother's sister's son's son). 2. he is my relative (mother's side).

hęnadoii (hęnaddoi) false faces.

henainhǫs (hené:nhǫ:s—my son-in-law) my son-in-law (used by both parents of wife).

hesgagǫt dęsgaǫdǫt (hęskagǫ:n dęsgaǫ:dǫ) the last time they will eat together.

hęswasǫdahe (haswasǫdohe:) 1. the chosen eve has come. 2. ten-day feast (after death).

heyadre (heyá:dre'—my grandson) my grandson.

heyohe sanǫste seyadre sęniyote is
    sehawak (heyohe sanǫhsde' sadre'tra' sę:nio i:s seháwak) 1. you are more stingy of your grandchild than your own child. 2. you love your granddaughter more than your own daughter.

heyǫwhadę (heyǫhwadę'—my nephew) 1. (m.s.) my nephew; spec. sister's son; also the son of any female cousin. 2. my nephew; male's sister's son.

Hodinǫsǫni (godinǫhsǫ́:ni:—Longhouse people) people of the Longhouse.

hodiwhiostǫ (hoiwi'sto) Christians.

hodiyanesǫ (hodiyanęsho') 1. Confederacy lineage chiefs. 2. the chiefs.

hodraswha'h (adrá'swa'—luck) his luck.

hodrihǫt (hodríhǫ:t—faithkeeper; agent) male faithkeeper; (com.) that is what he does/occupation.

hoksot (hehso:t—my grandfather) my grandfather (short version).

honadrihǫt (honádrihǫ:t—they are male faithkeepers) male faithkeepers; (com.) that is what they do/their occupation.

honasesęą'h (ogyá'sehshę') members of the two sides of the "fire" in the Longhouse; moieties.

Honatahyǫni (Hotahyǫ:ni:—Wolf Clan) the Wolves; they are of the Wolf Clan; (com.) they (males) are wolves.

honatsi friend; ceremonial friend.

honawędaǫ ahǫwadinha (honawęndao:' ahwadinha) the dead were hired (to do a bad deed).

hǫsakie whasę (hǫsakayehwashę:) 1. it has come ten. 2. it is now ten days (after death).

Hǫwatsadęhǫ (Hǫwatsadę́hoh—He Is Buried, He Is Dampened) Oneida Bear chief title meaning They Are Putting Mist on Him.

hoyaneda'h (gaya:ne:da'—chief title) 1. chiefly office (office and title being synonymous). 2. chief title.

hoyane'h (hoyá:neh—[he is] a chief; Confederacy chief) 1. a lineage chief. 2. a chief.

i'hdesgwayǫ'h ągisak sąnhǫ skąnǫ ahanǫdǫnyǫ'hhak (ętisagoh ngęsęk sęnho skęnoh ahęnohdǫniyohęk) 1. she should look for ways to make him comfortable. 2. you have left it up to me to look for ways to make him comfortable.

Kadiyo male lineage name belonging to Hǫwatsadęhǫ, Big Bear lineage, Oneida; meaning Good Forest.

Kahnawake Caughnawaga, Quebec.

Kaiawass female lineage name belonging to Hǫwatsadęhǫ, Big Bear lineage, Oneida.

Kanesetake Oka, Quebec.

kasiisdʌ (ksisda') 1. pestle 2. large wooden pounder used to make corn flour (used with ganikdah).

kdjiʌ (kehjí'ah—my older sister) my older sibling (agedjia'h [long form]).

kegędji (kegéhjih—my wife) my old lady/wife.

kegęę'h (ke'gę́:'ęh—my younger sister) my younger sister.

kehawakʌ (keha:wá:k'ah—my niece [maternal]) 1. (m.s.) niece; spec. brother's daughter or the daughter of any male cousin; (f.s.) niece; spec. sister's daughter; (o.l.) also the daughter of a parallel female cousin or daughter of any cross cousin; now often applied to a daughter of any cousin. 2. (f.s.) sister's daughter; my niece.

kehawʌk (kehá:wahk—my daughter) my daughter.

kenǫksǫ (ǫdę́nǫhksǫ—kin) my kinsfolk.

keseiǫ (kehse:yǫh—my daughter-in-law) my daughter-in-law.

keyadawę (keyá'dawę—my brother's kids) 1. (o.l., f.s.) brother's daughter; also classificatory brother's daughter (e.g., the daughters of ego's parallel male cousins: father's brother's son's daughter and mother's sister's son's daughter) 2. my relatives on my mother's side.

keyadre (keyá:drę'—my granddaughter) my granddaughter.

keyǫwhadę (gakeyǫhwá:de'—my brother's children; my nieces and nephews) 1. (m.s.) my niece; spec. my sister's daughter; also the daughter of any female cousin. 2. my niece; man's sister's daughter.

Kįdais female lineage name belonging to a non-chiefly lineage (see fig. 2).

knoha (knó:ha'—my mother) my mother.

knohaʌ (knóhá:'ah—my aunt [maternal]) my mother's sister; my "little" mother; my aunt.

knosę (knó'sęh—my uncle) my uncle; (spec.) my mother's brother.

knowhakiono (knhwakiǫno) 1. matrilineage of spouse. 2. all my spouse's mother's family.

kogiwe (kohgí:we:) 1. female dead feast officer (may officiate for own matrilineage feasts for the dead and/or yearly longhouse feasts for the dead). 2. she belongs to specific group in charge of yearly feast for the dead.

k'sot (kso:t—grandmother [term of address; term of respect for an old person]) 1. all relatives of grandparent's generation and above. 2. my grandparent (agesot [long form]).

Nagwadęni female lineage name belonging to Hǫwatsadęhǫ, Big Bear lineage, Oneida.

ne gai whaniyata ęsninyak (ne gai hwanidakwa węsniniakwe) 1. they endorse it. 2. this binds your marriage.

negodriwhade ąyenadjaniyǫtak it is her responsibility to hang the kettle from now on (household duties are hers from now on).

netaditadide (netadędatadidę') 1. they stand equally high. 2. they are all of equal status.

nigahnesa (nigęhné:s'ah—a short length of cloth) 1. cotton print cloth. 2. a short piece of cloth.

Nofrǫgyǫ female lineage name belonging to a non-chiefly lineage (see fig. 2).

ǫdatrewa'hdǫ (adatrewáhdǫ:'—repentance; punishment) 1. confession or repentance. 2. act of repentance.

odihgrǫfrah (adí'grǫhsra'—shyness) shyness.

odǫnhetra (sadǫnhe'tra'—your soul, heart, spirit) 1. spirit; soul; life. 2. life/heart.
odǫnhetrot gotgwęsage (odǫnhé:trat gotgwasage) 1. the spirit or life is in the blood. 2. there is life in the blood.
ǫdwęnǫgotanǫ (ǫndwęnogohta:no) 1. medicine rites. 2. passing of personal feasts.
ǫgedjia (kehjí'ah—my older sister) my older sister.
ogęhęge watnadaǫt (ogęh ęgǫwatna'da:'ǫ:) 1. corn bread cooked in ashes for deceased. 2. bread cooked in ashes.
ǫgeseyǫ (ǫgehsé:yǫh—[f.s.] my mother-in-law) (f.s.) my mother-in-law; my husband's mother.
ǫgesot (ǫgęhso:t) my grandmother (long form).
ǫgwaihǫwaika onǫ'hgwatra'h Indian medicine.
ǫgwanǫskǫ ǫgwadęnǫksǫ (ongwanǫhsgǫ ǫgwadęnǫhkǫ') our relatives within our own house.
ǫgwasotsądak (ǫgwe'soję:ndak) 1. ancestral spirits. 2. our ancestors; the grandparents we used to have.
ǫgwayada gęnhafra (ogwaiyada gai:háhsra') 1. power of tobacco over supernatural entities. 2. for our good; for our well-being.
ǫgwehǫwe (ǫgwehǫ:weh—First Nations, Indian people, Aboriginal, Native) real people; native people.
ǫgyagyo'h (ǫgyá:gyoh—my brother-in-law, sister-in-law) 1. (f.s.) brother-in-law (husband's brother, sister's husband); (m.s.) reciprocal wife's brother and sister's husband. 2. (f.s.) my brother-in-law; my husband's brother.
ǫgyanyę (ǫgya:nye:') 1. (m.s.) sister-in-law (wife's sister); (f.s.) reciprocal husband's sister and brother's wife. 2. my sister-in-law; my husband's sister.
ǫgyase (ǫgyá'se:'—we two are cousins) 1. preferred usage (1958) for cross cousins (mother's brother's child and father's sister's child); sometimes used for parallel cousin (father's brother's child). 2. my cousin; we are cousins.
ohdraswha (adrá'swa'—luck) luck, well-being.
o'hdyęhakǫfra (dehagǫ:sra') a feast for the dead.
O'hgiwe (Ohgí:we:—Ghost Society Dance) 1. ceremony for the dead (may be in behalf of individual, lineage, or community). 2. yearly ritual for dead (special songs).
o'hhnyagwįi (hnyagwái'—bear) bear.
O'hhnyagwįi Gowa Big Bear lineage.
O'hhnyagwįi'kya'h (Hnyagwái:' geha:'—Bear Dance) medicinal bear feast.
o'hna'h (ohna'—grease, oil) 1. anointing oil. 2. lard, oil, grease.
ǫhsidagewata (see also gadjisa) (we'sidagiwe'da:) on which to wipe one's feet; a mat.
o'hwhadjiʌ (ohwají:ya') 1. family (may apply to nuclear family minus the father, to sublineage, or to matrilineage). 2. the family; (com.) it's family.
o'hwhadjiadade (gahwajiyá:de'—a matrilineal family) 1. family line. 2. the family lineage.
o'hwhadjiagwęnio (ohwajiyagwe'ni:yo:) the main family.
o'hwistowęnes (ohwistowa:'nes) red mullet (food fish).
ǫkiwhaganǫnyanih 1. they inform the people how they should be. 2. they regulate the rules and matters for our (the people's) good.
ǫknenhǫs (ǫkné:nhǫ:s—my [a male's] mother-in-law) (m.s.) my mother-in-law (my wife's mother).
oksot (okso:t—my grandmother) my grandmother (short form).
onędodaǫ without roots (a tree just appeared).
onęhę (onęhę:'—corn) corn.
onęhę onada'h (onęhę' oná'da:'—corn bread) corn bread.

onęhogwa'h (onęhogwa'—lyed corn soup) corn soup.

One'sa'hen' (Oa) (Ohné'draę:'—Onondaga chief, the Best Soil Uppermost) Onondaga chief title meaning In the Middle of a Field or the Middle of a Hide.

ǫngwadąnǫksǫ a group of relatives.

onǫ'hgwatra'h (onǫhgw'atra'—evil, weeds) medicine.

onǫ'hgwatrahetgę'h (onǫhgw'atraihetgę') bad medicine; the medicine is spoiled.

onǫ'hwhet (onǫhweht—love medicine [restricted]) love medicine (usually to control someone).

osaistagowah (osháihsda'go:wah—large snake) 1. mythical great serpent. 2. large snake.

otgǫa'h (otgoa:) 1. small shell beads, symbols of corporate groups or symbol binding marriage or other contractual agreement; wampum. 2. wampum.

otgǫ'h (atgǫ') 1. power within a charm to do ill. 2. poison/charm piece.

otgwęsadagyeh (otgwęsadadiye) bloodline.

otsinnagęda'h (otsinǫhgę'da') 1. originally a hunting charm, now associated with witchcraft. 2. a charm.

owęna'h (owę́:na'—a word) the word; its word.

ǫwhądjageha gaiwhio hodriwhagehǫ (ǫhwęnsageha:' gaihwi:yo: hodriwagai:yo:) 1. both earthly and heavenly duties lie before him. 2. the message of Peace lies before him here on earth.

owhędjageka (ohwęjage:hka:) 1. worldly things. 2. belonging to the earth; earthly.

oyadadrǫk (oyatadrǫ) 1. ghost. 2. of a scary body; it has a scary body.

oya'hda'h (oyá'da'—a body) body; its body.

oyę'hgwaowe (oyę'gw'áǫweh—Indian tobacco [ceremonial, home grown]) 1. Indian tobacco. 2. sacred tobacco.

saetkajn godǫnisę (sę' ehetkan godǫnishę') 1. in your own rectum. 2. from the rectal area.

sagatga'h hoyǫda is ęsriwhaganǫni (sagatgahoyo'onda is ęsrihwagano:oni) I release my body for you to make the proper arrangements.

Sagogǫha (Shogǫgęhe'—He Is Seeing Them) Onondaga chief title meaning He Sees Her/Them Occasionally.

sahǫwędrǫhʌs (sahǫwahndrohas) 1. to put another in his place. 2. they give him a replacement mate after death of his spouse.

saǫdadatga'h (sagaesáhtga:'—they released you, fired you, let you go) she released her; she gives her freedom again.

saǫtiyǫdaisʌt (sahatǫyǫndaisat) she releases the body; she wastes the body.

sedwa'hdjia hoskęęn'hgeda gowa'h ądeka gagwa (Shedjwahjí:'ah Hosgę'ęgehdagǫ́:wah ga:gwa:gye's—our older brother, the Great Warrior, the sun) 1. our elder brother, the great warrior, the sun. 2. our elder brother, the great one, the sun. (Some people interpret the great "one" as the great "warrior," since this was once the general status ascribed to men, just as horticultural pursuits were ascribed to women, while others consider the term "warrior" to be antithetical to Deganawida's message of the Great Peace.)

sęhodę hoyądʌk (sohodę' hoyędak) his possessions; what he had/owned.

Sęnayewhas female lineage name belonging to a non-chiefly lineage (see fig. 2).

skanikwat (sg'anigǫhá:t odǫ́'ǫh—one mind) one mind.

Skanyadaiyo (Sganyadáiyo—Handsome Lake) the prophet Handsome Lake.

skanyadiga (sganya'dí:ga:'—heron) heron.

Sǫgwayadisǫ (Shǫgway'adíhs'ǫh—he is the creator [of our bodies]) the Creator; He that made us; He that made our bodies.

soheka o'hnida (sǫhehká:' ęhní'da:'—moon) the moon; a sphere of the night.

tadigǫstoais (tadigǫhstǫ:is) 1. long whiskers; feast for dead white ancestors. 2. they with long beards.

Tadodaho (Tadodá:ho'—Entangled) Onondaga chief title meaning Ensnarled.

Tahyǫni (Hotahyǫ:ni:—Wolf clan) 1. Wolf lineage. 2. Wolf clan.

tatiataita'h (dadiyadęda') they are holding a wake; they are awaiting the morning.

tęhdegayahdǫt (tę'degai:yado) 1. the disembodied spirit of death. 2. it doesn't have a body; without a body.

tęhdehayada'h sęgawhadjiade (tę'dihayadaso kwajadi) he is not part of the family.

tęhdeskot hądǫ tawaddǫ (tę'deskat hadǫn tawadǫn) 1. there shall be no master in the house. 2. no one shall be the head one (the boss).

tę'hdewadǫta dasaitgwęsadeni (tę'dahwadǫnta setgwęhsadé:ni') it is impossible for you to change the bloodline.

tiyaǫt (teáǫt—muskrat) muskrat.

tiyǫgweyę (tiǫ'gwaiyę) 1. parents-in-law avoidance. 2. we avoid.

todraǫ (todrao:) 1. wasting sickness. 2. he caught sickness from someone.

tonadatǫde (tęnadatǫdek) they listen to one another.

tsigawhadjiią'h (tsigahwajiya'yę:) a family was left behind.

wadęsǫ o'hdjigwah (ojíhgwa'—porridge; mush) roasted, sweetened corn mush; special food for hadoii.

wihowanę geiniyiwhage (wihowá:neh) principal ceremonies (Midwinter and Harvest) directed by chiefs and male faithkeepers involving the four great matters.

wiwhawędenyǫ (wihwawęhdę'nyo) 1. appendage ceremonies (female responsibility.) 2. matters (ceremonies throughout the year attached to the principal ceremonies) directed by female faithkeepers; (com.) matters or ideas alongside or attached to.

References

Beauchamp, William M. 1905. *A History of the New York Iroquois Now Commonly Called the Six Nations.* New York State Museum Bulletin 78. Albany, New York State Education Department.
———. 1907. *Civil, Religious, and Mourning Councils and Ceremonies of Adoption of the New York Indians.* New York State Museum Bulletin 113. Albany.
Canadian Labour Congress. 1957. *The U-I-A, Its Rights and Obligations.* 3rd ed. Ottawa.
Clark, Joshua V. H. 1849. *Onondaga: or Reminiscences of Earlier and Later Times; Being a Series of Historical Sketches Relative to Onondaga; With Notes on the Several Towns in the Country, and Oswego.* 2 vols. Syracuse NY: Stoddard and Babcock.
Colden, Cadwallader. 1747. *A History of the Five Indian Nations.* London.
Cooke, Charles A. 1952. "Iroquois Personal Names: Their Classification." *Proceedings of the American Philosophical Society,* 96(4). Philadelphia: The Philosophical Society.
Deardorff, Merle H. 1951. "The Religion of Handsome Lake: Its Origin and Development." In *Symposium on Local Diversity in Iroquois Culture,* ed. W. N. Fenton. Smithsonian Institution Bureau of American Ethnology Bulletin 149, 77–107. Washington: Government Printing Office.
Department of Citizenship and Immigration. 1957. "The Canadian Indian: A Reference Paper." Ottawa.
Dominion Bureau of Statistics. 1921, 1931, 1941, 1951. "Agricultural Census." Ottawa.
Dunham, Mabel. 1945. *Grand River.* Toronto: McClelland and Stewart Ltd.
Eggan, Fred. 1960. "Lewis Henry Morgan in Kinship Perspective." In *Essays in the Science of Culture in Honor of Leslie A. White,* eds. Gertrude E. Dole and Robert L. Carneiro. New York: Thomas Y. Crowell Co.
Fenton, W. N. 1946. "An Iroquois Condolence Council for Installing Cayuga Chiefs in 1945." *Journal of the Washington Academy of Sciences* 36(4):110–27.
———. 1950. "The Roll Call of the Iroquois Chiefs: A Study of a Mnemonic Cane from the Six Nations Reserve." *Smithsonian Misc. Coll.* 111 (15). Washington.
———. 1951. "Locality as a Basic Factor in the Development of Iroquois Social Structure." In *Symposium on Local Diversity in Iroquois Culture,* ed. W. N. Fenton. Smithsonian Institution Bureau of American Ethnology Bulletin 149, 35–54. Washington: Government Printing Office.
———. 1952. "Factionalism in American Indian Society." Vol. 2, *Tirage a part; Actes du IVe Congres International des Sciences Anthropologiques et Ethnologiques,* 330–40. Vienna.
———. 1953. *The Iroquois Eagle Dance: An Offshoot of the Calumet Dance,* with "Analysis of the Iroquois Eagle Dance and Songs," by Gertrude P. Kurath. Smithsonian Institution Bureau of American Ethnology Bulletin 156. Washington.

Fenton, William N., and Gertrude P. Kurath. 1951. "The Feast of the Dead, or Ghost Dance at Six Nations Reserve, Canada." In *Symposium on Local Diversity in Iroquois Culture*, ed. W. N. Fenton. Smithsonian Institution Bureau of American Ethnology Bulletin 149, 139–165. Washington: Government Printing Office.

Fortes, Meyer. 1940. Introduction to *African Political Systems*, eds. M. Fortes and E. E. Evans-Pritchard. London: Oxford University Press.

———. 1949a. *The Web of Kinship Among the Tallensi*. London: Oxford University Press.

———. 1949b. "Time and Social Structure: An Ashanti Case Study." In *Social Structure: Studies Presented to A. R. Radcliffe-Brown*. Oxford.

———. 1950. "Kinship and Marriage Among the Ashanti." In *African Systems of Kinship and Marriage*, eds. A. R. Radcliffe-Brown and Daryll Forde. London: Oxford University Press.

———. 1953a. "Analysis and Description in Social Anthropology." *The Advancement of Science* 10(38):190–201.

———. 1953b. "The Structure of Unilineal Descent Groups." *American Anthropologist*, 60:17–41.

———. 1958. Introduction to *The Developmental Cycle in Domestic Groups*. Cambridge Papers in Social Anthropology No. 1, ed. J. R. Goody. Cambridge: Cambridge University Press.

———. 1959b. "Descent, Filiation, and Affinity: A Rejoinder to Dr. Leach: Part II." *Man: A Monthly Record of Anthropological Science* 59:206–12. London.

———. 1962. Introduction to *Marriage in Tribal Societies*. Cambridge Papers in Social Anthropology No. 3, ed. Meyer Fortes. Cambridge: Cambridge University Press.

Goldenweiser, A. A. 1914a. "On Iroquois Work, 1912." *Summary Report of the Geological Survey [of Canada]—Department of Mines for the Calendar Year 1912*. Sessional Paper No. 26, Anthropological Division, 464–75. Ottawa: C. H. Parmelee, 1914.

———. 1914b. "On Iroquois Work, 1913." *Summary Report of the Geological Survey [of Canada]—Department of Mines for the Calendar Year 1913*. Sessional Paper No. 26, Anthropological Division, 365–72. Ottawa: J. De L. Tache.

———. 1937. *Anthropology: An Introduction to Primitive Culture*. New York: F. S. Crofts and Co.

Goody, J. R., ed. 1958. *The Developmental Cycle in Domestic Groups*. Cambridge Papers in Social Anthropology No. 1. Cambridge: Cambridge University Press.

Hewitt, J. N. B. 1895. "The Iroquoian Concept of the Soul." *Journal of American Folk-Lore*. 8:107–16. London: Houghton, Mifflin and Company.

———. 1902. "Orenda and a Definition of Religion." *American Anthropologist New Series* 4(1):33–46.

———. 1910. "White Dog Sacrifice." *A Handbook of American Indians North of Mexico*. Smithsonian Institution Bureau of American Ethnology Bulletin 30. Part 2: 939–44. Washington: Government Printing Office.

———. 1916. "The Requickening Address of the League of the Iroquois." *Holmes Anniversary Volume*. Washington: Bryan Press.

———. 1918. "A Constitutional League of Peace in the Stone Age of America: The League of the Iroquois and Its Constitution." *Annual Report of the Board of Regents of the Smithsonian Institution Showing the Operations, Expenditures, and Condition of the Institution for the Year Ending June 30, 1918*, 527–545. Washington.

———. 1929. "The League of Nations of the Iroquois Indians in Canada." *Explorations and Field Work of the Smithsonian Institute*, 201–06. Washington.

———. 1944. "The Requickening Address of the Iroquois Condolence Council," ed. W. N. Fenton. *Journal of the Washington Academy of Sciences* 34(3):65–85.

Hunt, George T. 1940. *The Wars of the Iroquois: A Study in Intertribal Trade Relations*. Madison: University of Wisconsin Press.

Maine, Sir Henry S. 1920. *Ancient Law*. London.

Morgan, Lewis H. 1851. *League of the Ho-de-no-sau-nee, or Iroquois*. Rochester.

————. 1870. *Systems of Consanguinity and Affinity of the Human Family*. Smithsonian Institution, Contributions to Knowledge. Washington.

————. 1878. *Ancient Society*. New York.

————. 1881. *Houses and House Life of the American Aborigines. Contributions to North American Ethnology*. Vol. 4. Washington: Government Printing Office.

————. n.d. "Laws of Descent of the Iroquois." Rochester.

Newhouse, Seth M. 1885. "Cosmology of De-ka-na-we-dah's Government of the Iroquois Confederacy." Ms. in possession of his daughter, Mrs. Lillian Henhawk, Six Nations Reserve, Ontario.

Noon, John A. 1949. *Law and Government of the Grand River Iroquois*. Viking Fund Publications in Anthropology No. 12. New York: Viking Fund.

Parker, Arthur C. 1912. *The Code of Handsome Lake, the Seneca Prophet*. New York State Museum Bulletin 163. Albany.

————. 1916. *The Constitution of the Five Nations*. New York State Museum Bulletin 184. Albany.

Putnam, Donald F., ed. 1952. *Canadian Regions—A Geography of Canada*. London: J. M. Dent and Sons.

Radcliffe-Brown, A. R. 1931. "The Present Position of Anthropological Studies." *British Association for the Advancement of Science Centenary Meeting*. Section H. Anthropology. London.

————. 1950. Introduction to *African Systems of Kinship and Marriage*, eds. A. R. Radcliffe-Brown and Daryll Forde. London: Oxford University Press.

————. 1952. *Structure and Function in Primitive Society*. London: Cohen and West Ltd.

Reville, R. Douglas. 1920. *History of Brant County*. Brantford, Ontario: The Hurley Printing Co. Ltd.

Smith, Raymond T. 1956. *The Negro Family in British Guiana: Family Structure and Social Status in the Villages*. London: Routledge and Kegan Paul.

Snyderman, George S. 1951. "Concepts of Land Ownership Among the Iroquois and Their Neighbors." In *Symposium on Local Diversity in Iroquois Culture*, ed. W. N. Fenton. Smithsonian Institution Bureau of American Ethnology Bulletin 149, 13–34. Washington: Government Printing Office.

Sparks, Jared. 1848. "Samuel Kirkland." *Library of American Biography*. Vol. 25. Boston.

Speck, Frank G. 1949. *Midwinter Rites of the Cayuga Long House*. Philadelphia: University of Pennsylvania Press.

Stites, Sarah Henry. 1905. *Economics of the Iroquois*. Lancaster PA: Press of the New Era Printing Co.

Stone, W. L. 1838. *Life of Joseph Brant, Thayendanegea*. 2 vols. New York.

The Indian Act. R.S.C. 1952, c-149, as amended by 1952–53, C41; 1956 C40. Office Consolidation. Dept. of Citizenship and Immigration. Ottawa.

Unemployment Insurance Commission. 1959. *Worker's Handbook on Unemployment Insurance*. 13th ed. Ottawa.

Warner, Beers and Co. 1883. *The History of the County of Brant, Ontario*. Toronto.

Wraxall, Peter. 1915. *An Abridgement of the Indian Affairs Transacted in the Colony of New York, from 1678 to 1751*, ed. Charles Howard McIlwain. Cambridge: Harvard University Press.

Zeisberger, David. 1910. "David Zeisberger's History of the Northern American Indians," eds. A. B. Hulbert and W.N. Schwarze. *Ohio Archaeological and Historical Publication* 19:1–189. Columbus: Fred J. Heer.

Index

The Comanches: A History, 1706-1875
By Thomas W. Kavanagh

Koasati Dictionary
By Geoffrey D. Kimball with the assistance of
Bel Abbey, Martha John, and Ruth Poncho

Koasati Grammar
By Geoffrey D. Kimball with the assistance of
Bel Abbey, Nora Abbey, Martha John, Ed John, and Ruth Poncho

The Salish Language Family: Reconstructing Syntax
By Paul D. Kroeber

Tales from Maliseet Country: The Maliseet Texts of Karl V. Teeter
Translated and edited by Philip S. LeSourd

The Medicine Men: Oglala Sioux Ceremony and Healing
By Thomas H. Lewis

A Dictionary of Creek / Muskogee
By Jack B. Martin and Margaret McKane Mauldin

Wolverine Myths and Visions: Dene Traditions from Northern Alberta
Edited by Patrick Moore and Angela Wheelock

Households and Families of the Longhouse Iroquois at Six Nations Reserve
By Merlin G. Myers
Foreword by Fred Eggan
Afterword by M. Sam Cronk

Ceremonies of the Pawnee
By James R. Murie
Edited by Douglas R. Parks

Archaeology and Ethnohistory of the Omaha Indians:
The Big Village Site
By John M. O'Shea and John Ludwickson

Traditional Narratives of the Arikara Indians (4 vols.)
By Douglas R. Parks

Osage Grammar
By Carolyn Quintero

They Treated Us Just Like Indians: The Worlds of Bennett County, South Dakota
By Paula L. Wagoner

A Grammar of Kiowa
By Laurel J. Watkins with the assistance of Parker McKenzie

Native Languages and Language Families of North America
(folded study map and wall display map)
Compiled by Ives Goddard